Writing Design Fiction

Writing Design Fiction

Relocating a City in Crisis

TONY FRY

BLOOMSBURY VISUAL ARTS
LONDON • NEW YORK • OXFORD • NEW DELHI • SYDNEY

Bloomsbury Visual Arts
Bloomsbury Publishing Plc
50 Bedford Square, London, WC1B 3DP, UK
1385 Broadway, New York, NY 10018, USA
29 Earlsfort Terrace, Dublin 2, Ireland

BLOOMSBURY, BLOOMSBURY VISUAL ARTS and the Diana logo are trademarks of Bloomsbury
Publishing Plc

First published in Great Britain 2021
Paperback edition published 2023

Cover design by Eleanor Rose
Cover photograph © Tony Fry

A catalogue record for this book is available from the British Library.

Library of Congress Cataloging-in-Publication Data
Names: Fry, Tony, author.
Title: Writing design fiction: relocating a city in crisis / Tony Fry.
Identifiers: LCCN 2021011485 (print) | LCCN 2021011486 (ebook) |
ISBN 9781350217300 (hardback) | ISBN 9781350217348 (paperback) |
ISBN 9781350217317 (pdf) | ISBN 9781350217324 (epub) | ISBN 9781350217331
Subjects: LCSH: Design–Methodology. | City planning–Climatic factors. |
Narration (Rhetoric) | Experimental fiction.
Classification: LCC NK1505.F795 2022 (print) | LCC NK1505 (ebook) | DDC 745.4–dc23
LC record available at https://lccn.loc.gov/2021011485
LC ebook record available at https://lccn.loc.gov/2021011486

ISBN: HB: 978-1-3502-1730-0
           PB: 978-1-3502-1734-8
           ePDF: 978-1-3502-1731-7
           eBook: 978-1-3502-1732-4

Typeset by Integra Software Service Pvt. Ltd.

To find out more about our authors and books visit www.bloomsbury.com
and sign up for our newsletters.

Contents

Preface

Driven by the desire for recognition, the project of establishing design as discipline and professional practice has been an ambition pursued by many design educators and designers over many years. The result has been that design has been defined and widely perceived as a restrictive practice. This has created two serious conditions of limitation. The first is that it undercuts a wider recognition of the ability to design being intrinsic to our species that, as such, should have been cultivated as a skill and hermeneutic capability within everyone's education. In this respect design(ing) needs to be understood as an ontological characteristic of our being that remains for most people an underdeveloped life skill. Saying this in no way suggests that design would not be selected by some as a vocation. The second limitation is as design's presence in the world is unbounded, thus having the ability to recognize its omnipresence is integral to being able to make sense of the fabricated world, within the world, in which we all live. Fundamentally design does not own design, nor designers designing.

It is against this backdrop that design often gets trivialized and reduced to object, style, method and process. Likewise, design has become disengaged from history by design history itself (here is the distinction between design in history vs the history of design). Changing circumstance are starting to make clear, to those willing to look, that design as a means of prefiguring 'the forms of the form' of the future has to become much more important. For instance, the futural implication of living the age of the Anthropocene are profound. What this implies is not just living with the still unfolding relational complexity of a changing climate, a major crisis of biodiversity and even greater difference of our 'species being' driven by inequities and technology, but with a massive imperative to adapt our collective and plural modes of being in the world.

This view of design, and of emergent world circumstances frames the thinking and content of this book. Second order design fiction aims not only to redirect the relation between speculation and design but also how a complex design project is directed. Equally, it is a break down and break out of design from a disciplinary condition of limitation. Put in the simplest terms, it arrives with no clear distinction between writing and designing.

Tony Fry,
Launceston (Tasmania)

Acknowledgements

Thanks to D Wood for her textual insights and help, Yan Yan for her drawings and Madina Tlostanova and Anne-Marie Willis for their encouragement. I also want to credit the knowledge gained from working with the Gällivare city movers group, and alongside architect Jim Gall. The city drawing and all the photographic images are my own.

1

An Extended Prologue

Plato told us that we see with our mind, our eyes being mere optical instruments. By implication all that is seen is framed by memory.

Second order design fiction draws on the thinking and term 'second order cybernetics' as a method of observation of what has been observed. What this means is the production of the fiction as a recursive exercise of critical observation and reflection that returns what is learnt from the fictive process, and what it creates, to its designer/author. It does not mean that the process will exactly mirror 'second order cybernetics' as such, nor does it completely bond to systems theory, but rather certain lessons of observation have been appropriated from it.

The fiction is not produced just as a projection to an audience to, for example, provoke dialogue. Rather its creation is predominately as an object for interrogation, from which other iterations may follow, that in the end inform a design brief. This process of review, revision and brief authorship can obviously be conducted by an individual or a group and observed by an audience who may be consulted. However, their role is secondary.

The scale of second order design fiction will not necessarily correspond with the prior use of such fictions that are certainly more likely to be attached to products, services and technologies. The second order approach is more directed at projects, structures and environments and may well be more linked to political, rather than just economic ends. Likewise, the motivation for these fictions' creation may often be to assist in the advancement of the autonomy of architects and designers, and thus go beyond service provision. So said, there is no way they can arrive within mechanisms of restricted use.

The example of moving a city (which implies transporting material fabric, in contrast to just a more general notion of relocating a city) was selected for three reasons. First, its scale and complexity illustrate the extended reach of a higher order of design fiction, spanning many design practices, while also demonstrating material that invites a recursive re-engagement in the context of an already known imperative and faltering early attempts to move cities at risk. Second, it illustrates possible future actions in the context of increasing climate change impacts. Third, its realism links theoretical knowledge and practical experience – this via the author's direct experience of working on a city move and other related projects, as well as his research and publication on a city move and cognate topics (see the Appendix at the end of this book).

This work is a hybrid creation. It divides into four parts. **This part** introduces the concept and argument for 'second order design fiction'. It then places this in the context of a critique of the current practice of the creation of design fictions, followed by making the case for elevating the status of the practice to engage far more contemporary worldly imperatives. **Part 2** is an elaborated example of the application of second order design fiction thinking where the example is of moving a city under conditions of crisis. In doing this, the fiction's narrative will be articulated by multiple voices. These voices allow for significant shifts in perspective on a range of issues and provide the basis for the elaboration of dialogue with different characters and narrator. **Part 3** critically reviews how the example of moving a city, the strategy it communicates and topics it critically addresses, illustrate ways such thinking can be developed and brought into possible forms of engagement with other and actual challenging issues of the present that are evoked. This includes reflecting upon how and where second order design fictions can increase the situated efficacy of design theory and autonomous and redirective design practice in the current age. In **Part 4** the objective in using the design fiction is presented as a developed design process based on 'designing back from the future'. Thereafter the fiction and its review form the critical context out of which a moving city brief can be created.

What this means is that the fiction is not projected as a solution or end-point but as a means in the production of a condition of exploration, applied research and learning that combine to enable the creation of an informed brief for the topic it addresses to be created.

The metanarrative of second order design fiction

The overall narrative communicated by the combined content of the narratives of the four parts shows that design fiction can contribute to redirective practices, gaining a level of efficacy that would give them increased transformative power. The aim is to counter the defuturing conditions produced by structural unsustainability, and the relational impacts of climate change.

Redirective practice can be understood as one of the key means to take design beyond continued attempts to constitute it as a restrictive practice, as evident in it as discipline, history, theoretical discourse, educational programmes and a profession. At the most general, design also needs to be understood as a pervasive activity intrinsic to the prefigurative actions of our being in and of worlds as they ontologically constitute a specific world. As such it is elemental to all forms of ordering of our actions to imagined predetermined ends. Redirective practice acknowledges and engages the worldly presence of design and its potential to be taken beyond its conditions of limitation. Writing can also be viewed as a profession and a domain of education, but unlike design it is not as constrained and widely recognized as a pervasive material worlding practice. As will be shown, second order design fiction acknowledges a commonality between design and writing. As a practice it aims to demonstratively constitute a discernible bridge between both practices.

Design as more than 'design'

What follows is based on what has been learnt from selectively revisiting and reviewing much that I have written on design theory, design history, architecture, cities, materials, war and the political over the past few decades. Two very basic conclusions have been reached. The first is that the presence of the agency of the designed in the world, past and present, is not reflected in the partiality of the design discourse (that is the sum of its theory, history and practice). The reason for this is simple: the majority of things material and immaterial that are designed are not done so by a designer. Architects do not design most of the built structures in the world, industrial designers do not design most manufactured products of the world, fashion designers likewise don't design most of the clothes the world's population wears (most clothes are not 'fashion' anyway) – and so on. Next, professional designers of all types who provide a service, which is the majority, do not make the most important design decisions about what is to be designed. It is their client who makes these decisions. Then, the basis of what our species materially needs in order to have a viable long-term future is negated by the prevalence of market-dominated design products and services that are about the maximization of consumption to maintain or increase economic growth. Rather than being a force that futures our life as a species, and biological life in general, such an economy defutures by constituting all that relationally and structurally increases the unsustainable. Yet notwithstanding these conditions of limitation, design's economic function and its environmental, cultural, social and political significance have never been anything like as important as it is now as an appropriate means of redirective affirmative change. However, this is only true and possible with the qualification that design itself must be totally redirectively transformed in theory and as a materially grounded praxis toward making the worlds of human habitation, elemental to the biophysical world, futural. Although urgent, this transformation is not going to happen quickly, nor as a grand programme. It will happen in fragmentary ways and it will take time to create convergences and consolidation, not as a result of a day of awakening but as a reactive response to situated changing global circumstances. Such change is not a dream but a slowly emerging reality of sustainment, as an acted upon imperative, to which second order design fiction can be constituted to contribute.

Meanwhile academic design research mostly continues to embrace 'the design process' by researchers inwardly focused and dislocated from a world of deepening crises. For them design, and 'design thinking', are un-problematically instrumental, and articulated to industry and the economic status quo. They view design as having no ideological attachments or political agency. Yes, there are a few progressives moving across disciplinary boundaries to develop a post-instrumental mode of design practice. But they are scattered, small in number. Their work continually runs against the institutional grain, for which they pay career consequences.

Fortunately, the design fraternity does not completely determine the nature and fate of design. Design, designing and the designed are now gaining interest from elsewhere. Philosophers, anthropologists, literary theorists, sociologists, psychologists and others are becoming interested in it and thereby exposing the field to other concerns, epistemological inquiries and forms of situated analysis. Counter to this positive is the negative of a substantial dimension of design's association with the digital domain subsuming it to technologically predetermined functionality.

The contradictory character of design reveals itself in other ways. Having visited a good many design and architecture schools over recent decades, what is clear is that some students, often the smartest, arrive at the end of the degree course recognizing the importance of design but contemptuous of the discipline they have been inducted into. They know they have been educated for the past and not the future. The best wised up and then educated themselves. Here one asks, what is a good design education? Certainly it's much more than just being able to design and to gain and please clients. It is actually to have learnt what design is and does as an endless learning. It is to have discovered the world in which we live – as a design-transformed cultural pluriverse + biosphere + hominoidosphere (the ethno-corrected 'Anthropocene') – that is a complexity beyond our comprehension that nonetheless we have to struggle to understand in general, but also in terms of the continuous ontological agency of design. Design is implicated in creating vast numbers of defuturing problems that constitute the condition of unsustainability, as well as conversely being able to be critically viewed and redirected toward sustainment. The redirection of design takes action contra to ill-informed practices claiming to deliver 'sustainable solutions' that actually sustain the unsustainable.

If one could gather all the enviro-climatic, geopolitical, politico-social, conflictual and inequitable unsustaining defuturing problems of 'the world' into one bundle and place design before it, the inadequacy of design, as it is, would be immediately clear. As would the reason why design as currently understood is of marginal transformative importance. But being in this situation is exactly why its actual omnipresence and ontological agency has to be made present and thereafter the importance of design as 'worlding' can start to be fully recognized. The question is, how and by whom?

If there is an answer to this question it cannot arrive instantly, from one person or without a considerable expenditure of time and effort, recognizing that: (i) an idealist answer is no answer; (ii) a pragmatic/instrumental answer is no answer; and (iii) whatever the answer is, it will be an accumulation of tested critical actions and voices. So said, and to indicate a thinking not disabled by nor disconnected from the views above, the following case for second order design fiction is put forward for consideration, contemplation, contestation and for a continuous conversation.

The metanarrative of the design fiction overarches all the elements of the work, and it functions to enable the elements to cohere into a project beyond any directly addressed content. The epistemological basis of the story and review of moving a city exceeds the specificity of the topic to define the greater project illustrative of design and designing as a relationally complex agent of worldly creation and transformation.

The work

The immediate aim of this work is to present the development and redirection of design fiction as a contribution to the advancement of design as a counter-force to the unsustainability of the designed and designing world-within-the-world of our species' creation. This negation does not apply to everything designed, but rather to design as defuturing, evident in the dominant character of its history. This situation arose not by intent but because designers (understood in its broadest sense) lacked an awareness of the consequences of their actions – the worlding or unworlding agency of what they enabled to be brought into being.

It is against this backdrop that the case for moving many of the world's cities, as sea levels rise over this century and beyond, will be made by the use of a second order design fiction. But before this is possible a critique of existing design fictions needs to be put in place, along with an outline of the approach of a second order fiction as an iteration of the first. But first, qualifying comment needs to be made on three familiar terms – *the designer, design fictions (existing) and speculation(s)* – which will frame how this critique will be enunciated.

1. It is common in the rhetoric of design discourse to evoke **the designer** as generic, and thereafter claim they all possess the same unifying general qualities and a shared ontology. But while there are creative, visionary, forward-looking designers, there are equally many who occupy the subject position 'designer' who lack some or all of these attributes. There is no unified 'designer' subject.

The distinctions between an inherent ability of our species to prefigure action and to acquire the facility to become a design professional have been blurred, by: childhood induction (within cultures of privilege) that inflates the belief that creative expression and designing capability, by default, form an adult with an illusory self-image; economies that reify, valorize and commodify creativity; and technology that facilitates user-choice 'creative outputs' by means of basic templates through to sophisticated designer software, which simulate the appearance of the actions of an independent creative subject. None of this is to say that there are not creative children, or cultural commodities that contribute to advancing creative capacity, or technologies that enable creative expression. However, the difference has been made harder to discern, not least in the design professions where the banal, the trivial and, above all, the servicing of defuturing hyper-consumptivity are elevated as evidence of creativity. In truth, the numbers of designers who act to counter those forces that maintain the extension of the homonoidosphere are extremely small. Dominantly, design creativity is still a handmaiden to a defuturing economy and its associated cultures of mostly unrecognized everyday destruction.

2. Existing **design fictions** are a creation, with an extensive undocumented past, and a name and presence often attributed to Bruce Sterling as voiced in his book *Shaping Things* (2005). However, the way he and almost all authors address the future is inadequate and assumes that how it is understood is self-evident, whereas the future is not a void: it is neither empty nor full, or open to be filled with infinite possibilities. Rather the future is more akin to an 'obstacle course', one created by what our past and present actions have thrown, or are throwing, into it, and their material effects upon a continual arrival in the present. The most evident manifestation of this process is seen in ecological impacts of the pollution of the land, oceans and the atmosphere, which is now especially being experienced as the consequence of a changing climate resulting from atmospheric emissions over the distant and recent past and present. In this respect much of the future already exists in the inchoate present as it arrives from that unfolding past active in the everlasting time of now – *jetztziet* (Benjamin 1973: 263).

In very many ways, and globally, we are all being affected by events we know and feel will arrive. But they always arrive in the specificity of a 'here', which is to say 'the future' is always 'the now of somewhere'. But clearly the future is also subject to change (including by our own actions) that may or may not be known with any degree of certainty. Of course the possibility of the unexpected ever remains present.

The more one thinks about the future the more one realizes it carries substantial epistemological problems. Certainly there is no 'general and universal knowledge' about it, nor is any 'general knowing subject' contemplating it: all cultures, theologies and cosmologies lay claim to a particular view of 'the' future, the known and unknown, the fixed and change, the expected and the unexpected. Just as the future mostly (and certainly Eurocentrically) goes unconsidered, so also does time, history and the ontological agency of design as worlding. The futures that 'design futures' conceptualize, propose and narrate are almost always disarticulated from complexity and from those futures already present, unfolding and disconnected from the counter-forces of futures of difference. Walter Benjamin's oft-cited reading of Paul Klee's painting, *Angelus Novus*, while written in the middle of the twentieth-century, ever resonates with critically viewing how the future is understood (1973: 259–60):

> His eyes are staring, his mouth is open, his wings spread. This is how one pictures the angel of history. His face is turned toward the past. Where we perceive a chain of events, he sees one single catastrophe which keeps piling wreckage upon wreckage, and hurls it in front of his feet. The angel would like to say, awaken the dead, and make whole what has been smashed. But a storm is blowing from Paradise, it has got caught in his wings with such violence that the angel can no longer close them. This storm irresistibly propels him into the future to which his back is turned, while the pile of debris before him grows skyward. This storm is what we call progress.

Linear time is but one mode of representing the future in the medium of time; the everlasting now (the only moment of time open to experience) and the circular time of biological systems are equally significant to acknowledge. Certainly there is no singular desired future. So said, the point is to keep 'the future' open to plural exploration in cultures of difference. The future of our species, and life as it is currently known, is finite – this is made clear by our age being defined as that of the 'Anthropocene' (an exclusive anthropos 'universal' grounded in an epistemology indebted to modernity, hence its displacement of hominoidosphere) and the announcement by evolutionary biologists that this moment marks the commencement of the planet's sixth extinction event.

Almost all design fictions currently existing, mostly unknowingly, are situated in a context wherein the form of the future is being contested by those forces striving to continue with 'business as usual', supported by a technocentric notion of salvation, as opposed to those who, by degree, recognize that without fundamental directional change, our future, and that of many other species, are being continually delimited and being increasingly placed at absolute risk.

3. Design fictions are speculations and thus understanding **speculation** is crucial if design fictions are to have any agency with foundational substance. Central to this understanding is the anchoring of speculative thinking in 'experience' as opposed to being interpreted (Whitehead 1978: 3). As such,

experience is viewed as an actual occasion (an event) and thus existentially situated in specific conditions of relational complexity, thereby able to be rendered as an object of critical reflection or projection. This means that what will be thought is *a view of experience placed outside its conditions of limitation*, which can only possibly arrive for critical examination if the contextual conditions are interrogated relationally.

Alfred North Whitehead's seminal work, *Process and Reality*, was based on a series of lectures given in the late 1920s that detailed and demonstrated the application of Speculative Philosophy. While Whitehead is seen as a key figure in establishing and developing the significance of speculative thought, the concept preceded him. The American educator William Torrey Harris founded *The Journal of Speculative Philosophy* (a quarterly publication of the Philosophical Society) in 1867 and edited it until 1893. Influenced by Hegelian dialectics, Harris saw philosophy as a relational way of thinking able to 'transcend all natural limits' (Moffat 2019: 2).

Speculation is a term that does not glide across contexts with anything like a common meaning. The term usually arrives in the worlds of finance and gambling as taking a risk, buying stock, making a punt, placing a wager; in common parlance it names a wondering about varied possibilities and questions of 'what if'. But philosophically/theoretically it arrives as an object of serious enquiry and as a particular methodological address to epistemology. In this respect, use and meaning are open to being contested. For example, consider this statement (Wilkie et al. 2017: 8):

Speculation is not a matter of determining what is, and what is not, possible, as if possibility could always be ascertained in advance of events, that is, from the impasse of the present. By contrast, speculation is here associated with a sensibility concerned with resisting a future that presents itself as probable or plausible, and to wager instead that, no matter how pervasive the impasse may be, it can never exhaust the unrealised potential of the present.

From remarks already made, it's evident that such a view gives the future an independent voice whereas it, like history, is always expressed from a particular point of view. Moreover, the future is not experienced as universal (the abstraction has no content), 'we' existentially do not all occupy the same present. So while the present may always have an unrealized potential, the defuturing events of structural unsustainability significantly quantitatively diminish it.

Against this backdrop, the global struggle for decoloniality by the neo-colonialized peoples of the world is not so much for an alternative future but rather against the continuation of an imposed present, together with gaining a condition of autonomy that would make contemplating and realizing another kind of future possible (Mignolo and Walsh 2019). Creativity, inventiveness, visions and fictions are not enough; neither are appeals to resistance from the margins and the marginal against the combined now multi-cultural forces of the behemoth of late modernity that still steers global futures. The starting point is not with creating a vision of an alternative future or a design fiction, but with a conjunctural analysis of the directive force of the status quo, and the specific conditions of limitation coming from an identification of the ontological conditions and intellectual resources held in a situated present. Thereafter, the political leverage in which transformative agency can be strategically constituted and directed can be contemplated. Contrary to arguments that try to find and constitute the means to create an alternative future assemblage in the ruins of the now hegemonically instrumentalized academy, and within the institutions of now debased social democracy (Diprose 2017), the locus of the construction of progressive action, as will be argued, is in the formation of borderlands (cultural, political, epistemological) by the marginalized, oppressed and intellectually alienated.

Speculative research, as linked to future-casting, reveals an instrumental reduction of speculative thought that directly connects to its use in risk analysis and management (both economic and environmental). Speculative design has been touched by this appropriation, and more generally by speculative product and market developments in the service of corporate capital. But more positively it has also been linked with 'new materialism' (Meillassoux 2012: 72; Moffat 2019: 3) with its understanding of 'the life of things' (a partial reworking of Heidegger's notion of the 'thinging of things'; 1971: 163–87), and similar to a contemporary understanding of ontological design (Willis 2007: 80–98). While speculative design is presented as 'a method' with the promise of engaging substantial global, socio-cultural or meta-design problems, it so often spirals down to 'solutions' delivered by new products and services, and 'speculative techno-visions' aiming to go beyond the perception and limits of existing technology. In turn these 'innovations' degenerate into gizmos, like a wallet that provides banking details, a devise that tracks and monitors diets and health indicators or an artificial biological clock.

Design fiction positioned

Design fiction is yet to be fully developed as a means of research in and beyond design, which means not necessarily by design theorists. It has a place in fiction yet to be recognized, and not as a 'poor relation' to a literary elite. Rather it is a form of writing able to add to a tradition of literary works with political intent. In doing so there is no implication that such novels' potential transformation design agency is in any way compromised.

Fiction, the fictive and design fiction

At the most fundamental level, design fiction is not a recent innovation but is grounded in the very origins of the meaning of the word 'fiction'. Etymologically it comes from the Latin *fictionem,* a fashioning from the meaning of *fingere* to shape, form, devise; and also from *fictilis,* made of clay, a factor (maker) or moulder (evident in the seventeenth-century English usage of *fictor* as sculptor). By the thirteenth century there is the word *ficcion* (French) meaning invention, fabrication; then two centuries later, *ficcioun* is an invention of the mind. By the sixteenth century this meaning extended to prose works created by the imagination and then in the seventeenth (English) *fictum* means deception, fiction. In contrast, the meaning of design is modern, with its origins in the sixteenth-century middle French, *desseign.*

The fictive: the imagined world of the fiction

The fictive, ficlif (seventeenth-century French) and fictivus (Latin), exists in almost every form of imagined fictional, cultural expression and production. Yet the imaginary itself does not signify the fictive but 'rather the positing of new forms' (Castoriadis 1997: 84). Although the form it takes is different according to the medium in which it is expressed the fictive has 'no status in ontology' (223). It therefore is not contained by those things that directly identify themselves as fiction. Fiction is equally irreducible and in terms of fundamental representational forms (like life and death, and biological and social being) all such forms can be seen at 'the beginning' of their creation and thus arrive as representations of 'the real' (Agamben 2006: 105) – a clipped echo of 'in the beginning was the word' (John 1.1). It should be added that neither the fictive nor fiction are culturally universal categories with common or contested meaning.

Second order design fiction as conceptually outlined, and as will be exemplified, is the fictive given a particular narrative form and function, one with a specific aim of presenting a believable future to a designer/reader that their imagination can occupy and elaborate. Specifically, the narrative of the second order design fiction is produced by weaving two narratives together: an account of the need to move a city due to rising sea levels; and the description of an event in which the process of moving the city is described. In common with many other text-based fictions, while the moving city fiction will be known not to be true, or carry truth claims, its fictive qualities should and do strive to evoke a thinkable reality. Thus, aesthetically it can be understood to operate within a realist literary paradigm in which truths can be recognized. However, this does not mean that what has been imagined may or could not actually occur. In this respect it is more than a descriptive scenario because it invites a reader to identify with worldly conditions and the created world as constituted by fiction's literary form and elements: plot, setting, temporal events and characters. What this means is that it will have to be well crafted with seductive power that propels the reading of a fictional text. Obviously, this requires design fictions sharing stylistic characteristics with literary texts, while not sharing the same literary ambitions.

Clearly such a fiction also exists with a design function that reveals, and can be viewed by, the construction of a narrative centred on fictional representation – one that provides a credible simulation of a possible or even probable future. Foundationally the narrative would not be based on pure invention but on situated fictional elaborations of known facts, trends and risks about emergent contexts and circumstances. Thereafter, subjective reflection and critical review would be brought to a demand for design to prefiguratively respond to especially negative futures.

While a second order design fiction can be considered as an addition to advancing a futural design process, it can equally be seen as a means of extending the existing reach of a designer's imagination – this recognizing that design itself is a fictive practice that prefigures *a something yet to be made present*. Likewise, it may also prompt research. In this respect it is not just extension, supplement or compliment to a visual representation but a generative source.

How is design understood, nascently appropriated and engaged?

Design ontologically is not something that has been created. Rather, it is a cognitive capability intrinsic to our species' being, manifest in the ability to prefigure the desired form of the outcome of an action. As such it became elemental to the practice of making as the idea of the form and function of the made that went ahead of its creation, which may or may not be modified in the process. The activity of conceiving, directing and ordering eventually became formalized by a representational practice integral to the act of making. Design as designing became reified when this practice was disarticulated from making and was given an independent status and named (in various ways in different languages) as 'design'. Design can be directive of things material and immaterial. The practice and discourse of design in no way embraces the worldly totality of design as enacted and realized.

Design does not end with the arrival of the designed – object, product, structure, image. As the consequence of its coming into being, design itself has designing effect(s)/affects, be they functional, aesthetic, social, cultural, economic or environmental.

Design is a means by which fiction becomes fact

Design arrives in a specific world in the specificity of a particular form. It is not, and cannot be, universal. This is because what something is deemed to mean is cosmologically and culturally inflected. So qualified, difference in meaning can be major or minor and is not held in 'the thing itself'. Instead culture brings meaning to the thing. The dominant mode of address to design is Euromodernistically grounded, and as such it fails to recognize global inequity and differential understandings of fact and fiction. All of these differences are evident in, for instance, the relation between science and 'magic and the magical'. 'Sophisticated' cultures present themselves as having transcended the power of magic, whereas it has been recoded and appears rhetorically constrained in both science (in relation to materials and properties that seem to defy reason), and in religion (in relation to belief in the power of 'God' underscored by theology). Fiction, so framed, is deeply embedded in mischaracterization. It is posed as the binary opposite to fact, to truth and the possible, whereas it can be, and often is, implicated in a process of transition/transformation to a realization in fact. This is very different from the ethos of the political right, especially in recent history in the United States, that upholds an Orwellian inversion of meaning: 'received truth is asserted as a lie, and the delivered lie is proclaimed as the truth'. This process not only negates the binary division but also renders governance dysfunctional as American history has demonstrated.

Fiction can be in the service of truth. Mediated by design, fiction has the ability to create the conditions that make the seemingly impossible possible as an actuality or appearance. Second order design fiction has no predetermined or particular form. It can present the past as the future, the present as the past, the future as now or the future as futural. All of which says it can do the same as any other form of fiction. Whatever it produces can never be universal in conception or perception. Moreover, no matter the ubiquity of what is brought into being it can never be universally perceived as the same and neutral. The perceived locus of its point of origination is as much a part of what is encountered as its form and content. The agency of a design fiction will always be conjunctural – it will thus always be situated somewhere. Such fictions can appear to be utopian (meaning that by being able to be realized they are not truly utopian, since the inability to be able to be brought into being is the fundamental flaw of utopias) or as dystopic (fated conditions of negation, disaster and helplessness) or even as heterotopias (that which is otherwise, disorientating, strange or confounding).

Having no given form or purpose, but always with form being posited, a second order design fiction can be progressive or regressive. It is always of an economy, predicated upon an exchange relation, but never just reduced to a monetary transaction. These design fictions can equally create or expose an illusion of reality, or disrupt particular forms of their construction or projection. They can also acknowledge the *ontic* as an absolute affirmation of the real as unreachable reality.

Adding to understanding of the 'truth and fiction' relation, it has become indivisible as a result of digital representational technologies – photography, video, sound. What is seen and heard can now never be assumed and taken to be true at the level of a correspondence between referent and representation. Yet life is now lived by many people, in this age of a post-semiotic condition of the image, without knowledge or recognition of this situation. Neither the photographic image nor the video can be taken to be true, so that viewers dwell in a state of akrasia, which is to say they know they cannot believe their eyes but fail to act on the basis of this knowledge. Prefigured by Marshall McLuhan's writing in the 1960s, and by Jean Baudrillard's in later decades, the real was made to disappear. This became evident in the rise and construction of hyper-reality: 'that which makes it possible to give an equivalent reproduction of the same as displacement' (Baudrillard 1983: 146). Hereafter, the real arrives as simulation; the unreal is taken to be real, making it the hyperreal. Mostly what can be learnt from McLuhan and Baudrillard has been rendered banal, normalized, dismissed or forgotten. In many ways their thinking, as it foresaw the coming of the contemporary media environment, was ahead of how it is now seen and taken. Against such a backdrop, design fiction needs to be understood as a contribution of a means to be able to discover and explore appropriate pathways to ethically futural action, but in conditions that are uncertain. It can be deployed to explore the acuteness of a crisis in order to directly critically respond with a mode of imagination and modes of action that may (or may not) offer forms of adaptation or 'solutions'. Here, and in general, there can be no unqualified appeal to imagination.

Richard Kearney (1988), from a Eurocentric universalism, announced imagination exhausted and in its wake taken to the present, his teleological account has been overtaken by a more complex view in the recognition that imagination is globally and culturally situationally relative (Fry and Tlostanova 2021). There is no common form of appeal. Any claim to a master narrative of imagination is a fiction, but one in continual use and based on the assumption that, like thinking, imagination is intrinsic to the mind. But unlike thinking, which does not exist independent of epistemological difference, imagination is taken as a variable quotient of the same. What such an assumption does is disarticulate imagination from its worldly placement geo-culturally and techno-semiotically. The 'stuff' of imagination comes from what one's being-in-the-world has been exposed to as the basis of what the imagination assembles, transforms and reacts against in its process of prefigurative construction.

Thus, the individuation of the imagination of an individual, as difference within a cultural commonality, is authored by the sum of an individual's ontologically formative worldly experiences within their own and external conditions of limitations and possibility. Taken to imagining a future other than the one that is already present, inchoate and seemingly determined, what is formed is an imagination that is situated, and as such different from that of an Other.

None of what has been outlined occurs in conditions of neutrality. For the vast proportion of the global population, the formation of imagination is politically contested and in numerous ways colonized, albeit ideologically, economically, epistemologically or culturally. This process, which is clearly not a singular organized conspiracy, has become elemental to the being-in-the-world of most of us. One overt example of an instrument of the process is capitalism's appropriation of 'creativity' in establishing the 'creative industries' to colonize the imaginaries' imagination for economic ends. Within the standardized world of difference of the culture industry is the intent to establish, by default, a consumer-desired similitude that overrides and erases imaginaries of difference (Jullien 2014: 13), namely a commodity looking different in order to be the same (tattoos being a literal example). By bonding to hyper-consumption not only has this 'development' taken Adorno and Horkheimer's thesis of the deception of 'The Culture Industry' (1972) to a higher order, but has further subordinated culture and colonized imaginaries to defuturing wherein acquisition advances negation.

Placed in a larger frame, what is being described is part of the 'already here' of the afterlife of a neoliberal view of the world (the North co-opting the South) in the pragmatic post-globalism of the end state of non-realized late Euromodern and world-ordering attainments. But this as a fading order attempting to maintain economic hegemony in a situation of growing dysfunction and national and international instability wherein substantial repeatable short-term crises, like COVID-19, fold into long-term ones, as with climate change. The conditions created by a neoliberal economic hegemony and its associated ontologies aimed to erase an ability to think, act and imagine in any other way of being. This is nowhere more evident than in governance globally, nationally and locally. Data-driven policy and metric-driven economic determinism arrive in forms deadened by a political imagination of difference (Tlostanova and Fry 2020). Digital technology arrived to accompany and support this political economy of conformity especially evident in corporate culture and education from kindergarten to doctoral level. Contrary to claims that this technology liberates imagination, it is destructive of it in the restrictive form it authors. The digitally constituted ecology of the image creates a condition of absolute saturation. What results is a simulation of imagination where what is imagined is a product of the already imagined as montaged, hacked, repurposed, reformed and re-constructively appropriated. The product of this imagination is a simulacrum: a hyperreal, an ungrounded copy of an unoriginal original (Baudrillard 1983: 3).

Dominantly the address to imagination dislocated it from cosmologies of difference. The appeal is to a discourse that is ethnocentric. The very notion of imagination is universalized and the plurality of its form flattened with its inherent process of change sought to be arrested (Fry and Tlostanova 2021: 156). As suggested, it is as if imagination was a quality of mind common, by degree, to everyone everywhere, whereas it is plural, diverse and differentially culturally formed: 'to be imagined' arrives out of different worlds. Kearney's genealogy of imagination, while originally progressive from a Eurocentric perspective, can now be seen as inadequate. Configured at the largest scale, imagination operates in the circumstances of a community as it is constituted, replicated or transformed. Individual acts of imagination have always been integral to this differential context and our species' ability to survive. The ability to imagine things as other than they are and then move to change them politically are the bedrock of imagination.

Evidence of a widespread and current lack of political imagination is discernible in the environ-climatic and geopolitical crisis of 'now'. It is expressed in the impetus to attempt to stay the same in a situation that demands substantial redirective change. Re-enforcing this disposition is a particular form of instrumental restrictive imagination that posits technology as the means of salvation. Not only is this techno-utopianism but, even if it were viable, it folds into the abandonment of all those nations unable to afford such technology. Even more dramatically, this view goes to a willingness to abandon the planet itself – an imaginary fed by science fiction fantasies visualized and globalized by Hollywood. The nihilism that accompanies this predisposition exposes a willingness to write off the sustainment of 'what is' in the expectation of achieving a utopian (likely dystopic) future elsewhere. Thus '*the what* that is imagined' negates the imperative of imagining that worldly change needs to be imagined.

Understanding that life is now lived in a pluriverse of bio- and socio-cultural diminishing diversity presents fictions with an ethical challenge that fold into the imperative of sustainment, with an aim of negating actions destructive of the natural and socio-historical processes that create diversity. Here is a significant project to which design fiction can be directed to respond in common with other generative forms of fiction, including literary. It also links to the seeding of difference by the production of desired imaginaries with realizable potential. Here then is a realism that sits between utopianism and dystopic imaginaries that may well deploy heterotopias.

The implication of these remarks shifts the emphasis placed on fiction in design fiction to counter the relation underscoring a good deal of technocentric and object-centred approaches to extant design fiction.

Anthony Dunne and Fiona Raby in *Speculative Everything* (2013: 69–88) sojourned across the media of fictional worlds, concluding that they preferred 'backdrop over narrative', and posing design as between cinema and literary fiction – saying cinema makes little demand on imagination whereas literature makes lots. They went on to designate a difference between literary fiction and design in that for design 'its medium exists in the here and now' (a view that attracted criticism (Tonkinwise 2014) that is totally at odds with the need to learn how to 'design in time'). Moreover, they want a contemplated future to be manifest in 'everyday life'. There are several fundamental problems with this kind of thinking. First, it rests with a restrictive view of design associated with institutional and disciplinary confinement. Design elementally directs, in some form, the entire constructed world our species brings into being. This is not to say design is everything. It is to say everything is touched in some way by design. Second, design is not purely of the here and now; it is also in its ongoing agency a 'thing' with agency that futures or defutures. As such, in its temporality it extends or negates what our finitude creates. Put starkly: design as affect takes (our) time away, or extends it. The final problem is the reference to everyday life, which is a meaningless generalization. My everyday life is not yours: universally the only thing that is universal is difference.

Designing literary fiction

To make the argument clearer, here is a brief design fiction over-reading of a small selection of works of literary fiction, starting with Mary Shelley, famous for her authorship of *Frankenstein; or, The Modern Prometheus* (1818).

The imagination that produced this extraordinary work, published when she was twenty-one, was formed from induction into the influence of her free-spirited mother, the feminist philosopher, Mary Wollstonecraft, who died of a fever shortly after giving birth to her daughter. As a philosopher Mary Wollstonecraft was a foundational key figure in the creation of futural imaginaries for women. One can only speculate how Mary Shelley's imaginary and indirectly acquired knowledge of her mother formed her own sense of self and her imagination. Another factor was the influence of her father, a writer, philosopher and publisher of Wollstonecraft's *Memoirs of the Author of A Vindication of the Rights of Woman* (1798). Added to this was Mary's interest in science in the shadow of the attainments of the Enlightenment. Here then was a milieu out of which feminism, speculative thought and a futural imaginary converged to create the condition from which *Frankenstein* emerged and to foster her reputation as a founding figure of the vibrant genre of Feminist Speculative Fiction.

Ursula Le Guin and Margaret Atwood are perhaps the best-known inheritors of this tradition.[1] One example makes this clear: Atwood's 2003 dystopic novel *Oryx and Crake*. It centres around three characters: 'Snowman' (Jimmy, an advertising copywriter), Crake (Glenn, a bioengineer) and Oryx (a one-time porn star who becomes a teacher of 'primitive human-like creatures' and is Snowman's sexual partner). The trio's eventual disastrous relationship is set against the background of Crake's involvement with the activities of his employer, RejoovenEsense, a company that manufactures a drug that engineers the creation of the Crakers. Glenn also creates a Viagra-like super-pill named BlyssPluss marketed as producing health and happiness, but which actually sterilizes the people who take it. Even worse, once globally distributed, BlyssPluss's real function becomes apparent. It has been designed to cause a pandemic to wipe out the human race; chaos then ensues. Snowman realizes Crake had always planned to do this and that both were made immune, but not Oryx. The final act: Crake slits the throat of the dying Oryx and Jimmy the Snowman grabs a gun and shoots Crake. What this compressed summary does not convey is a sense of the progression of the arrival of a bioengineered future (captured in the book by a factory making headless and limbless chickens), and the precariousness of a future where a tiny mistake or malevolent act could lay 'the world' to waste.

The slippage between designing futures and defutures is a fine one so often predicated upon an underdeveloped ethical judgement. Second order design fiction placed in this context can be cast as the projection, narrativization and interrogation of the futural consequences of the design rather than prototyping the form, function, use, immediate impacts or market or user perceptions of the designed.

Literary speculative fiction has the ability to present the past as the future arriving in the present. Robert Harris's novel *The Second Sleep* (2019) exposes the challenges, possibilities and pitfalls of such fiction delivered by another dystopic but slowly unfolded narrative. It is based on an apocalyptic event creating a material condition of regression taking a society back to the conditions of the fifteenth century technically, socially and theologically, in which the archaeology of the past was the detritus of a destroyed modern world. The design future prompted in this kind of account is a projected designed future based on the recovery of knowledge, concepts and technologies of the ancient world remade now. There are already partial examples of this practice. For instance, over one thousand years ago during the Sung dynasty, buildings were constructed with interchangeable component elements (Fry 2009: 158–63). What this meant was a building that could be disassembled and reassembled in a different location in a different form. As a construction method this capability is in advance of current design for disassembly technology. There is a huge literature of the distant, and not so distant past, scattered in collections around the world with material that has the ability to feed the creation of design futures not around products (although there would be some), but as ideas in their difference, content or strangeness, prompting ways of thinking otherwise.

Three other novels can be seen as literary works with designing consequences. The first is obscure but in its crassness is interestingly so. The remaining three, while written several decades ago, still in different ways, have salience.

Somehow Crystal (translated), a novel by the Japanese writer Tanaka Yasuo (1980), is an explicitly designed work of fiction overly about designing consumer conduct.[2] The narrative is banal. It centres on the 'heroine' being separated from her musician boyfriend who goes away on a two-week tour. During this time she has a relationship with a boy she meets in a disco. The story unfolds around their patterns of consumption. They are walking down a street and there is a footnote interjection: 'if you feel like an ice cream the place to go is' – this followed by the naming of a specific ice cream. Whatever the product, where it can be obtained, the address of the business and its telephone number are given. The same pattern of narrative disruption occurs throughout the book. It is all about an ephemeral text naming the fashions and trends of the moment and designing of taste and conduct. Celebrated as an icon of postmodern literature, critics hated and panned it, but 800,000 copies were sold. The work can now be seen as in part prefiguring the current existence of social media influencers.

The second work is Tayeb Salih's *Season of Migration to the North*, first published in 1969, and reprinted in 2009. The novel is a work of post-colonial literature that in a certain way has been recoded as a result of the arrival of the discourse of decoloniality. In introducing the book, Laila Lalami writes: 'the persistent metaphor in the novel is that of colonialism as a disease – it spreads from one people to the next and from one continent to the next, leaving behind a steady trail of violence and destruction' (Salih 2009: xix). This infection is played out in the novel in the life of Mustafa Se'eed a brilliant Sudanese economist who had a stellar career in London that ended as a result of a disastrous relationship with one European woman. As a result, he returned to live on the edge of a village in Sudan on the Nile. What is played out in the novel is an auto-destructive ontological impossibility of betweenness created by non-acceptance of difference by the culture of migration (the North) and the culture of origin (the South) into which Mustafa literally totally disappears. He leaves tragedy behind him in both the spaces of his life. What confronting such a work makes clear is the vacuousness of so much call to, and rhetoric of, decoloniality in the global North. Like 'sustainability' the meaning of decoloniality has been emptied out by the generalized, loose and uncritical use of the term. This situation presents a political position (including in design) that not only recognizes that the conditions of postcoloniality have never been achieved, but colonialism has managed to continually reinvent itself, and be reinvented, even in the language that appears to critically engage it. At the most basic level, one challenge of design fiction is to explore, develop and reveal decoloniality as an ontology, sensibility and epistemological ground embedded in a practice that transforms 'betweenness' into a conceptual and material borderland space. In this space transformative agency can be created and (per)formed in situated projects as an 'acting back' on actors (as the ontologically designed) and an 'acting forward' (as ontological designing) of materialities.

The last is William Gibson's cyberpunk novel *Neuromancer* of 1984. It was hugely influential, specifically as a source of techno-futural ideas, which it embraced, articulated and amplified, in particular the exposition of a term he had already created – cyberspace. In many ways the novel contributed to the creation of the technoculture of Silicon Valley, a general source of the imaginaries of contemporary techno-romanticism, but above all as the generative force of a new techno-futural imaginary that has become elemental to twenty-first century culture in the global North and in large parts of the South. Not only is the prime narrative of the novel set somewhere in the future, the story centres on the end-career of Henry Case (a burnt-out hacker) taking him into a struggle against the force of artificial intelligence that, counter-productively, at the time was against the drift of the story. The contest that was central to the plot now resonates even more powerfully and ambiguously with the current technocentric age. Clearly here is another design fiction waiting to be (and in some ways is being) appropriated, resituated and elaborated.

Beyond the fragments

Design process, speculative design, critical design, design futures and scenario design are all examples of non-discrete, often confused and contested concepts and practices within the plurality of design as a discipline and profession. Moreover, invested ownership of terms, that constitutes a defence of sub-disciplinary positions, obstructs the very possibility of design critically addressing any kind of conjuncturally situated imagined futures that advance its affirmative transformative agency as practice and affect.

Rather than this situation being generalized, and then attempted to be resolved by logical argument, it will in actuality be altered as a result of particular circumstantial analysis, changes of thought and practice, and cultivated imagination. Bringing such an approach to the politics of decoloniality in the conditions of limitation of a former colonized nation, or to modes of cognitive colonization of particular technologies in clearly defined circumstances, I cite examples that invite such an engagement. Design so positioned requires to be understood as existing in a relational matrix that is always differentially constituted.

Currently the fundamental and dominant divisions of design, its thinking and practice, centre on a subservient relation to the economic status quo. As such they are defined by the conventions and research agendas of the academy and the marketplace, and while counter practices do exist, they are marginal or become incorporated (sustainable design being a clear example). The defuturing character and consequences of the designed and designing go largely untheorized, unthought and unnoticed. Decade after decade a hapless call to adequately reductively define design arrives. The discussion goes nowhere. Speculation *on* design is not informed by a framing based on 'a coherent, logical necessary system of general ideas' and the interpreted experience of its relational complexity (Whitehead 1978: 3). For most of the design 'community' solipsism, relativism and instrumental reduction are the norm. Design cannot be claimed as being under the ownership of any specific discourse (including its own) or epistemology. So, in its indeterminacy what can be said? To answer this question is to understand design as both something (the realized as object, process and consequence) and nothing (a reducible essence). In actuality, design is the one and the many as: 'an event' of prefigured becoming; an event of ontological determination; an event of imposition and direction; and an event of assemblage. Yet so much of the language, practice, promotion, study and, above all, divisions of knowledge of design conceal 'it' as an event. In the context of moving a city (the 'design fiction' to follow), cities are essentially seen and understood as (designed and designing) event(s) of redirection. Thus, so framed, the *moving event* of a city is a futural transformation of what a city is as a locus of (un)settlement and all that animates its life.

The narratives of existing design fictions are mostly exposited as a means to provoke and prompt dialogue with 'an audience' (be it general, a focus group, corporate, students and so on) and on specific design objects (in their widest and most particular sense). But a second order understanding, while not rejecting this intent, goes much further. Such a fiction can provide a specific, larger and more complex object of critical reflection and interrogation. In this respect the author(s) can equally, or primarily be, the audience – this especially when the author(s) are associated with an autonomous practice. When more broadly used as a heuristic, the fiction is a means of self-learning. As such these fictions enable the event of the onward (ontological) designing of the designed to be rigorously explored and directionally elaborated, thus facilitating the forecasting of possible consequences, which then inspire a back-casted revision of the designed.

Such narrativized design fictions become elemental to a data-informed and speculative practice of 'designing back from the future'.

Second order design fiction is not bonded to prototypes, or to technology. Prototypes are presented as objects of a pluralistic expansion of meaning as they have been extended to embrace any kind of examination of material or immaterial objects of projection and reflection. A particular kind of prototype has been 'invented' to serve extant design fictions – the 'diegetic prototype'. It has no material form, and exists to 'suspend disbelief about change' (Sterling 2011: 18). Sterling tells us that design fictions are about 'mutability' (25). They are equally claimed to be the stuff of 'popular imaginary more comfortable on the realm of Hollywood films, best-selling novels etc.' (Bleecker 2017: 28). The proposition is that there is a correct way the reader/viewer/audience should understand and engage the fiction, organized around narrative elements such as plot, form, structure and characters. Sterling's naming of design fiction in 2005 lacked a definition (Levin 2016: 1), and his later qualification,[3] and competing voices asserting meaning, have not resolved confusion. Likewise, the claim that design fictions are able to transcend disciplinary boundaries in their present form is overblown (Bleecker 2017: 31). Contradictory views of and fuzzy theorizing about design fiction simply expose the lack of, and need for, the creation of a sound epistemological base for the practice.

More specifically, the faith in technology and 'techno-humanism' as a basis of design fiction fails to grasp the extent of the overdeterminism of the ontological designing of instrumentalism. What this faith displays is what Carl Schmitt ([1919] 1986) described as 'political romanticism'. This is characterized by positing agency with transformative action conceived and deployed from an egocentrically constructed fictional view of the world. By implication, this means that the ground upon which a design fiction is constituted is itself a fiction, as well as a deceit. Such a critique also exposes the wider problematic of the subject position from which the future is viewed – one that is always from a synthesis of a particular epistemology and the experiential (which includes an ecology of culturally plural imagery). There is no overall and independent future. As already said, 'the future' is always 'the now of somewhere'. My future, as determined by my changing state and conditions of being, is not yours; Tasmania's future is not that of the Brazilian Amazon. Nothing can and does encounter and occupy the future as an abstraction, a totality or void. 'The future' is meaningless without it 'being now' and, situated as such, is plural. For 'us' the sum of the impacts of our actions makes our future materialize in the continual arrival of its situated difference.

Design fictions are intrinsically 'political' in the sense that anything aiming to influence the future is. But second order design fictions are explicitly political in that they contest futures. They are certainly not just about social interaction, innovatory products, possible technologies or worlds of unlimited potential.

Rather their intent is also to enunciate possible, needed and desired forms of sustainment that recognize the relational complexity of our age, while adding to knowledge that negates the defuturing forms of unsustainment in ways that, via critical interrogation, inform transformative action. By implication, these alternative forms can be positioned in opposition to design's support and servicing of the economy and culture of the anthropocentric, Euromodern, ethnocentric and techno-colonial status quo.

The second order of 'second order design fiction'

As stated at the start of this prologue, the term 'second order design fiction' draws on the thinking, and use of the term, from second order cybernetics. As such the production of the fiction is a recursive exercise of critical auto observation and reflection – the observation of observation that does not presume an external viewpoint (Luhmann 1989) that returns what is created, and how, to an author, so s/he can reflectively observe their observations, including on processes and objects of creation. The intent is directed toward a process of unlearning, new learning, redirecting or remaking. The production of the fiction of (the) design fiction, as a recursive exercise of critical observation and reflection, returns what is learnt from the fictive process, and what is created by it, to its designer/author. It does not mean that the process will mirror one of 'second order cybernetics' as such, but rather that certain lessons have been appropriated from it. The point of the process is to structure how articulating an understanding of a design problem is approached that does not take it as given, but interrogates the basis of its constitution and thereafter responds by creating a fictional narrative that poses a solution. This 'construction' does not take the solution as the resolution to the problem but treats it as an object of observation on the problem to be observed by a process of critical reflection. The point of the exercise is to identify 'the what and the how' of a design brief in order to approach the problem at a fundamental level – that is causally and not just as effect. At the most general this often means the exposure of the anthropocentric ground of the problem, and the problematic of anthropos embedded in Euromodernity.

Thus, moving a city is a propositional design problem that assumes the instrumental design problems of moving a city so as to task such an exercise within conventional divisions of knowledge. The design fiction approach, in envisioning design solutions, would reveal the prefigurative presence of design assumptions that critical observation would write out of design action, thus enabling the ultimate aim of a design fiction, the writing of the highly refined brief, for a well-defined and understood design problem. By implication this brief would not mirror the fiction but correct it and modify its proposal if appropriate. While such a fiction is not primarily produced to present to an audience it could be used to provoke dialogue. Used as a consultative instrument, this fiction is questionable as it could well be taken literally as a proposed solution of a known situated problem to an audience, and thus just be reacted against.

The scale of second order design fictions will generally not correspond with the prior forms of design fiction. They are certainly more likely, but not exclusively, to be attached to projects, structures and environments rather than products, services and technologies. They also could be expected to be more linked to political, rather than just economic ends. Likewise, the motivation for their creation could often be to assist the advancement of the autonomy of architects and designers, and thus go beyond service provision. So said, there is no way they can arrive with mechanisms of restricted use.

The main intent of second order design fiction begs restating as a process of elaboration, interrogation and recreation. It re-cycles itself as: another iteration, a changed form, a figure, or a theoretical extraction, an object of auto-pedagogy, or a mode of address to a restrictive audience that enables the possibility of a grounded theoretical exposition. By implication the 'why and for whom' of a second order design fiction does not necessarily correspond with readers of the prior forms of design fiction, but neither does it wish or seek to exclude them.

To advance their critical efficacy, second order design fictions are specifically conceived and directed toward conditions of criticality wherein the fate of some thing is able to contribute to securing viable enviro-social futures: irrespective of their form, something is always at stake. In doing so such fictions are, to restate, subordinate to a process articulated to a more rigorous engagement with the speculative. Likewise they are underscored by a complex understanding of time and the future. Above all, as indicated, as 'the designed and designing' they are viewed as 'events' (Fry 2017: 37–9, 258) directed against the still proliferating forces of defuturing (that is, forces that have been brought into being, in large part, by design), and as a means able to advance future conditions of sustainment.

Second order design fiction as fiction

A second order design fiction is a nascent genre in its own right. It tells a story, has a narrative, and a narrator, and is embedded in a particular theory of causality that conjoins design and text. As such it flows into a 'vortex around which other discourses orbit in ever closer proximity' (Richardson 2000: 169). It is constructed on the basis of 'narrative time', and works with a notion of plot, speaks with a particular voice, and addresses a reader's interest in and beyond the discourse of design. As such second order design fictions construct a series of related statements that expose the causality of design as an agency of world making and unmaking: this is done via the causal efficacy of narrative to transport the mind of the designer/reader toward a reflective understanding and potential worldly action. In this way design, as indicated, is understood and presented as 'event', and not merely as process or object. Here then is a convergence between the prefigurative agency of design as 'event', as a 'bringing into being', and the causality of narrative as a gathering of relational elements. This, in turn, forms a sequential (fluid or punctuated) account of narrativized occurrences, one that unfolds as temporal and causal.

The fictional representation of, organization and presentation of events go beyond a narrative that takes the reader to the end of the story. The bonding of a fiction to design and narrative concludes with an opening into an imaginary that can potentially initiate a design project, or more directly, reflection on the fiction being generative of a design brief. It follows that design and designing act to constitute and direct the interpretative scheme of the text. Thus, the narrative is historical (it draws on and recounts seeming occurrences of the past) while actually (as causality) being futural (as prefiguring a design 'event' of the future).

On the question of method

The specifics of the method employed in the creation of second order design fiction have to be selected for their situated particularity. But there are a number of methodological issues and transformational forces that can be considered when approaching such a form of fiction. Specifically:

- *setting, time and placement:* to be comprehensible and appropriately evaluated, second order design fiction needs to be seen as coming out of, influenced by, and functionally situated in relation to the forces and conditions of its context. In particular, this applies to the temporal conditions of exchange and relatedness in which it acts (this is what Whitehead calls 'prehension', and Heidegger names as 'worlding'). Nothing just is. Therefore, the starting point is never with the fictional projected 'thing' in itself.

- *all things created come out of a cultural context and go to a cultural orientation:* all that gives voice to, visually represents and animates the fiction needs to clearly express this.

- *exposure of the critical:* second order design fictions need to be based on an understanding of the critical conjunctural potentially of a transformative situation. This means grasping its significance as a critical agent.

- *epistemological basis:* second order design fiction requires making evident the epistemological base upon which it and its narrative are created.

- *unlearning, learning, heuristic value and learners:* one of the critical functions of these fictions is to prompt an unlearning of those modes of design that are directive of designing and the designed acting as a means of defuturing. This obviously implies a confrontation with one's habitus and the acquisition of a new learning through the creation, context and pedagogic substance of the fiction as produced by its author and its second order re-encounter as an object of learning.

- *conditions of limitation:* to counter the utopian propensity of design fictions there are conditions of limitation to which a subject should be acknowledged and responded to.

- *the political ambition and value of second order design fictions:* these require acknowledgement that is overtly expressed.

- *deploying the design fiction as prefigurative criticism:* one of the forms of agency of second order design fiction is to make the consequences of a proposed project evident, and specifically the subject of socio-environmental and socio-political criticism before it is actually created.

- *level of viability:* from a realist epistemological perspective a fiction begs consideration and appropriate exposure to criteria that test its viability.

- *process development:* the intent of a second order design fiction is not a matter of resolved prediction, that is getting 'it' right, but the development of a process centred on identifying what there is to think about, making this evident and using knowledge gained to create, direct, modify and remake directive action.

On the moving city fiction: a qualification

Over recent decades the difference between many cities has become far less distinct as corporate architecture, high-rise apartment blocks and new traffic systems have imposed themselves on, and in many cases overwhelmed, older cities with a more modest built fabric. In traversing the cities of the now 'old modern world', of which the USA is the prime example, what is discovered in, for instance, New York and Chicago is aging infrastructure and neglected structure behind facades. Many buildings of old and new cities expose the contradiction of contemporary building construction technology. While this technology is more advanced than at any time in history, the life of many of the buildings constructed is shorter than ever before. There are a number of reasons for this: building performance is given more significance than the quality of the built fabric; the economics of rapid construction time; and construction budgets based on specifications that keep input costs as low as possible while maximizing market value for the developer. These trends apply to both domestic and commercial building. But with the latter, building performance and appearance are especially given significance in the sale of the building and/or the marketing of space. There are two other factors affecting the life of commercial buildings. One is change in office design trends. Individual offices became 'unfashionable', as a mode of workplace organization when open-plan offices arrived. One of the implications of this change was that many structures with column spacing for individual offices were demolished and then replaced with buildings with clear-span space. Such change links to a pattern in the development industry that treats buildings the way the affluent treat cars. They are replaced on a regular basis by a new and more fashionable model. The restricted space of central business districts itself is used by developers to maintain this development pattern – Hong Kong being an extreme case of this. In a post-COVID 19 world another wave of change is likely to be seen. Segregated space and individual offices are going to return, home offices/spaces will become more like domestic architecture and some commercial builds will be retrofitted to be in whole or part residential.

The mode of construction outlined, while being predominantly of the economies of the global North and the wealthier 'newly industrializing nations', will influence urban development in some of the cities in the uneven economies of many poor nations of the global South. But along with this will be the other major dimension of rapid urbanization in these cities: a continued massive increase in the growth of informal settlements.

Most significantly, the form, built fabric, life and future of all cities everywhere on the planet will have to deal with the complex relational impacts of climate change. These will not just be environmental but will reconfigure relations within and between nations, alter geopolitical dynamics and create major issues of international security, plus having major economic consequences, and effects on food security and public health.

In Part 4 the focus of the move is on a fictional city called Harshon. In fact, Harshon is a composite place, loosely created from elements of some of the world's major delta cities, all with populations of multiple millions. Geographically, economically and culturally it is characterized by inference as a delta city. Harshon has been situated in a borderland between the periphery of a still-declining Global North and an even more unequal South of major powers with significant economies and failed states. In common with so many cities in the world, for historic, economic and logistical reasons, Harshon was situated and developed in an inappropriate environmental location. So introduced, delta cities are fed by rivers that often provide deep harbours. The silt of deltas (which often need dredging for shipping) is very fertile so agriculture flourishes. Originally this was one reason that deltas attracted settlement and commerce. Another reason was they are often fed by river systems that could be used to transport extracted resources to a port for export, long before the establishment of a road network. But equally, their advantages are also their vulnerability – they are prone to flooding, structures built on silt slowly sink and, with sea levels rising as a result of climate change, they are, and will increasingly become, at risk.

[FICTION STARTS ...]

2

The Story of Moving Harshon: A City in Crisis

Paul Auster writes In the Country of Last Things: *of a house that is there one day, but gone the next; of a street that you walked down yesterday, but is not there today.*

(AUSTER 1987)

Now, to introduce myself, my name is Carlos Rey. I am a 'rapporteur', a teller of stories: more about me later. When I agreed to tell the story of moving the city of Harshon I decided to gather together a group of people with specific knowledge on what I viewed as especially important aspects of the process. What they have to say, which took place at a special event, will be the main content of the story. Other elements of the event at which they spoke will put the moving city project in context. This document presents all of this material, with added comments from me.

As you will soon discover, moving a city is not about the transportation of built structures, although some structures can be moved in whole or part. Rather it is essentially about relocating, rebuilding, and recreating the life of an urban environment, its social fabric and diverse cultures so that people can sustain a futural and plural way of living productively, socially, politically, economically and culturally.

Setting the scene of the fiction

We arrive in a strange city; we look out of a train, bus, or car window as we move through its outer suburbs towards its centre. We are yet to smell the city, feel its air on our face, listen to its sound. Nevertheless, we look at the people on the street, at signs, shop windows and buildings – we form a first impression, make provisional judgements. It's not possible to drive you into Harshon but the wish that you form a first, but different, impression persists. Thus, its recent past and current present are given to the words below to realise.

Harshon profile

Like many delta cities, Harshon grew from a small port based on regional trade, and the commerce of traders and the attraction of its markets to the local and surrounding populations. People came bringing animals, produce and goods of all kinds to sell, or they arrived to buy. They came by sea, travelled down from the hills, or from across the flatlands. For almost a hundred years its expansion occurred in the shadow of colonialism and the economic power of the East India Trading Company. This period had a lasting impact on the planning and form of the city, the creation of ethnically diverse cultures therein, and the nature of its institutions, mode of governance, and obviously its economy. The spatial order imposed on the city during this period was extended by modernity as its port expanded, trade increased and industrialisation started to be embraced. Save for the old harbour wall and two churches, most of the architectural traces of colonialism have gone.

In time, the built forms of Euromodernism enveloped the city, in so doing it erased the old signs of the power of domination and replaced them with new ones. But inequity still was clearly evident. At one extreme were the signature 'world-architecture' tower blocks of multinational corporations and international banks, insurance companies and finance houses. The same aesthetic of 'envirotech' facades was also applied to the central retail hub, the city's two conference centres, four museums, three municipal art galleries, and airport, plus the two super-speed rail stations and twelve individual, family and commercial on-call solar-electric navigator (SEN) parking stacks (vehicles using any type of carbon based fuel were nationally banned in 2045). Then there was what the media called 'the ring of gold' – the high-end harbour-side and inner city luxury apartments.

As for the rest of the city it was made up of a small areas of old terraced and newer mixed medium-density housing, a scattering of low-rise mansions, a large area of cheap to expensive high-rise apartments, and the outer-ring high-rise estates. Like most reasonably affluent cities, almost all retail (clothing, pharmaceuticals, luxury goods, household goods, office supplies, dry and perishable foods and more) were acquired from 'big-box stores' via virtual shopping either online or from downtown display stores, informed by customer body-scan bio-metrics and a full data-profile selection. All purchases were delivered to the customer's stock box via auto or air trans-delivery. Local fresh-food marts, co-ops and farmers' markets had optional remote purchase and auto delivery services. As for green spaces there were many, and a few continue to exist, but under heat stress, and only by virtue of domestic and storm water that has been detained in local storage.

A decade ago many office buildings had only around thirty percent office occupancy. Most companies have a virtual interface, and many offices are virtual, and function in MIEDs (Multiple Integrated Electronic Domains). Not only do these facilities function operationally for meeting, tasking, finance, information-management and information storage but also in flexi downtime and work social time. The remaining office space was retrofitted for affordable housing, as well as for restaurants, gyms, clubs and so on. Structural change also meant that the dockland area of the city became less busy and scaled down. Fewer goods arrived by containers as a result of the major downturn in the global economy due to the huge costs of climate change impacts on national economies and industry. The local economy obviously reflected this situation. Production output slowed down, consumer spending reduced and unemployment became higher. Based on the evidence coming from the region and the rest of the world things are certainly going to get worse.

At the same time, in addition to all these changes, inundation from rising sea levels has had a significant impact. Over twenty-six percent of the industrial area of the city is under water. Over one hundred and eighty kilometres of roads have been lost. Houses have also been impacted: two hundred and forty-seven houses have been lost, and fourteen tower blocks have had the ground floor inundated, while nine are stranded and unable to be reached by road. Equally significant, property values have crashed, numerous businesses have been bankrupted or closed, and a massive amount of capital has taken flight.

It was at this moment that the political process commenced that led within six months to the decision to move the city – its economy, communities, social fabric and some of its material assets: much more on this later. So now back to first impressions. What would you see and think if you now visited Harshon? Three main things would be immediately apparent. The first would be a city partly underwater; second, a huge amount of the city would have been destroyed, and third a strangely functioning city centre, along with islands of economic activity, would continue stranded amid devastation. Overall, the likely impression would be a city in its death throes that is being abandoned. We shall be looking at the city beyond appearances, and to the city it gave birth to – the new city to which the old one moved.

Clearly the cost of moving a city is very high. The only positive aspect is that it employs a lot of people, and this keeps the local economy alive. It also creates the space to restructure toward it being far less dependent on imported materials and products. This change is set against businesses relocating from the old to the new city, as well as the creation of new city start-ups. All this has been positive for local manufacturing but conversely the retail sector has been hard hit. This sector has yet to fully establish itself in the new city and is running down in the old. More than thirty percent of the shops in the city centre have closed.

Old City. Illustration courtesy of Yan Yan.

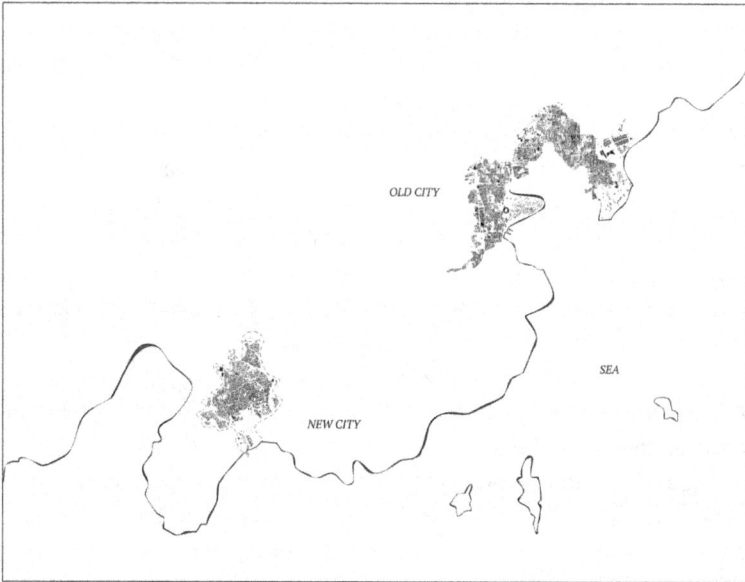

Two Cities. Illustration courtesy of Yan Yan.

Vox pop voices

Cities are as much defined by the people and their cultural life as by the built form, institutions and economy. To recognise and communicate this I decided to do a random sample. I stopped and questioned people over an extended lunchtime as they passed through the Seven Stars Plaza in Harshon on a sunny autumn day a few weeks before the event I organised that we shall soon encounter.

Because of its popular food court, supermarket and a cluster of popular shops the Plaza is the most vibrant part of what was otherwise a depressed city centre. I spoke to and recorded the comments of twenty-two people, and selected what I think are the most interesting of them. I specifically wanted to gain an insight into how these people view and feel about the city move and a sense of their general mood, as a way to frame how I was going to structure the event.

To put what follows in context you need to know that the city move process started with its planning in 2050. The move began two years later and is due to finish in 2080, although construction should be complete five years prior. Currently things are going well and approaching the last phase. The length of time the process takes is due to two factors: first the scale of complexity in every respect – material, social, economic, cultural and psychological – recognising that something had to be created to move to that was a viable social and economically functional living environment. This alone took over a decade. Second was the generational factor. Most young and working-age people were willing to move if there was something good to move to, but many old people wanted to die in the city that they had spent their lives in (there is more to say on this issue later). How this issue was managed was part of a more general trauma-minimisation policy.

The other crucial thing to understand is that moving was staged according to the city being divided into twenty-six graded segments, designated according to an impact risk assessment linked to a functional operational planning scheme – this to ensure that the old city remained functional at 'cluster levels' as it was gradually scaled down, unmade and abandoned. The new city obviously had to acquire an initial level of operational functionality before anyone could move to it. To add to the complexity the move was not a total transposition. Some people left to join family living elsewhere, others just took to the road. Quite a number of businesses, especially struggling ones closed down, and others had to move in stages, as did many institutions. Thus the new city had a significantly smaller population, footprint and more modest built form than the old one. Unsurprisingly, move management and logistics spawned a large local government department dedicated to it. The management of decommissioning the old city and supporting the creation of

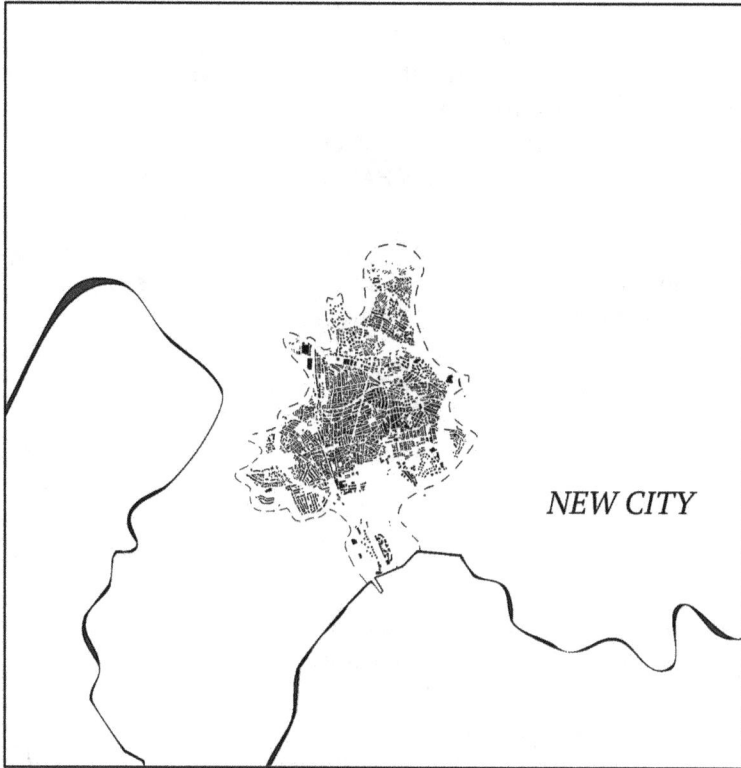

New City. Illustration courtesy of Yan Yan.

the new meant key elements of Harshon had to remain operative to the very late stages of the move: the city centre core being one of these. Now for the views of the people:

Max (28 years old, accounts manager): he told me his family moved to New Harshon four years ago, so I asked Max why did he stay behind.

'It was down to wanting to keep my job. The bio-electronics firm I work for is actually going to move in two months' time. I will go with them and stay with Mum and Dad until I find a place of my own.'

'How do you feel about this prospect?'

'Not good. Harshon is a dying city, it was never a great place to live, and now it's all but dead. As for the new city it has yet to come to life. I want to see a positive future and live in an exciting city, but I'm not sure it will ever happen.'

'Max, I really hope it does!'

Janet (54 years old, a para-legal): 'You have already moved to New Harshon. Why have you come back to the old city?'

'I came back to see my sister who still lives here, and this is the first visit since I moved with my family.'

'Well, what did you say to her about the move?'

'I told her that living in New Harshon was like living in an unfinished new house along with the builders. There is a lot to do and it's frustrating, but in time I know it's going to get better, whereas in the old city we all knew things would continue to get worse. I'm pleased it's been good for the kids, I like the feeling of being part of something new.'

'That's nice to hear Janet, thanks for your time.'

Kai (21 years old, University of Harshon student): 'I believe the UoH has just closed the last campus it had in the city. I presume you are going to move?'

'Yep, next week.'

'What are you studying?'

'Soil microbiology. I'm especially interested in bringing nutrient-dead and contaminated soils back into productive life, and with much higher moisture retention capacity.'

'Is this new?'

'No, work in this area has been around for decades, but what is new are advances in BMRMs, which stand for bio-replicating moisture retaining materials.'

'How do you personally feel about the move?'

'Well, pretty good. Most of my friends have already moved so I'm looking forward to it.'

'Thanks Kai.'

Jie (27 years old, chef): 'I was interested to hear that while you are a chef you don't work in a restaurant.'

'That's right. I work in the food research laboratory of Nutrafoods in New Harshon who make high-protein food substrates. On their own these foods have no flavour, so the lab does a lot with the creation of synthetic flavours. Also the food bases are not very attractive, so we add value by turning them into nice looking and tasty marketable products, like soups, sauces, pie fillings, cakes and more. Getting the products right means going through a lot of trial and error to make them look and taste good. I work in an experimental kitchen where this development work is done. Everything is measured and adjusted: exact ingredient quantities including colour additives, cooking times, tasting, sampling – it's all very scientific.'

'So why are you in the old city today?'

'I've just bought a townhouse and have come to collect things I left here in storage.'

'So things have worked out for you?'

'Yes, mostly, but not exactly as I imagined they would a while back. The money is good but my dream is to get a restaurant of my own in a few years' time.'

'Okay, Jie, I hope your dream comes true.'

Rena (36 years old, holographer): 'As I understand it, your company was commissioned a number of years ago to create a holographic record of Harshon, its built and social form, which you say you have been doing for the past five years.'

'Correct.'

'Why do you think this record is so important?'

'Well, there are lots of answers to this question. Here's three I feel are the most important. In a decade there will be just a levelled site where once there was a city – the holographic archive in the Harshon memory park will socialise the experience of remembering place; it will reanimate stories, not just the ones from the old to the young; and it will enable future generations in the region to view our attainments and failures, which is to say the archived record is as much an object of learning as it is of memory.'

'Thanks Rena, you're doing an important job. I'm really pleased to have met you today and found out about it.'

Rick (31 years old, tiler): 'Why are you still living here?'

'Easy. There's plenty of work for me here.'

'So what do you do?'

'I'm a tiler working in a tile recovery programme. The firm I work for has a technology that cuts tiles off walls and floors. We then clean them and resell them from our showroom in New Harshon and from our virtual store.'

'Does this mean an income alliance?'

'Yes, we get a percentage on the sale and so does the building owner whose property we strip them from.'

'How long do you think you will be doing this?'

'I'd say we'll be working here in Harshon, but in a scaled down operation, for maybe another three years. I expect to get work when I move to the new city.'

'How do feel about that?'

'I can't wait to get out of this dump, Carlos.'

'Thanks, and good luck, Rick.'

Mario (58 years old, welder): 'I believe like Rick you are in the materials' recovery business.'

'Yep, that's so. I cut steel out of buildings, in particular, pipes, RSJs, steel framing, roof trusses, whatever.'

'What happens then?'

'After the steel gets inspected, as either scrap or is recertified for reuse, it can't be sold until this is done. All the scrap goes to the super solar-arc furnace and then the caster-line to be turned into new steel construction products. All reusables and new products get transported to our yard and storage sheds in New Harshon.'

'How about you and your life?'

'Well, I'll be doing this work until I retire in a few years. I've a small block of land on the edge of New Harshon, on which I have a small old caravan. I'm gonna build a small house there with the help of my two sons, who both have families and work on construction projects in the city. I'm on my own, my wife died in the flood of 2072.'

'Mario, it was a pleasure meeting you. May good fortune shine brightly on you.'

Greta (40 years old, hairdresser): 'So what keeps you in Harshon?'

'First my mum, next my boyfriend and then my lovely clients. I have a contract with home services and I have a list of ladies. I visit each one of them every two weeks to do their hair. Some are still in their own homes, but most are in aged care. The worst thing about the city move is the loss so many old people feel. These ladies are really important to me. They see my visit as a spark of life in a world that for them is ending.'

"That sounds very sad, Greta.'

'It is, but for a short while for them it is not. They like to tell me about the good times in their lives, how they met their now-departed husbands, and their grandchildren, or even great grandchildren. I have eight ladies who are over a hundred. I call them my superstars.'

'Greta, you are something special, bless you.'

Greg (63 years old, project manager): 'You tell me you are the project manager for Harshon sector 17. What does this mean?'

'When it was decided to move the city, it was divided into 24 sectors numbered according to risk. Prior to 17 I was responsible for sector 5. I have a team of twelve guys and gals and we have four main tasks: to assist people to migrate to New Harshon – of course, some go elsewhere; to assist with businesses and other organisations to migrate to the new city; to decommission all building and work sites; and supervise decontamination where needed and material extraction, which can only be done by accredited and licensed organisations under my direction. All empty buildings are secured and monitored by an ultra-vibration alarm sensor we install that if triggered is instantly registered by all security and police patrol vehicles. Then, lastly, the final act of extraction is to level the remaining buildings and remove all steel – structural and roofing steel and rebar – from concrete and then plastics and composites, and then crush all concrete, blocking, and bonded brickwork. Not a thing is wasted; everything goes to the reconstruction storage yards in New Harshon. Last of all we certify the levelled site as safe. This after the removal, remediating or sealing of areas of detected ground-held toxins. With the expectation of future inundation, you will understand how important this action is.'

'Wow, Greg, that's quite a job. I thought I knew a fair bit about the city move, but you've given me another perspective. Much appreciated, thanks. I hope we catch up again.'

Lu (14 years old, school student): 'Hi Lu. You're here in the city to visit your Nanna, who you said has refused to move. Do you know why?'

'I don't know all the reasons but I know two. My Granddad died last year and was buried in the cemetery at St John's Church. He was buried next to their daughter Carol who died when she was six years old. Nanna says she will never leave them. The other thing is that she was born in the house she still lives in and says she will never leave it and says she wants to die in her own bed. She is 86. Mum and Dad have argued a lot with her in the past but have now stopped. We know if she were forced to move, she would just stop eating and die. It really upsets me. She is so sweet and kind. I feel helpless.'

'Lu, I can see how hard it is for you, but I know you are helping. I'm sure you are making your Nanna's last years of life worth living.'

'I truly hope so.'

'It was a pleasure meeting you, Lu.'

I did not hear anything that really surprised me. Overall the mood, even with the sadness, was positive, but I also knew this was not a true reflection of the raw reality of the move for those people it hit the hardest. The city centre was not the place where one was likely to meet 'the battlers', the disaffected young, older unemployed workers, the poor, and I am sad to say, the broken and psychologically fragile. There have been, and are, a significant number of people who have been unable to cope with the trauma of crisis, including financial disaster and an associated family breakdown. They simply join the ranks of the desperate. Having said this, the overall feeling I have gained over the past few years is that most people have risen to the challenge of the move and, like those I spoke to in the Plaza, are getting on with their lives as best as they can. The scale of the transformation of people's lives is so hard to communicate. Everyone who was born into a comfortable way of life now lives a life of hardship, it is now basic. So those who were born into hardship are now desperately struggling to survive. Many left to look for work in other cities where they found vast numbers doing the same thing. Those that have stayed are better off; some have got low-paid jobs; many others squat in abandoned buildings, and are sustained by soup kitchens.

The story of the move (transcribed from a public event)

The story of the move is going to be told by a group of people who, in different ways, played a part in making it happen. The reason for this is to give a pluralistic perspective in contrast to trying to construct a single narrative. Of course, these people do not collectively speak for the entire project – nobody can. But what they have to say does provide a means by which its complexity challenges and potentially can be recognised. To help the story unfold I will be raising issues, posing questions and developing a dialogue with them. Occasionally they will also be talking to each other. The whole event was recorded, transcribed and translated. Before starting I need to say a little more about my values, my role as 'rapporteur', and myself.

As a journalist and former manager of Harshon Newsnet I have been an observer and reporter of the environmental destruction and the relocated remaking of the city of Harshon for over two decades. During that period I reported on politics and urban affairs, interviewing thousands of people from every possible walk of life. My wife is from the city, and my children were born and grew up here. To see and experience a city die is very painful. My role over the past sixteen months has been to find and work with those people I chose to speak at the event, to host it more like a master of ceremonies and 'rapporteur' rather than chairperson, and help tell the whole city move story. Finally, it was my job to gather the material, write what needed to be written, oversee the transcription of the event presentation and edit and organise the production of this publication. I can say, in contradiction, that what has been produced is modest and, for us, weighty. It is a very significant marker of where we have come from and where we are going.

Like all moved cities around the world, the human cost has been huge. Our age has been marked by a lot of regress and not much progress. Likewise, to see the city remade, mostly from destruction of the old one, has not been easy. In so many ways the new city is less than the old – a lot has been lost. The new city is an expression of different times and circumstances, but for all that it lacks it is a beginning out of which difference will grow. That we have a city with a future is something for which we are eternally grateful. The fundamental lesson I have learnt, as have many of my, and later, generations is that the past that was once called the modern world does not provide anything that can be seen to give us a model of the future. It gives us a material resource, but the form of that future is what we alone have to create. No matter what we do it has to be guided by all that now constitutes a modest way of living. What has been true for the entire history of our species is now truer than ever – we depend on each other and, in many instances, scarce resources.

Cities are never finished – they arrive, grow and change over time. Many of us have now learnt, as others have before us, that all cities, in the end, are destined to perish.

Before the creation of the nation state, and in an age when the global population was much smaller, so were cities, but they were also more autonomous. Industry was local, as was most trade. Food and material resources in the main came from the surrounding regions. The rule of government was, for the most part, remote. This past now appears, in a remade contemporary form, to be cities' future. However, these cities did not arrive in a bucolic idyll or as the realised utopia of a counter culture. Instead they arose as a condition of lived necessity – all captured by the concept, creation and reality of an 'essential autonomous future'. Against the backdrop of failing states, economies, eco-environmental disasters and continued climate chaos, together with high levels of 'population unrest and conflict', cities have now no choice but to find ways to protect, feed and support themselves. This is especially so for those mega-cities with populations of the size of small- and medium-sized nations. But it was easier for smaller cities like ours to undertake a transition as our presentation shall show.

The creation of an autonomous city centred on three critical factors: the making of it to be as materially self-supporting as possible; establishing it with futuring capability (which means securing the means for it to sustain itself over time in an affirmative form – this includes having the ability to protect itself); and having a form of governance, with a forward planning regime, able to respond to regional and global events that will arrive and affect the local situation.

The idea for the telling the story of moving Harshon did not come just from me, but also came from Eric Fontenille, the CEO of Displacement International, a think tank and publisher of several caster and audio-action journals. Eric's background is in population studies and international affairs. He has published widely in this area including seven multi-modal books. Eric is very supportive of projects like ours. He has been gathering information on many similar to and different from ours. He sees them as important, not least because he regards them as helpful for the authorities and people of other cities planning for, or in the early stages of, moving their city. Certainly our move team learnt a lot from reading material supplied by Eric. What it makes clear is that, in contrast to the earlier decades of this century, moving cities is a global phenomenon in this our age of mass population displacement.

Before actually talking about Harshon I thought it worthwhile to place its story in a bigger picture of what has happened over the last few decades, and is still happening, nationally and internationally. As we are all aware, news coverage from the world at large is at best limited and intermittent. However, regional and global enviro-climatic conditions continue to worsen and are forcing transformative action, including the necessity to abandon more cities or move them. As someone who has spent his working life studying these trends, I invited Eric, who lives in Canada, to write and record a short essay outlining the current situation, as follows:

Eric Fontenille – Overviewing the global picture 2078

I send you greetings from Canada. Carlos and I have known each other for a number of years and at my request he gives me regular updates on the progress of your project. Viewing it comparatively I can tell you that you have done, and are doing, very well. You should understand that what you are doing has a value beyond its worth to you. What you are doing is adding to a global pool of knowledge and inspiring others to follow you. So, here is my short overview essay.

We are all now living in the epoch of postdevelopment in which notions of continuous progression of modernity and globalised economic advancement are no longer credible. Not only is the idea of economic progress dead but the reality of regress is now the lived condition for the vast majority of humanity. Clearly, the lower the lived economic base at the start of this regressive process, the greater the hardship experienced as it progresses. Layered onto this situation, as will be outlined, is the inter-relation of enviro-climatic crises, conflict at various degrees of seriousness, multiple systems failures (technical, agricultural, economic and political), and the dysfunction of the nation state together with an associated breakdown of the international order. Clearly the impact upon cities has been differential but, in all cases, profound. Chaos is widespread, but uneven; the condition of unsettlement in its varied forms is normative; and disorder in many parts of the world is extreme. Yet there are various isolates where order has been created and imposed, plus there are some positive, and some ambiguous trends. Three in particular that are responses to the situation indicated will receive specific comment a little later: military enclaves, technopoleis and neo-city states.

The broadest characterisation of the 'state of the world' is its being in a critical condition of breakdown and suffering. This situation is reducing the size of the global population, but currently to an unknown number. Yet at the same time there are varied and scattered forms of reparative, reconstructive and re-creative actions happening. Some of these are directed, in varied ways, by organised and other groups of people thinking and acting futurally – all with pragmatic rather than idealist intent (idealism is a state of mind that has not in reality survived).

In reading the history of the arrival of a 'world of disorder', what was very clear was that in the early decades of the twenty-first century, problems were treated as discrete and resolvable by technical means. Most governments overlooked the scale and depth of problems, political and enviro-climatic, in order to continue maintaining social and economic 'normality'. In particular, climate change was dominantly addressed as it was defined by climate science, with solutions deemed as deliverable by technology. Likewise, pandemics were treated as medical and economic events rather than ecological. The relational complexity of this situation and its connection to a causal matrix of future-determining problems, and the deep relation between climate and culture, was just not grasped. While the notion of 'tipping points' was part of the rhetoric, the reality was that the dominant sensibility of problems progressing incrementally remained. Moreover, it was believed that the problems that threatened could be solved eventually by technology and legislation. Critical voices were ignored. All of this is now known to be thinking and acting in error. What certainly wasn't foreseen were the speed and convergence of events, and the complexity and scale of the problems that then occurred. These included climate wars and systems and market failures, with their ensuing panic and breakdowns. So before getting to contemporary responses to the aftermath of this situation and subsequent crises, it is important to acknowledge just how it unfolded.

The direct impacts of climate change are well known and documented: temperatures have continued to rise; warming was and is in the mid to high range; extreme weather events became and remain chaotic, increasingly frequent, and unstable; vast geographic regions are now 'dead zones' totally devoid of biological life. Large areas of the globe still experience daily temperatures of over fifty degrees Celsius for months on end. Now, for several decades, for us these areas have been completely uninhabitable. Likewise, while sea levels have continued to rise, and as ever pose mid- and long-term dangers, the most immediate and devastating impact has come from severe and frequent storms, storm surges and floods. As a result, coastal erosion and flood damage was and is enormous. Many villages, towns and cities were, and continue to be, abandoned. The amount of lost terrestrial and ocean biodiversity was, and will continue to be, huge. That the sixth extinction event is well under way is now taken as given. It cannot be stopped, but it can and must be slowed.

Besides the discernable environmental impacts of climate change the related wider consequences have also been enormous. Global food production has dramatically declined, while at the same time the nutritional value of food has lowered. The amount of malnutrition in the world has significantly increased, and this has contributed to lowering the general health of the global population. In particular, vector-borne diseases have become far more prevalent and mental illness has massively increased – this as a result of a whole range of factors including the failure of numerous industries, financial institutions, economies, agriculture and infrastructure systems. Conflict between nations over ownership of resources has proliferated and continually occurs as a result of mass crossings of national borders by people looking for food, water and shelter. Fortunately, although tactical nuclear weapons have been used several times, total nuclear war has been averted, but only just. There have also been major clashes between displaced people, urban populations and rural communities within nations. The condition of unsettlement has now, by degree, become the overriding physical and/or mental state of being in the world for everyone, everywhere. The very axis upon which life turns has changed.

Alongside all of this, nations have started to break up as the ability of governments to manage crises has diminished. Geopolitically, as conflict between nations has increased, the international order has broken down. However, some organisations have survived, and a few new ones have been created. Most importantly, autonomous regional, urban and local governments have become far more important actors in crisis management. The pragmatics of providing very basic services have in some regions expanded. Examples include the creation of: local energy networks; rural, peri-urban and urban foodscapes; shelter camps; essential public health services; and the formation of civil defence, engineering and reconstruction corps. Essentially, what is being indicated is that life in a postdevelopment world continues, but with hardship as a norm in the present and expected in the future, with the challenge of survival having to be met incessantly, if unevenly.

For many people one of the most distressing things to face has been the fragmentation of the human species where, in evolutionary terms, both regress and pluralisation have occurred. Many of the millions of the abandoned, who have experienced several generations of material and cultural deprivation, hostility and rejection, have become dehumanized. These ontological conditions have meant that their sensibilities and actions have become less human than those of their antecedents. At the other extreme are those completely instrumental cybordic beings that have become fully colonised by psychotechnologies that populate the techno-spheric lifeworld that they dominantly live within. Both the abandoned and the cybordic have become less than human in other ways. Detectable genetic changes in both groups have been reviewed by a number of independent scientific panels that have concluded that the human genome is significantly fragmenting with, at one end, what looks like, but is not exactly, a reversion to an earlier physical stage of Homo sapiens' development. And then at the other extreme, adaptation to an almost total technological environment is producing a marked evolutionary change that deviates from the variations in the characteristics of Homo sapiens that in the past were dominantly defined as 'racial'. Essentially it is now confirmed that 'our' species is fragmenting. Now to my next considerations.

Postdevelopment and transformed modes of settlement

As the numbers of remote, rural and urban environments became unliveable or seriously impacted, thereafter a series of different continuing trends became evident. Initially there was a first-wave flight of capital and people as the terminal condition of place became recognised – this was especially the case with people of means. Then there was a graduated abandonment as environmental circumstances worsened, this leading to a total abandonment once life in various environments became completely untenable. Associated with these trends, besides the identified breakdown of economies and systems, was violence and a considerable degree of panic. Likewise, large bodies of armed neo-nomads looking for places of temporary residence often had lethal encounters with controlling authorities or with resident communities. At the same time as these trends emerged so did adaptive responses. As acknowledged, there was the rise of predominantly three types of isolates: military enclaves, technopoleis and the larger variants of neo-city states and neo-regions (the context in which 'moving cities' will be discussed). Each of these will be considered in order. These isolates developed very unevenly around the world. In the once-developed world they were numerous, but everywhere else they were far more scattered. Globally the dominant form of existence was living in the surviving, but mostly stressed and declining, settlements of the rural and urban environments of the bygone global age. In this setting two clear trends were evident: a continual growth of the population of the abandoned, living extremely precarious and often violent lives; and transitional communities working to create futurally viable conditions of existence. The widespread practice of remaking cities, via 'metrofitting' and moving cities into new and sub-regions, as we shall see, is now the most significant example of this practice. Now to the three enclaves:

Military enclaves: these were initially created at the direction of government under the aegis of an expanded model of 'coming to the aid of the civil powers'. However, they developed and grew in conditions of national political instability and fell under the direction of a military council of combined forces. What this actually meant was that the command structure moved from being politically directed to become autonomous, with relational connections to all arms of military service. The implication of this arrangement was that the military council decided to whom, when and how the military aligned itself (in almost all cases this being historically influenced). The nature of these enclaves is far larger and more complex than military camps. They are socially diverse and include all military elements, plus supporting industries, schools and hospitals, commerce (business and retail), farms, energy generation and water storage infrastructure. Essentially they are large self-sufficient areas, policed by forces with extensive combat capability and who contract their services as outreach requests.

Technopoleis: developed out of the technology centres of the once global megaregions, from the fourth decade of the twenty-first century onward, they started to become interlinked 'super-dome clusters' of advanced technology corporations. The cluster content spanned environmental, renewable energy, communications, electronics, robotics, composite and nanomaterials, biotechnologies, and reproductive and medical technologies (including lifeworld-assisting psycho-chemistry), plus 'urbazones'. As time went by, and as worldly and local conditions worsened, technopoleis started developing laboratory grown protein and industrially manufactured food and the 'augmented realities' of what became known as re-naturalised life environments. Effectively what was established was a sophisticated totally technological-dependent mode of self-sufficiency. More than anywhere else these technospheres, and their functional instrumentalism, created lifeworlds almost completely disconnected from the world outside. For instance, inducted air was filtered and 'scrubbed', water existed in a closed recycling loop, sunlight radiation levels were 'safety screened', thermal conditions were set with seasonal variation, and lighting level was controlled at a summer and winter daytime constant, with artificial supplementation if needed. Education and culture were equally delivered artificially, by 'programme implants', OKIRs (operational knowledge instructional robots), and by the 'plug-in pleasure dome'. Even after several generations, adaptation to this environment was, as said, contributing to the creation of the basis of a clearly posthuman species. In the first two decades, around forty percent of the 'founding population' left, but of the generations born into this environment, ninety-seven percent stayed. The relation to the world outside was managed by 'spaces of controlled exchange' policed by fully automated weapon systems, the tech-polis security service, and 'protection contracts' awarded to military enclave forces.

Variants of neo-city states and neo-regions (looser forms of enclaves): these emerged with the dysfunction of many nations, and/or the partial abandonment of parts of nations because of heat, salination and flooding. The need to abandon cities, or in some cases move them, produced two different political and land-management actions. One was to establish self-governing regions to which cities could be moved; the other was to create a new kind of city state (essentially a compressed self-governing city where everything from homes to factories and retail spaces are scaled down along with a very large scaled up peri-urban area, with urban foodscapes, to enable the city to reduce per capita consumption and to feed itself). While the environmental impacts of climate change have played a large part in these developments the other factors have been: the collapse of the international financial system; the cost of climate change impacts; the flight of capital and investors; the breakdown of stock markets and the banking system; and widespread conflicts. All this has meant the rise of very basic local and sub-regional trader economies. These are based on the exchange of labour for goods, food and services, where labour is valued in variable credits, according to unskilled, skilled, trades and professional service grades. Local currencies have also been created, but they have no value outside their circulation area.

Here then is the context of moving a city. The overall situation of the 'state of the world' is harsh, but it is not totally apocalyptic. Certainly the risks of major conflict are high. Likewise, the fragmentation of humanity brings another condition of uncertainty. However, the emergence of functional isolates in what seems now to be stabilising conditions of dysfunction offers something more than hope. What this has meant is that the overall lower level of natural resource, industrial and domestic consumption, as well as full-spectrum methane and carbon twelve emissions which are now at an all-time low for this century. So in the pain of this postdevelopment world there are a number of possible contested futures with one of variable desirability (from my position), which clearly favours moving cities in the context of neo-city states and neo-regions.

The event

Eric's overview provides and informs an important and disturbing backdrop against which to view our moving city project. We must take serious note of his comments, though I am sure we all found them very unsettling. Some of what he said is familiar, while some of it is new. I think we can all agree that although we live in an unsettled world you can never fully get used to being unsettled. By degree, while our city has been touched by some of the worldly changes Eric discussed, it's also clear that, in our economically privileged position, we have been sheltered from some of the worst impacts of these changes. But I also know some of them will be coming our way in the not too distant future. It is worth saying a little more about unsettlement. I believe it is something that we need to have a common understanding of.

From what I have read and discussed it can be understood in three ways. First, it names the current state of the world literally and metaphorically. By the middle of this century over seventy percent of the planet was urbanised. But then enviro-climatic events started to undo this process of settlement. More and more people started to become displaced. This created conflict in some parts of the world, and this situation made already bad things worse. The ongoing process of mass population unsettlement continues. Second, unsettlement is part of our experience. We have been physically unsettled and transitioned to resettlement. So unlike hundreds of millions of people around the world, in this city we are lucky. Third, unsettlement is a state of mind. We feel it. We are unsettled by the state of the world in which we live in a global and personal sense. This psychology affects how we see and act in the world. Many people cope with this situation, but vast numbers of others don't.

My view, in some respects, differs from Eric's. To prompt a more personal way of thinking about the critical futures in which we exist and are acting, I am going to say a little about a memory of my school days (circa 2031). I'm in Year Nine of Ramos Ferrara Public School in São Paulo (it is my final year in Brazil). The situation in the country was bad in so many ways. The impact of the COVID-19 pandemic was huge and, rather than addressing the problems, the ruling dictatorship just acted to protect its immediate interests. One of the problems that Brazil shared with many other countries was the critical number of youth suicides. On the particular day I'm remembering the head teacher called a special assembly to talk about our future. He tried to tell us that while times were bad at the moment they would improve, 'they always did', and that we should 'look forward to better times'. He did not mention suicides, but we knew this was what the event was all about and that his platitudes were crap. Now forty-seven years later, objectively things are much worse for the young and people in general, but for them it is 'normality' – there are still suicides, but far fewer.

The way I feel, and I think the group of people I have gathered together also feel, is that we have to face, redirect and remake a viable way of life in the 'normality' that is now not new. Unavoidably we still live in an unfolding horror wrought on a world abused unwittingly, but sometimes knowingly, by so many past generations. Even so, the choice by tens of millions of people to embrace affirmative change is now making some difference worldwide. There is not a shred of utopianism in this action. Life is and will continue to be hard; division and fragmentation will continue. The past attempts to avoid hardship and sacrifice have been causally part of what brought the conditions now being experienced into existence. Effectively past generations of privilege were willing to disregard the impacts of their actions on the future in order to retain their way of life in the present. For us, affirmatively making and remaking values and meaning out of our conditions of hardship are recognised as the only way to view and direct life futurally. Faith in the gods and technology as a means of salvation have clearly both failed us. So said, we cannot survive without building and reasserting faith in ourselves – this in all our differences, and acknowledging the 'technological beings' that we are but, at the same time, also reconfiguring our understanding of, and relation to, technology.

Their city, my city – old and new – is located in one of the most high-risk delta regions of the unsettled world in which we live. Of these regions it was not the first or the hardest hit. For us the numbers of people that have been displaced has been small. While there has been some violence in our region our two cities have not been touched by it. Yet judging from news from elsewhere there is a risk. In the world in which we now all live the sheer volume of the dispossessed means among their numbers are many people from the armies of broken nations damaged beyond repair in their economic ability. An already dangerous world is currently being made even more so. Depleted environmentally and economically, nations struggle and compete to survive. In the midst of seemingly endless conditions of tragedy there are signs of another future, but it is fragile and everything remains in the balance.

Moving perspectives: eight voices

These voices come as transcripts of interviews recorded during the Public Event, at New Harshon (the new city), on August 7–8, 2077.

The accounts are from people who played key roles in moving the city of Harshon. Of course there were very many other people who over several decades made important contributions. I spoke to lots of them over several months. Those who were invited to speak at the event were from a list that resulted from suggestions made by these people. I actually ended up with a list of twenty-eight people. At the same time, I, and the other event organisers, had an image of the kind of event we wanted to create. It was to be intergenerational, broad in scope and reflect that contributions were made from the diversity that constitutes our community. We ascertained that one full day was the most appropriate format. On this basis eight people were selected.

I should add that the presenters and I had a meeting after the transcripts had been completed and read. While we were all happy with them, apart from a few minor changes, we felt that something was missing. It was hard to name: the feeling, spirit, mood, ambience, emotion, pleasure, pain – it was all of these things as felt and seen on people's faces, and heard in the chatter during the breaks. We looked at photographs of the event but they looked like most other images of a convention. Then we started proposing words that went some way to conveying what we wanted to communicate. The view was that this might work if they were well chosen, but where to put them. At this point someone suggested images from the area to capture some of what we wanted. Finally it was agreed we would try to put appropriate words and images together. So here they are in this document.

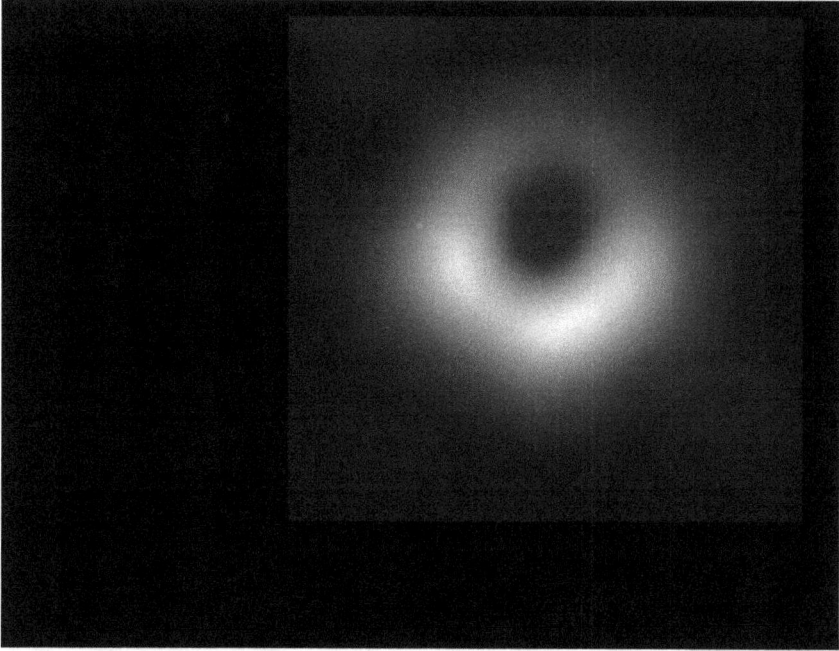

We looked at what we lost and felt empty. There will be something else, but it will never fill the void.

1. Grace Ebu (ex-Mayor, now the retiring transition commissioner) – On the city

The city is not just where I live, for the city also lives in me.

'I would like to introduce Grace Ebu who knows more about the history of Harshon and the move to the new City than anyone else I know. For four decades Grace has worked in a critical environment holding crisis at bay without being defeated by the trauma that accompanies the death of a city. She is truly a remarkable person. This remark is not a mere superlative but an empirical fact. Grace is incredibly focused. Her determination is legend, her kindness extraordinary.' (*Applause*)

'Thank you Carlos, your generous words are appreciated. What you say makes me very aware of the difference between a retrospective view of one's life, how others see you, and the daily experience of living, whereas in public office you simply deal with what has to be dealt with as best you can. For me there was and is nothing I feel to be remarkable about myself. I was just doing my job as best I could. I'm still doing this.

'I was born in the city of Harshon. I was totally committed to the city as it was, but now I'm totally committed to the city as it is being relocated. This is more about the spirit of the people who create the place than it is about buildings and businesses. I'm going to start by saying a little about the history of the city, its people and how it grew from a fishing village to a large modern metropolis.

'Originally the people of the region were water nomad fishers; they caught and ate fish and traded them for other foodstuffs and goods. In the early seventeenth century, because of harassment from pirates, many of these people abandoned their traditional way of life and established fishing villages on the shoreline. To protect themselves from pirate raiding parties they built walls around the villages. Slowly a more diverse economy was created, this initially from small farms. The more this settlement developed the more trade became an active part of the way of life. Hereafter the most successful villages were destined to become small towns. The most insightfully led of these towns built a port so that vessels larger than small riverboats could visit. In turn more goods started being brought to the town for sale. Then the trading company arrived: timber, animal hides, sacks of rice and varied grains were exported, with spices, farm tools, cooking pots, woven fabrics and more imported. By the mid-nineteenth century this port town had grown to become the city that, by the end of the century, was known as Harshon. For almost two hundred years the city flourished, until the impacts of a changing climate started to seal its fate.

'The first signs of a problem, fifty years ago, were when trees and crops started to die on the low-lying land south of the city. With this happening in other parts of the country we knew this a result of soil salinity due to seawater entering ground water. By 2035 food production in the region had fallen by twenty percent. Over the next decade this loss had risen to forty-eight percent. Large areas of agricultural land became inundated, as well as some of the industrial areas. Flash flooding became a regular occurrence in some suburbs as the storm-water outflows to the ocean failed due to sea levels rising and the rate of discharge decreasing. While in theory people had known that the city was at risk it now became visibly and unavoidably clear. The result was the start of what became an ongoing financial disaster. Property values dramatically fell; corporations stared to move out, as did capital, building and infrastructure development; all construction stopped; and unemployment massively increased. In just a few years the once-thriving city, like so many others around the world, became a 'basket case'. The only thing that grew was crime.

'On July 11, 2052 the City Council convened "The Future of the City", a one-day convention to which all the city's industry, political, social, cultural and religious leaders were invited. At the end of the day a motion was proposed by the then Mayor, Gordon Kee, that the "City of Harshon should commence a process of orderly abandonment and be moved to a new location, and that a special commission be formed to oversee this process." It was decided that the Mayor's motion, passed by the Council and supported by the commission, required endorsement by a clear majority of the electorate in a referendum. A motion to this effect was put to Council and was passed with an absolute majority. The referendum was held on August 16 after a major public information campaign and massive local media coverage. The result was posted at 2.00pm on August 17 – sixty-seven percent of the population supported the move. The fate of the city was sealed with many tears.

'Gaining a clear understanding that the moving of the city had to be done as peacefully and painlessly as possible was a prime objective and message of the Council. But implementing the decision, planning and developing the move process, and dealing with all the legal problems and implications of what had been decided were very challenging. As was acquiring a new site for the city – all of this took several years. Meanwhile, sea levels continued to rise, the material damage got worse, dysfunction grew, crime, especially theft, became a major problem, and suicide of the young increased. For me, the scale of poverty was especially upsetting. The sight of malnourished children broke my heart and will stay with me forever. There was also a small resistance movement of "stayers". They were more a nuisance factor than a substantial disruptive force. This was the state of the city when I became Mayor in 2064, a position I held until 2072.' (*Extended applause*)

'I think this is a good moment for me to chip in with a question, Grace.'

'Fine Carlos, go ahead.'

'Let me start by asking how did you manage to run the city in such circumstances?'

'I could not do this, nobody could. It wasn't possible to "run" a city in a condition of dysfunction and partial chaos. All you could do was try to find the means to reduce a descent into complete disorder, minimise what suffering you could, and try to speed the transformation process as much as possible. It was exhausting. I just learnt to take it one day at a time. What sits in my memory, above all, was a feeling of helplessness, especially when there was a food crisis and children were going hungry. But the turning point for me, and I think for everyone, was when people started to move to the new city, which was the opening of the possibility of a future.'

'What has surprised me over recent years has been the emergence of a functional everyday life out of dysfunction. How has this become possible?'

'Well I think there are several reasons. First, as more people have moved the pressure has reduced. Second, somehow everyone has learnt to adapt to changing circumstances. Another factor is more abstract to describe but very real as lived. It is that the dying city started to become a process more than a place. Dying was a process whereby the city and the old people who wanted to die with it became one. The work of mining the existing city for reuse in the new city was a process. The working life of the people supporting the city in its dying days was a process. At the end when the process had almost exhausted itself and the time of the last acts of the destruction started to arrive, there was nothing of value to destroy. We knew the feeling of deep sadness would be with us until we died. Future generations would not remember the city but they would feel the loss.'

'How about you, Grace? Seeing and, in several ways, overseeing the death of the city has been a very significant part of your life. How have you coped, how do you now feel?'

'Carlos, you can see the sadness on my face. I feel physically and psychologically very, very tired. Spiritually I look back into the darkness, the black hole that once was the place to which I belonged, but I also see a light. This is what emanates from the new city. What this light illuminates is a new way of life, a new future very different from the past. I am proud to have done my job and what we have achieved. I am proud to have made a contribution to the new city's creation but it's not my future. Yet it allows me to live out my days, now that my working life is all but over. For all the sadness I feel for what has been lost here and in so many other places, I am buoyed by the energy and commitment I have seen in the makers of the new city. It really is a monument of hope. I am not bitter. I still have hopes and plans for myself.' (*Applause*)

'What are they?'

'Carlos, I am not going to tell you! After years in public life I aim to have a private one, except I will tell you one thing I want to do. Although I have no children of my own I do love children. Seeing children die in the worst ways in the end years of the city really did break my heart. So I decided a long time ago that when I retired one of the things I would do would be to work as a volunteer a couple of days a week on a child-related project. I am about to choose which one.' (*Applause*)

'Grace, we have known each other for a long time. A lot of people are going to miss you. I want to thank you for your insights. As always, it's been a pleasure hearing what you have had to say.' (*Extended applause*)

'Thank you, Carlos.' (*Applause*)

We either accept being placed with the labour of another beginning, or drift into the company and space of the abandoned.

2. Lena Arikan (fieldworker, National Relocation Department) – On the displaced and the move

In the face of tragedy we only have two choices. Either we give up or rise above it. I will never give up. I say this knowing I am not alone because I am part of a community of courage committed to overcoming.

'Before introducing Lena, and linking back to unsettlement, I want to say a little about the issue of population displacement, and the issue of moving cities in this part of the world. As you know, we have lost some of the largest cities on the planet. Combined with other environmental impacts this has resulted in more than three hundred million people being displaced. Very early in this crisis there was a meeting of the leaders, and their ministers of environment and foreign affairs, of all nations in the region. One of the major decisions made at that meeting was to attempt to keep displaced people within the borders of their own nations.

'This has mostly been achieved – the retention rate of internally displaced people (IDPs) has been around eighty percent. While there have been a few problems with mass illegal border crossings generating conflict, they have been resolved without massive violence, which has not been the case in many other parts of the world.

'We have dealt with some thirty million IDPs in our country alone. This has been a monumental challenge economically, politically and socially. It has not been easy. Mistakes have been made, people have suffered, but lessons have been learnt. The dividing line between managing large numbers of IDPs, holding chaos at bay, and the imposition of a repressive regime of control is not always clear. Of all the lessons learnt the most significant has been that pre-emptive action creates a place for the displaced to go before they are displaced. Obviously this is the context of moving cities. But as you are aware this has not always been possible, especially so in cities destroyed by fire, or in those parts of the world where during climate and resource conflicts many complete cities have been totally levelled. The pain of the world is so clearly visible in these conditions of functional dislocation and abandonment. What is being highlighted is the graduated reduction of political control that was prefigured and evident at the birth of this century for those who cared to look. Essentially complexity and dangers were dramatically increasing globally, while nationally and internationally political leadership was totally entrapped in ideologically myopic and situationally dislocated pragmatism.

'So this is the contextual background to my introduction to Lena.

'The National Relocation Department (NRD) is on the ground working in conditions of crisis. It is a decentred organisation with a number of divisions. Department fieldworkers and their teams have a lot of power. Notwithstanding the breakdown of so many arms of government, this department continues with budget support from an impoverished national purse and from some of the nation's larger city councils. When I was consulting the people I mentioned earlier, at least twenty said "you must invite Lena Arikan". The most common comment about her was that "she is truly amazing". So it's a pleasure to meet you Lena. I'm looking forward to hearing what you have to tell us.' (*Applause*)

'Thank you for that introduction, Carlos, and especially for your kind words that set the wider scene in which I work. Let me start by saying a little about myself, and my team, which is in the cities division. I have been a fieldworker and team leader for seven years. By training I am an anthropologist and spent five years working as such in a team before my current appointment. There are six other people in my team: Kennard, who is a lawyer; Eli, a geographer; Mia, a sociologist; Nachun, a psychologist; Mika, an urban designer; and Akira, an economic planner. Having introduced them I immediately need to point out that we work in a totally interdisciplinary way; this means we don't stay in disciplinary boxes. Any person can input into any issue, and all the decisions made are by the team as a whole. (*Applause*)

'Before giving a picture of what we actually do there are two things that need to be understood. First, what we represent is a new order of public services. We do not sit behind a desk making decisions based on fixed policy and writing rulebooks. While our activity is framed by policy, how it is implemented is completely based on situated circumstances. Second, our role as a small team is not to direct all the listed activities in our terms of reference, but mostly to facilitate the people faced with the numerous challenges that displacement poses and to help them organise themselves to meet them. Key to such facilitation is our ability to bring lessons learnt from the experiences of others who have been through the same process. Our relation with the people we work with is not hit-and-run but sustained over years. We worked with Grace over many years and, as I think she will confirm, what we do works.'

'Yes, Lena, I certainly offer that confirmation without reservation. Besides all the practical aspects of working with NRD what really stands out in my mind is how having the knowledge of the team available on so many occasions acted to break through an impasse of what, at the time, seemed an intractable problem. The fact that they came bringing knowledge from the outside, but were working with us on the inside to overcome an immediate problem is what made this capability possible.'

'Thanks, Grace, that's a really helpful comment. So now let me tell you about our terms of reference. The first goes to the issue of site selection within the regions of the country designated by the government. This is not purely a geographic decision. Rather, it has to be informed by understanding the nature of the community, an evaluation of their needs, and "contextual knowledge and skills capacity". To illustrate with a crude example: it would be clearly unwise to move an industrial city to prime agriculture land in the expectation that it is going to instantly become a farming community. Instead the expectation would be that the moved city would continue to be industrial, albeit with likely changes in the form of the industry. The question thus becomes one of the relations between the use of low production land, the logistics of the city in the context of a supply chain, and the desirability of the location to the community. Two qualifications: selecting the most appropriate relocation site and a visualised concept of the new city are crucial in enabling a successful move. Minimising the distance between the old and the new city has to be an attained ambition whenever possible.

'Although emissions from H-trucks are no longer an issue, moving high-volume heavy loads takes a lot of time and is very disruptive of traffic flows. Before saying more about the NRD and moving cities, I need to be more specific about what we actually do to give a better sense of the organisation. At the most general we are tasked with responding to multiple areas of action.

'Unexpected impact events: these can be anything from the urban impact of a devastating extreme weather event, or a major wild/bush fire to an act of war. The obvious priority in these circumstances is dealing with the medical emergency with the help of medical services, and providing temporary shelter, food and clothing for the displaced. Once done, we organise an assessment team to examine the impact zone and then undertake damage and risk assessment reports. Thereafter, it becomes possible to produce a provisional strategic plan.

'Our main activity, of course, centres on moving cities. Our entry level of action is helping with making the decision to move. There are many factors to consider and hard decisions to make. What fate awaits the city and when? Can the city be saved by being metrofitted which might mean some or all of the following: partial abandonment and new extensions, raising levels, the retrofitting of many structures and infrastructure services, protective architecture, or downsizing? Does the will, motivation and organisational commitment to move exist? There have been examples of cities that have started the move process but have stalled and failed. This outcome always has a combination of factors: disagreements on key decisions by organisers and a lack of faith in, and support for, decisions made by the most qualified and able members of the community who leave in the hope of finding employment in another city or country. This happens to some degree in all cities but once numbers become high the loss of this critical mass seriously diminishes the economic viability of the moved city. Qualified and able people are very hard to replace. Few people will move to a fated city. And the jobs the new city will need to fill are yet to exist. Another issue is demographics: cities with a very high ratio of older people have less chance of success. Many of them will not want to move, and because the move process takes time, many of the slightly younger ones will be past retirement age by the time the new city is at least partly established. These are just some of the issues that have to be assessed prior to gaining approval to move a city.'

'Sorry to interrupt, Lena, but before you finish could you say a little about the work of these divisions, as there may be some people unfamiliar with them?'

'No problem, Carlos, will do. Just to wrap up on the supporting decision-making, I will say a few words about two variants. There are some cities that want to create a move plan and strategy long before impacts on the city arrive. Reasons for doing this include: to enable businesses to establish transition planning; to create the ability to lower the problems of psychological adjustment; and to build the capacity to create a viable future, which shifts the focus of the move from it being an end to it being seen as a means. At the other extreme are cities that leave the decision to move until the moment when impacts are creating major levels of dysfunction. These are the worst circumstances to deal with because they require approaches based on crisis management. Only a few of these cities gain approval to move, most have left it too late. Which means the speed of the arrival of impacts exceeds the speed with which it is possible to move a city.

'These remarks address the issue raised by Carlos on the divisions within NRD. There are five: spatial, organisational, legal, social and economic. Each of the team managers represents one of these five areas. But the reality is that we work as a team and leadership shifts according to the situation. A good deal of our time is spent troubleshooting. Trouble is never simple and usually involves all of our areas of concern and crisis. In this situation we act as the assessment and coordination team, which means we identify what resources can be called upon and then how they are enabled to work together in the crisis. What is important to understand is that the nation state in our current age is a shadow of its past. Resources are very limited. For this reason, troubleshooting, which is the last thing we actually do, is the hardest task of all. Often it's at an interpersonal level, the most common being youth and mature adult suicide. When a young person takes their life the impact on the family is obviously huge in and beyond it. For young people the past is the provider of the future they desire. It was "cool", replete with sounds and images of a world of desire that no longer exists. For so many, the world of now looks poor and grey. The cost of climate impacts has been huge, not just economically but also psychologically. So when the prospect of moving a city arrives it looks like another emptying out of the future. To get young people to see it as a condition of possibility where their power to make a future can increase is difficult. Argument does not work. What does is interacting with them in a group to make something futural. This itself takes a lot of time, energy and learning. While it works for some it does not for all. Thus depression is widespread, and a suicide, when blame comes into play, is one of the causes of family breakdown. For older people the loss of a job or business in current circumstances is felt as the end of their life. The future is seen as completely empty. Again, the impacts on a family, and also on a business, can be devastating.

'Overarching so many family breakdowns is the loss of wealth, because it's linked to loss of status, a past standard of living, and employment opportunities, all of which so often produce depression, alcohol and drug abuse, and domestic violence. Frequently guilt and blame are evoked, felt and present in the social context of breakdown. These problems are widespread but become amplified by the stress created by the prospect of moving the city you live in.

'The reason our team specifically confronts these conditions of breakdown is because they affect a wider circle of people. The cohesion of the social fabric is of vital importance in the move process. This especially pertains when it involves the loss or dysfunction of a person performing an important role in the process and upon whom other people depend. In this situation we have to find someone to fill the organisational gap. This can be very hard to do.

'Now I want to particularly focus on the practicalities of moving a city. The order of these activities entirely depends on the project. Usually a city will have a group of people, often councillors and business leaders, who have come together to talk about moving their city, but they are not necessarily the most appropriate, qualified or skilled people to manage the task. Additionally, the expertise for such a task is not just technocratic, not least because it's a very socially as well as technically complex task. In getting the best possible team we have a process based on time spent learning about the city and its population. After this the first thing we do is write a brief based on previous experience, local advice acquired from multiple community interests, our own situational assessment and review all the knowledge gained. This allows us to project the types of people needed within an organisational structure concept and the key critical factors the move will face. Feedback is then invited. Thereafter, the brief, the organisational structure and membership criteria are published. Nominations are invited and shortlisted and interviews conducted. The result is always a surprise. There are people who have been part of the power structure of the city but there are always many others. Overall, two domains are very clearly delineated: that which needs to be managed; and those who will do the managing. A major lesson from the history of moving cities is that the community needs to be continually informed about what is taking place, when and why. What this means is the media have to be inside the process and not just external observers who are fed media releases.'

'Lena, as a media person who has been "on the inside" for many years I just want to interject to underline just how important what you have just said is. The media must be on the front line because, as you know, the prospect of moving a city generates a huge amount of anxiety and even fear. So working closely with the media is vital in dealing with this.'

'Carlos, your remarks are apt and appreciated.'

'Staying with this issue for another moment I want to return to what I said about the creation of desire for the new city. It's hard to build, but even so, as a counterweight to insecurity and anxiety the task is essential. Perhaps, even more important, is projecting a positive future while honestly confronting the problems to overcome to get to it. Clear truthful information is one of the few things that can be provided to offset the resistance to moving that is always present especially from older people. Key to dealing with this is spelling out the process in time. The earlier the process starts, the less resistance. Some old people realise they can see out their days in the city they may have spent their whole lives in, others have time to adjust to the idea.

'Not too distant from what we have been talking about in the early stage of moving is a social impact evaluation. This addresses how the news has been received and the consequences, be they political and hostile toward the decision makers, economic unrest over the impact individually and commercially, or psychological in terms of depression and suicides. All of the reactions are relative to the conditions that precipitate the need to move, and the clarity and desirability of the designated move location. On this latter issue, the quality of life-futures, imaging and its presentation directly correlate to how people will feel. Linked to this activity is the need to identify and communicate job opportunities created by the move process and the construction of the new city, and thereafter the form of the city as a place of attraction. Many of the suggested future employment opportunities will require training programmes. Introducing such training early has again to be seen as having a positive influence.

'Strategic planning and risk mapping are crucial actions in securing the future of the new city. This security requires having a very clear idea about the operational form of the future city, including what key economic functions of the old city are viable and sustainable that can be continued in it. For Harshon this was immediately identified as having a port. So in terms of relocation this meant a shoreline location with an appropriate topography. The implication of this decision was to construct a port that could be moved back from the waterline in many years' time if sea levels continued to rise with the city behind it on higher ground. Thus the economic strategic significance of the port to the city and regional economy could be retained with a smooth transition by a gradual decommissioning of the old port and commissioning the new (eighty-five percent of which would be constructed from the old port). While to do this required some landform reshaping it was practically and economically doable. Just as important was the creation of a sense of socio-cultural continuity. This was of enormous importance to Harshon's population. Thus this feeling generated the name of the moved city – New Harshon. Four specific strategic determinations of the city to direct its character were selected.

'The first was and is modesty, applied to almost every aspect of the city, from the size of its footprint on the land, to the size of its buildings, resource demands and ways of life. Linked to this is the foregrounding of utility as practice and an aesthetic. In both cases the spirit of these applied values, modesty and utility, was not a moralism but an economy, realism and honesty of appropriateness to available means and of the times, all done with elegance. Without an imitation of style or ethos the approach was inspired by Shaker architecture and construction. Rather than being underpinned by a theology, the foundational moral value of New Harshon was the constraint, and what this meant was reversing a culture of consumerism. Practically this meant a material world designed to have a long and useful life, to be able to be repaired, and to display craft skills and knowledge of making. Again, none of this was an expression of utopianism, but a futural regime of realised possibility in conditions of circumstantially imposed necessity and constraints determined by a dramatic reduction in the scale and output of extractive and manufacturing industries. All combined with a substantial investment in the cultivation of renewable resources. In this context what reverse consumerism implies is an investment in skill and labour over purchased commodities. More than this, while the construction of such a city does not arrive foreseeing any future need to move, a large percentage of New Harshon (being designed for disassembly) is able to be moved and reassembled in the future if circumstances dramatically change. The city in its arrival and form is a marker of the variable speed at which the nomadism of our age now operates. A sense of permanence has been replaced by one of unsettlement, most evident in, but beyond, the vast numbers of displaced people whose temporality is the temporary.

'Coming back to the question of loss, such a world would be seen by the young and old alike as a condition of depletion. To recognise this is to grasp that an explicit response is required at the very same time as the lifeworld of the city is created. Socio-cultural richness has to be laid onto an environment of seeming austerity. One immediate action is colour – natural, surface applied, and by the use of structural fabrics. Another is sound – the city needs sound: wind installations to generate it; places of music; and environments designed to attract birds. A third is image – projected, applied, fixed and changing, linked to colour and light. All of this suggests an extremely dynamic way of thinking, designing, creating and seeing the urban landscapes and foodscapes of a city. Foodscapes are the result of an ecology of the city that fully uses its organic waste and harvested water for the totally pragmatic reason of the city contributing to feeding itself. So the city becomes understood, seen, heard and felt as not just a place but also an event that constitutes a mood, desire and experience.

'Another dimension of adding socio-cultural richness to the city is by inviting, exploring and developing education based on the culture of learning for the form, structure and content of a progressive future. This is not learning confined to the classroom or the electronic environment. Rather, it is learning by experiment and discovery; by the invention of a new discourse by which to define the city; and the formation of new community and collective forms of cultural production that express the desired identity of the city as a place of seriousness and pleasure. Implicit in such thinking is that new cities produce new futural subjects, an idea that goes directly to the crisis of young people to counter their view that the future is a wasteland. It is incumbent upon us to make cities ontologically as designing events that carry their populations into the future enabled to confront the certain challenges that are going to arrive. More than this, such a designing needs to provide populations with the means that prompt and enable people to create and experience conditions of cultural richness that sustain their minds, imaginations and spirits.

'Finally, I just want to say a little about the complex legal and economic issues associated with moving a city. This is dominantly the responsibility of our legal division, but our team does have a responsibility to scope out problems and needs. This action has to be seen against the backdrop of several decades of transformation of land tenure and a major shift from a national economy to a regional economy – this is still a work in process. A moved city clearly has a key role in this economy, especially with a focus on meeting local needs as comprehensively as possible while contributing to regional economic sustainment. What this means is that in moving a city the economy is not being moved as it was but is understood to be as much an act of remaking as the material and social fabric of the city itself.'

'Lena, that really did give us an incredibly rich, if complex, interesting picture, that raises many issues that I know other presenters are going to take up. So I am going to sit on most of my questions and see if they get resolved as things unfold. If not, I will bring them up at the end of the session. But I do have two organisational questions that have been passed to me that I would like to put to you.'

'No problem, Carlos, fire away.'

'Lena, these questions are related to your team. The first is from Kerry-Anne Myer. This is what she wrote, "Most city move projects span several decades as the planning, design and transition process takes a lot of time if done in a socially and economically responsive and responsible way. It would be unlikely for team membership to be unchanged over that process. Recognising the amount of knowledge and relationships any team member would have built up over the years, how is the succession to a new team member managed?"'

'Carlos, it's a tricky process and is divided into two parts. The first is, obviously, membership does change. New member orientation consists of meeting the team, and being interviewed and briefed over two or three days. Every new team member comes with a ten-page profile, which they submitted as part of the selection process. All team members read this and their job description changes as they and circumstances change over time. They then each nominate five key project reports from their case files. We then collectively review these and make a selection, sometimes adding more material. The new member then has a month to read this followed by an informal team re-interview to test their level of understanding. This event always generates more reading which has to be done in their leisure time. Part two is a three-month field probation period, within their probationary year. They normally spend a week with the person who is leaving if circumstances permit. In order to leave, every employee has to serve a "notice of intent to leave" at least one month before serving three months' notice. It is still a year before a new team member is fully independent of additional support beyond a culture of support intrinsic to the team. Speaking from my own experience of joining and leading a team, it's hard. I think you will agree it's a very rigorous process. We have only added one person since I have been a team leader and this is Eli, our geographer, who joined us two years ago. Eli perhaps you could say a few words about your experience?'

'Sure, Lena. Well, it was the hardest thing I have ever done. Much harder than anything I did at university and in my previous job. There was so much to learn and not much time to learn it. But the most difficult part of all was gaining the confidence of Caroline's client group. She was the person I took over from. Although it was never spoken, I knew that I was being measured against her. Having said this I should add that everyone in our team was super supportive. I can't tell you how many times they threw me a lifeline.' (*Applause*)

'Thanks, Eli, I felt the same way as you when I arrived. Okay, Carlos, what's the second question?'

'This is another basic question and comes from Mi Ling. She asks, "How does your small team deal with several projects at a time?"'

'Well, at the moment, while we would rather have two, we have three projects, and it's a juggling exercise. We really need a team three times the size, but the money to employ extras is just not there. So what we have to do is often split the team. Depending on circumstances we usually spend two days a week with each project. So one project will get a full team visit while the others get a partial team, usually of two to four members. All we can do is plan week-by-week, trying as best we can to respond to needs. Once a project is well under way and its management has become experienced it's not too bad, but in the first year or so it's super stressful.'

'Lena, I was brought up Catholic, and while I lost my faith along the way I never stopped believing in miracles. Why? Because of you! I've seen you arrive at a meeting where all hell is breaking loose with people almost coming to blows. But then two hours later it's as calm as a pensioners' tea party. Thank you for a super presentation.'

(*Cheers and extended applause*)

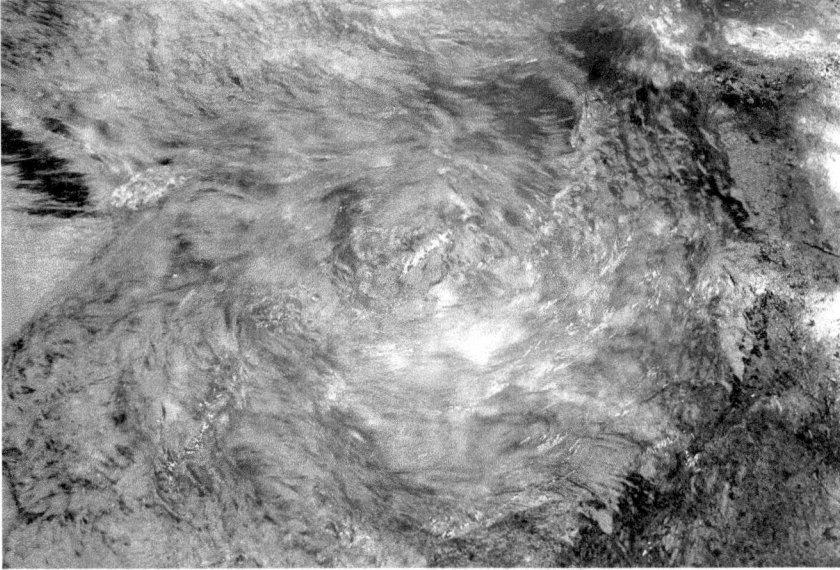

Can you imagine falling into a whirlpool and either spinning around and going under, or being thrown out to find yourself in another world?

3. Kendrick Jensen (move planner) – Stasis and unsettlement

Historical anthropologists tell us that our species was nomadic for tens of millennia. We still are, and are increasingly becoming so. In this situation the real and the critical issues are the speed of our movement, where we move to and the impact of our arrival.

'I now want to introduce Kendrick Jensen, a friend of mine and an NRD consultant anthropologist who I know meets with Lena's team on a regular basis, and whenever she introduces him he gets named as her mentor. I can tell you Kendrick is a mentor to many. Like a lot of people in my life I first met him as result of being asked to interview him. After we finished I took him to lunch and we talked until 4.00pm. We have been meeting on a regular basis ever since. I can say that he changed how I view the world and the people who populate it. As always I have a series of questions for him, but first I would like Kendrick to say a little about his history and how he views our project.'

'You said you were my friend, Carlos, and you know that as far as talking about myself is concerned, I am a snail who prefers to withdraw into its shell.

But having a dutiful nature I will do as you ask with my head lifted toward the world and with a smile on my face! (*Applause*)

'I grew up in Norway and developed a dislike of the cold at an early age. (*Laughter*) Fortunately my father, who was a lowly diplomat and remained so in the service of the nation all of his career, got posted to warmer climes. The best was when I was twelve years old. He was sent to work at the Norwegian Embassy in Buenos Aires. My mother, sister and I followed him to Argentina eight weeks later. We lived there for five years. I loved it. They hated it.

'I attended the International School. Again I loved it, but my sister, who was a year older than me, hated it. School finished at 4.00pm, my father's workday at 5.00. The Embassy was only a block away and we would meet our father outside the school at eight minutes past five every day and travel home by bus with him. Like many other children, after school we went to the library and did our homework or read. One day, I think just after I turned fourteen, I sat down to do my maths homework and saw a book left on the table, obviously old, with a strange name and a striking cover. The title was *Tristes Tropiques*, its author Claude Levi-Strauss. I started to read it and did so every day over a few weeks. To tell the truth I hid it on a shelf behind a collection of dusty books on world religions. I was pretty sure it would not be disturbed. After I finished it, I left it on the table where I found it. From *Tristes Tropiques* I gained a picture of what it meant to study another culture. This fascinated me. From that moment on I knew that above all I wanted to be an anthropologist. The book had sealed my fate.

'Fast-forward five years: I am now at the University of London as an undergraduate studying anthropology. On one of my courses' reading lists is a book by James C. Scott, *The Art of Not Being Governed: An Anarchist History of Upland Southeast Asia*. The fusion of anthropology and politics that was promised by the back cover blurb appealed to me. I read it. The Uplands were a mountain region spanning seven countries of the region that Scott called Zomia. It was a place of refuge for millions of people with a long history of rejecting being incorporated into the state. These people took flight from all efforts to control them. They defined themselves as stateless, and this was the core of their chosen identity. Scott's book focused on the past, but I read it as an account of the coming future, and in so many ways it was. We are now in a world of circumstantially forced social autonomy, not because we rejected the state but because it has effectively abandoned us. I went on to do my PhD on the Akha, the purest of autonomous peoples of Zomia. They occupied places in the mountains, as I learnt from Scott, where they were least accessible to "soldiers, bandits and tax collectors". I spent four years trying to make sense of their world. If asked what I learnt it would come down to an indivisible relation between three things – movement, freedom and resilience – that for the Akha was the singular essence of their being. Without the ability to freely move there was no freedom. Without being able to surmount whatever obstacles or hardships that one encountered on life's journey there was no freedom. Without freedom there was no life.

'After a number of short-term and casual positions at several universities I gained a position at the University of Harshon as an Assistant Professor. Thirty years on and a mountain of publications later I am still the Professor and Chair of the Department of Anthropology. I would now describe my work, an area of study and passion, as the understanding and contemporary advancement of "the cultures of self-organised autonomous societies" in conditions of planetary crisis. I have argued more forcefully over the years that in a world where the costs of the environmental and geopolitical impacts of especially climate change and related effects, like sea level rises and reduced biodiversity, have broken the financial backs of even the wealthiest of states, such self-organised societies are the future. We now all live in "shatter zones" and exist in "the broken" in conditions of impending flight, be it slow or rapid. We tend to forget that our species has always moved and adapted under the force and extremes of a changing climate. In one cycle the world turned to ice, in another the heat turned forests and grasslands to desert.

'Settlement allowed us to make a world within the world, combusting its stored energy to do so. Metaphorically, for many centuries we ripped up the floorboards of our home to burn to provide heat and to capture and productively use energy at a planetary scale. Eventually the atmospheric effects of our actions were of such a magnitude that they altered the behaviour of the climate, and as a result the very conditions of life on Earth changed. The name Anthropocene was given to this age. What it demanded was that our species again globally redistribute, and adapt to an altered environment, as our ancient ancestors had done. But at the same time we had to dramatically reduce the impacts of our world making. However, now that we are so many, so divided, and so anchored in place, our ability to move has been severely restricted. What this means is, irrespective of whether "we" are technoids moving toward complete artificiality, or we are residual Homo sapiens, our resilience and freedom have been diminished. In various natural and unnatural ways a global population "correction" has been under way for many decades. You and I are part of that distributed collective that are striving, to date mostly unknowingly, to survive that correction. Our species has never been in control of its fate. As planetary conditions change, our ability to survive always rested with the ability to move to more convivial conditions.

'In the unavoidably chilling setting I have outlined, I view moving cities as an important action. But it is not a solution. Rather it's a step toward one. What relocation affords is movement toward establishing societies based on forms of self-organised autonomy and governance in our conditions of political abandonment and structural uncaring. In truth there is nothing that cares for us other than ourselves as we gather together to secure a future for our futural being. Cities and societies in the world like ours have no prospect of utopia, yet they resist a capitulation to dystopia. It's almost impossible to imagine life beyond an existence in hard times, but notwithstanding this it is essential we strive to make the best possible worlds for ourselves that we can, and for all who come after us. This is what the moderns aimed to do, but as we know, in doing so unknowingly and without material constraint, they completely lost their ability to be futural.'

'I hope everyone now understands why I asked Kendrick to say something about himself and how he understands our situation as it converges and digresses from Eric Fontenille's. (*Applause*) My first question, which actually follows on from what you have been saying, is how has the meaning of settlement changed?'

'Carlos, I would like to change the question before answering it to "why does the meaning of settlement continually change?" The short, but rather abstract answer is because the very ground of our existence continually changes. Any sense we collectively had as a species that roots could be put down and that where a settlement was established would be forever was always an illusion, an illusion that persisted and was held no matter the ravages of war and nature. For over ten thousand years our species has occupied a world of relative stability. But this was never, nor will it be, the normative condition. Our planet is a place of continuous and sometimes violent change. Dramatic climate change played a major role in the global distribution of our species over tens of thousands of years. Put in its simplest terms, unless you moved you died. Such was the impact of the ice age that the total world population of hominoids diminished to a few thousand. We are the children of the few. So the normative condition is unsettlement, and it is one we are in and likely moving more deeply into. Clearly unsettlement of body and mind unsettles most of us. But being unsettled has always been part of the human condition, as confirmed by numerous examples, like the people of Zomia, the Bedouins of the Sahara and the Sami of Lapland. Over the two hundred thousand years of our species' existence nomadism was the norm.'

'Kendrick, your answer certainly gives us a lot of food for thought, and my next question goes to the issue of the activity of moving itself, in a world where vast numbers of people are on the move, many by choice, but so many others by being forced to do so due to environmental conditions, conflict and coercion. In these circumstances, and with a global population of 9.2 billion people, how do we appropriately think and approach movement now? Does a new nomadism give us the means?'

'Carlos, that's a really tough question. I can say a few things but certainly do not have a complete answer. Let me start with nomadism. It was never one thing. The people of Zomia, the Bedouins and the Sami I mentioned never all moved in the same way, or had the same way of life, or functioned at the same speed. But they all did so under the rule of one discipline: the law of the load. It was not possible to move beyond the limits of what you could carry. Nomadism centres the issues of the selection and form of transportation at an individual and mass level. Here then is a critical resource and design problem. Next, nomadism does not have a final destination. It is recursive. Thus, the key question concerns the selection of points of passage – shelter in particular seasons, water, trade and grazing, being some traditional norms.

'In contemporary and emergent societies supportive of nomadism the model of desert nomads could perhaps be recreated in a new form. What they did was pass through settled places and trade where they could, for example exchanging goats for dates and water at an oasis. More substantial were the trader nomads of the ancient world, like those transporting silk and spices on the "Silk Road" between China and Arabia who were replenished in the city of Petra. In our age this could look like an economy of service settlements between cities which nomadic traders passed through to access services like health. The context for such a culture needs to be seen in conditions of neglected infrastructure and dangers from raiders. No doubt such a culture of larger family groups able to protect themselves and travelling in all-terrain independent power input vehicles with extendable lightweight structures could be possible. From such modes of transport, supporting technologies, and economies, convergent groups could form transitory villages and towns.

'The harder questions are the politics and management of movement. Regulation, direction and control negate the very freedom to move integral to nomadism. But tracking where people are, and having the ability to communicate with them, could help counter border incursions being treated as an invasion and an act of war. Another possibility in a world of continued severe environmental impacts is itinerant communities of repair that occupy the city they repair until another city requires their equipment caravan, labour force and trade expertise. All this is to say that the scale of the task of making such a complexity work socially and legally is acknowledged. These ideas are not posed as solutions but rather as feeds toward conversations of possible research.' (*Applause*)

'Kendrick, there is no way I can respond to what you have said. There is so much to reflect on. But what I will say is that I see direct links between what you have been saying and post-move life in the new city and interactions with an emergent world around it. I really do get a sense that we have to start to go beyond the pragmatics of the city to a more complex process of worldly engagement. Certainly an exploration of many of the things you have been talking about is a useful entry point.'

'I absolutely agree, Carlos. Lena and I spend a lot of time talking about this possibility.'

'Now I have two final questions. The first is on the issue of security. We live in dangerous times globally, nationally and regionally. The only thing we have any power to address is regional. So far we have escaped attack from nomadic raiders. We already have had, as you know, a few small group warehouse raids. What are your thoughts on the issue?'

'This is another hard question, Carlos, but one I have done some work on as a member of a counter-conflict research group. What is clear is it's an issue that cannot be ignored. Naturally I am disposed to a "deter and defend" approach rather than hiring or creating a counter-strike force. This does mean a considerable investment in surveillance and asset protection technology. You can't afford to look like an easy pushover, which means forming a rapid reaction paramilitary unit within the police force. The existing civil defence volunteer force would be wise to increase its size and train more rigorously and strategically. You certainly don't want to turn the city into a fortress but you do need to make your defensive intentions evident. This means having some visible high-profile surveillance technology, a well-armed defence capability, plus regular and very observable defence action drills. These are just indicative possibilities. What you actually need is expert advice. I have a couple of people I can suggest to the city security committee.'

'Thanks, Kendrick. What you have said is helpful and depressing. I will follow up with you on your suggestion. My last question goes to an issue that we have spent many hours talking about: how to deal with the unmoveable – those mostly old people who refuse to move?'

'We all agree forcing especially old people to move would be counter productive. It would kill some of them, cause huge family problems and division within the community. This is, as far as I understand it, the thinking to date. But the issue is always open to positive change. There is a consensus, when possible, to let the very old who refuse to move live out their lives in the old city so long as it is contains a level of function and services. This will create the issue of some being presented with the choice of moving within the city to a serviced old people's facility or to the same in the new city or to their family, if they have one, there or elsewhere. Younger healthy people who refuse to move, of which there are only a very small number, will be served notice on or before the date the building in which they live is transferred into Council ownership by the requisition authority. If they are tenants, they will be evicted by bailiffs and lose their housing relocation entitlement. All cases so far have never come to this point. The people have left of their own accord and been relocated. Building owners who refuse to move and are forcibly evicted will lose their "transferable title rights" which gives ownership of the building selected from the pool of options in the new city. Again as far as I know nobody has got to this point. The last group are the old but still active refusers. They will be subjected to a staged process. They will be given an extension to stay subject to their location. Once this expires they will get a "notice to move", a copy of which will be sent to their family. One month before the due date they and their family will be summoned to attend a family/Council conflict resolution meeting. If no agreement to move is gained the forced eviction process will be put in place. None of this is ideal. I do not know anyone who wants to expose the elderly to forced removal. Moving a city is a huge emotional trauma for almost all whose lives have been invested in a place. I know that whenever it can be avoided it is, and will be.

'I don't want to end on the sad and tragic consequences of moving experienced by some of the city's oldest generation. Instead I want to say a little about the New Harshon Museum of Memory and Oral History where anyone who arrives in the city from Harshon can deposit small objects of historical significance, and printed, painted, drawn and photo images are to be archived, as are all forms of recorded moving images. There is also a recording facility with a focus on oral history, where a home recording service is also provided. The primary objective is to create an account of the culture and life of Harshon as an object of memory and study. I believe this to be anthropologically and historically important. Obviously older people are especially encouraged to contribute. There are two other things to say about the Museum.

'First, the building material recovery programme has deposited an amazing collection of objects: sculpture, building plaques, architectural carved stone, stained glass windows, and there is more to come. The programme is also responsible for the removal of all tombstones that will feature in a park of remembrance with a multi-faith chapel built with doors removed from every religious building in Harshon. Likewise, many businesses have donated objects, antique tools, a printing press, historic advertising signs and posters and more.

'Second, everything in the Museum is electronically documented and entered into a curated format. This material is to be available to all universities, schools, and other educational institutions as well as the public at large. Sorry for this long and wandering answer, but I judged that at least some of what I have said offsets any impression that the old is to be forgotten and the past erased. I'm told that formal recognition of this will be an annual Harshon Day public holiday with a parade and public open-air concert.'

'Kendrick, what a picture you have painted over the course of your presentation. So many challenges and images conjured up, so many colours of light and dark, and so many feelings that envelop us. You really have given us a lot to think about. Warmest thanks.' (*Extended applause*)

We arrived at a point when all we saw when we looked toward the future was an unclear shape hidden in mist.

4. Angela Leung (psychotherapist) – Life in the end times

For so many people they feel that their world has died. They know they cannot live in the past or the future, but hate the present.

'I met Angela at a party a few years ago. We had one of those "what do you do" kind of conversations that took an unexpected turn. She told me that the day before she had gone to the funeral of, sadly, one of her former patients, or should I say clients, a seventeen-year-old girl, who had committed suicide. For Angela this had been the third such event so far that year. Angela described her frustration at her own practice being ineffective in preventing such deaths and her equal despair at the nihilism that led young people to end their lives. She also said that she had colleagues who had experiences worse than hers and that some of them were self-medicating on anti-depressants. Angela then said she was determined to find a way out of her impasse. Knowing that youth suicides had started to rise again when I was planning this event, I thought it worth giving her a call to see if she had made any progress. She then told me some headway had been made and a little about what she had done. At that point I invited her to speak at this event. I was delighted she accepted. So now let me extend a warm welcome to Angela Leung.' (*Applause*)

'Thank you, Carlos. I am worried that you have created the impression that I am about to become a miracle worker when all I have done is to make a few baby steps. Before I start I should say that since so many people have been affected by such a tragedy, if anyone thinks they will, or does, find what I am going to say upsetting, they can leave whenever they like. So here we go.

'Common among young people is calling where they live, no matter where it is, the deadlands. So what, as far as they are concerned, is dead? Well, there are certainly many things around them that are dead. The path to extinction is littered with many dead animals, as the global loss of biodiversity continues. Dead trees are everywhere; the number of birds and bees are but a fraction of the numbers of my childhood. You know all this just as well as I do. But what else is dead is what they call "techusions". They use this word to name the past illusions of technological salvation be it by a "sustainability" techno fix or the madness of an AI technology reaching a point of "singularly" where it is able to download our brains into a machine and so discard our bodies. Then there is the ghost of history where what has gone looks so much better and haunts the future. All of us have felt some of what they feel. Lastly there are two killer questions they ask themselves and each other: first, why go on having children? To which the stock answer is "because we want the human race to continue". The reflex answer immediately follows: why? To which no answer is ever sufficient. Question two is why bother to study so I can spend my life doing a worthless busywork job? Claims that the job puts "food on the table" or is "socially useful" just don't wash. The issue is actually not about work at all, but rather goes to a death of meaning based again on a feeling that the future is negative, it has nothing on offer.

'At this point I want to remind you of something Lena said a little while ago when she talked about loss. She said responding to it required taking action at the very same time as we create the world of the new city to which we move. I quote: "Socio-cultural richness has to be laid onto an environment of seeming austerity. One immediate action is colour – natural, surface applied, and by the use of structural fabrics. Another is sound – the city needs sound: wind installations to generate it; places for music; environments designed to attract birds. A third is image – projected, applied, fixed and changing, linked to colour and light. All of this suggests an extremely dynamic way of thinking and creating urban landscapes." Not only do I support what Lena said but, I would like to let you know that what I am saying and trying to do echoes exactly the same sentiment. My version goes like this. The messed-up world we live in is not a condition of impossibility. There are things we can't change, but there are many things that we can, but don't. Mostly we expect someone else to change things. So what do we do? Do we make a mimetic city? Yes, but not by as a pretentious architectural statement. Even if this was a good idea we cannot afford it. Rather we set out to create an affirmative place and way of life, this by using an architecture of improvisation that we hope will inspire others and be copied. But what about the young, are they being inspired? The answer is no. Why? Simple: they have not been part of the making!

'By implication this means bringing young people into the space of making the city as a futural event – of our own and becoming — open for people elsewhere to copy. So, yes, we can and should inter-generationally make a city of colour, sound and re-naturalised environments. But it has to be more than this. It has to offer zones of retreat, places where a seeming flow toward an ever-diminishing world is broken. These are an interruption in the daily passage of time. From my perspective they are about going back to a point that redirectively enables a way to move forward. This is a journey of discovery requiring a particular kind of new learning. It is a task to be done, not a solution to be given and receive. For this to be possible it follows that these zones have to be placed outside the rhythm of everyday life and its activities. Such places in the past were created as spaces of the sacred and worship underwritten by a theology. Our zones of retreat offer nothing but nothing. The sacred is not to be found there. The zone is what each individual brings to it, what is there to be discovered. It replaces loss, not as a something, or spirit or transcendence but as a meaning of enablement posited by a self in one's world. As Charles Darwin knew, life arrived without meaning: it is simply *life* given meaning by us. It is our creation and our loss. Meaning was first made and socialised as myth, and then transformed into religion, despite all the efforts of all theologies to conceal the fact. Thereafter, myth and religion co-habited with fetish objects, material and/or immaterial, posited with the power of making spirit present by faith. But for all but the very few, faith has gone away. What is not lost is the leftover world of a future to be remade, and a demand for faith in ourselves and making with care, and the gaining of an essential knowledge to ethically define the distinction, and relation, between destruction and creation.

'Self-discovery in the zone of retreat enables a re-creation of meaning. There is no life for us without meaning: we cannot find it. It has to be made. It is the loss that kills. But it cannot be made in and of itself. It is posited with that which carries its reflective production. For it to have a life affirming capability, meaning has to have a transcendental potentiality that, in the circumstances of our age, can overcome knowledge of our species' reduced finitude. Meaning now has to be futural. It has to be constituted by bonding hope to futural action, not to realise a dream, utopia or transcendence, but to simply make everyday life meaningful. I have not succeeded in prompting this action. What I have done is create an abstraction that has to be concretised as a place from which to make another start, but not by me alone. This is not the project of an individual but that of a change in culture.

'Here is a short imaginary into a start-up process toward such a culture of place: a mimetic city.'

'The work of the working group

My name is Leffie. I am one of the founding members of the mimetic city working group. We are one year into the project and aim to complete it within five years. The idea is not to create our city to imitate its form but as a reproducible event out of which meaningful and different lives can be made. This is to say created meaning will be plural but the function it performs will be common, namely: living with a futural intent and thereby "making time in order to be". Life so lived would counter the nihilism so common these days. Our development process is experimental insofar as we discover what works, or does not, by doing things. Obviously events have to be orientated to different interests, to the socially adventurous as well as to the more culturally conservative. So here is an invented list of events that would be stream-cast to various profile collectives. They would arrive as a daily announcement when the day is switched on. Such events would arrive in real time with levels of support and interest measured. The immediate objective would be to establish a critical mass of viable ongoing events. The longer-term aim is for process to become self-generative within the animated life of *our* city producing a futural culture that many others would appropriate and strive to emulate. So here is what a trial and error programme might look like as a block.

Hi! I'm Leffie and I will be introducing the events happening today and later in the week. They are from the general mix and those matched to your social profile.

Street life: today's urban colours are tangerine and green grass. Laser colour projection illuminating our CBD and places of culture starts at dusk and ends at midnight. Other colour attractions are the flag-path walk, the city square lunchtime fashion parade, and the memorial park fountain.

Music: we have two free concerts. The **City Youth Orchestra** will perform Rolando Mie Wa's *Requiem for Ship Starlight* at 7.00pm at the City Concert Hall, and the wave three jazz quartet, **Singerman**, are playing at the Hole in the World at 9.00pm. The theme of this year's June **drum festival** is "beating the blues".

Music: a day to learn to play: this week it's the cello – see what you can learn in a day. If you like it sign up for "learn free" at the Music School on Sundays 2.00pm–4.00pm – bring a packed lunch. Call Auto-register 900 41 40 46.

Serious Entertainment: this event is at the Futures Institute at 7.30pm and is a debate between Carston Harrison and Olga Kruss on the value of unfinished books in higher education. For you unfamiliar with these books they are reprogrammable playback and self-recording books to which you listen and then record a finish. Carston and Olga will be talking for between one and two hours. The bookend has to be done in no more than four days. The prize is an audio book recording contract. These books were created as part of the imagination development programme of New Harshon Pluriversity.

Food: the Pluriversity farm "diggers and pickers" weekend is on the 2nd and 3rd of September this year – all welcome. The autumn and winter farm volunteer programme opens on the same weekend. The listspeak number to record your name and interest is Auto-register 900 41 41 44.

City Forum: this regular Saturday morning discussion will this week focus on the Civil Defence Command Detachment proposal to extend the citizen civil defence service requirement from eight evenings and two weekend training sessions, to ten evenings and three weekends. The overall service commitment remains the same: once every four years for all genders between the ages of twenty and forty.

Education: The new one-day-a-week work release day is open to all full-time employees. There is free choice of a multitude of subjects, all with free enrolments. Last year fifty-three percent of the workforce enrolled in at least one subject.

Work tour of the week: this week it is at J.W.G. Ceramics: is this a place you would like to work? Do they make things you would like to buy? Do you want to enter the paint-a-pot exhibition pool and prize-winning competition? If so, come along and pick a pot to paint and submit it for judging.

Read day: actor Jarr Whyle will be reading the short book *Bartleby the Scrivener* by Herman Melville, the famous author of the classic 19th century novel *Moby Dick*. Sunday afternoon from 2.00–4.00 at the City Library Open Space. Call Auto-register 900 48 41 43.

Friends of the Zone of Retreat – autonomous design workshop: conceptualising places where a "seeming flow toward an ever-diminishing world" is broken. These are an interruption in time. They are about going back to a point that enables a move to another timespace. If you think you have something to contribute do so by attending or by postEmedia. Call Auto-register 900 48 41 43.

News outside the news

- Jo Kee has just been appointed as the new head of the City Craft Repair Centre
- The City ConstructCorp has just opened eight new apprenticeship places

- Theatreworks has announced that audition dates for its production of the musical, *The Housebreaker*, will be posted today

- Work on stage two of the groundwater storage plant has been completed

- The City Night Run's "inspired runner of the week" was Lucy Jong who completed her 200th run and held her first place record in her 60–65 age class. If you can run, come! Every Wednesday evening at 6.15pm at The Mill Pond.'

(*Extended applause*)

'Angela this was not only an interesting presentation but also positively challenging, by which I mean the challenges you posed are very positive. They invite being risen to. So let me ask you this. Every city has a city life, and has events. How far do you have to go to be perceptibly different, and is difference itself sufficient to create the momentum that would produce the mimetic effect?'

'That's quite a question, Carlos. I wish I had the perfect answer, but I don't. What I can say is I believe that out of this low-budget materially simple, and unpretentious city of ours we can make something special, something futural. I cannot be certain that other cities will be inspired by what we do and copy it, but we are truly going to try.'

'Angela, you really have given me, and I am sure all of us, a lot to think about and hope for. Thank you so much.' (*Extended applause*)

An ancient philosopher once said that nothing is weaker than water and nothing is more powerful. We are a water city.

5. Gerda Krauss (doctor) – The world of health

Clearly being healthy in the diseased world that we all now occupy is really hard, and sadly in many ways this is increasingly becoming ever more so. This situation demands new kinds of intervention and action.

'Not only is Gerda Krauss my GP, she is also head of Medtrax, which is the health monitoring project established in the region by the Department of Health twelve years ago. She is the person who has educated me more than anyone else on the seriousness of the situation we are in for the long-term health of our species in general, and, particularly, the very young and old. So I did not have to give a moment's thought to deciding whom to ask to speak on this issue. Welcome, Gerda.' (*Applause*)

'Thanks for that intro, Carlos. I also count you not just as one of my patients but also as a friend.

'I aim to do four things. First, make some general remarks on health in the age of a changing climate that I will link to the moved city. I'm sorry, but the only way to do this is as an information dump. I will then talk about three important health action areas being introduced into New Harshon: the

Monitor Me programme, the Toxex Centre, a facility called Talking Places, and the Living Food Programme. Some of what I have to say may be familiar, but I think you will also hear new information. I will start with a review of physical impacts.

'As many of you already know, heat and air pollution, especially from wild fires, have a very significant impact on heart and lung disease. Heat of itself stresses the heart and lungs and can be, and often is, fatal for people suffering pulmonary and cardiovascular disease. Obviously, when combined with smoke and the particulates it carries, the effects on the body are even greater. Smoke also causes premature births and weakens the newborn, and clearly is very dangerous for asthma suffers, who are, along with allergy sufferers, exposed to higher pollen levels created by increased temperatures. Smoke from fires is thus particularly harmful; moreover, it can burn the lungs, plus carry mercury and carcinogenic particulates and neurotoxins into the body. Babies, children, older people and pregnant and nursing mothers are all at high risk. Heat also leads to dehydration, electrolyte imbalance and thus to kidney problems, including failure. Likewise heat and burning sunlight cause and aggravate skin diseases, not least cancer. Heat also affects bacteria carried in food and water and thereby increases the risk of gastrointestinal problems and digestive illness from salmonella and campylobacter. The relation between heat, rainfall patterns and water (both stagnate and floods, and during drought) increases vector-borne diseases – insects spread malaria, dengue, Lyme disease, West Nile virus, waterborne cholera, Zika virus and cryptosporidiosis. Many of these diseases lead to neurological problems.

'More indirectly, drought impacts food security, reduces supply and increases the numbers suffering from malnutrition, which in turn stresses the body and weakens the immune system and exposes the sufferer to any disease to which they are exposed. Added to this, extreme heat reduces the nutritional value of plant crops: protein, zinc and iron levels all drop. Mental health has already been mentioned in this event in terms of living with the feeling of a world without a future. But research has shown a direct relation between heat and mental illness. Those already suffering from it get worse; stress, depression and anxiety all increase. As does conflict and violence, both among individuals and groups.

'System impacts can be and are huge, obvious and concealed. Besides injuring people, extreme weather events – cyclones, floods, tsunamis, wild and bush fires, landslides, ice storms – bring down power systems, sever water supplies, and create chemical and other radiation hazards. Hospitals and their life support systems fail, emergency services become inoperable, and communication systems break down. Consequently, people die in numerous ways in the trauma, but then there are the invisible impacts. Like, for instance, the breakdown of the supply chain of critical medicines, and the effects on drugs exposed to high heat.

'It is not hard to recognise that any combination of these climate/health events can and do have huge immediate and enduring social impacts. The greater the impacts the more we beings are at risk. We travel toward risks as they travel toward us while climatic conditions continue to worsen. Future impacts are assured. We need to see the city against this backdrop. As a condition of population density, cities are locations of risk from infectious diseases and extreme weather events. Conversely they are places where we seek to create protection and security. As you will see this is not a simple matter of steel and concrete but equally of health systems.

'I need to take a deep breath before I carry on; maybe you do too; so let's all do it. Okay, stand up. Hands on hips, deep breath in, hold it, breathe out, and again, now once more. Good! Have a shake and sit down. Now for the programmes I mentioned.

'**Monitor Me:** In response to growing risks to health being created from the relational impacts of climate change, *Monitor Me* is about to be introduced as a free automated risk reduction technology. To look at, it is simple. All you see is an attractive composite material necklace with a small stainless steel sensor cartridge. It comes in black, white, red, yellow, blue or green and is issued by your GP who activates it with a personalised code. The sensor has the ability to monitor a whole range of body functions and conditions: heart rate, temperature, respiratory function, level of hydration and so on. The information it stores gets automatically picked up from anywhere in the city and reviewed. Any abnormalities go directly to the issuing GP who will send a "request to visit" notice. It will be made clear to all issued with the necklace that such a notice does not mean an immediate health crisis, but rather it is early detection of an abnormality that needs to be checked and, if significant, treated at this early stage. Although wearing the necklace is not compulsory it is highly recommended and it comes with an incentive: a free visit to the GP for a response to a "request to visit" notice and a twenty percent reduction of the costs of all other visits.

'**Toxex Test Caravan and Unit:** many environmental events like smoke from fires (which can be vast distances away), exposure to dust from damaged buildings, chemical and gas releases from industrial plants as a result of a disaster, or road spills and contaminated flood waters can produce ongoing negative physiological and neurological consequences and cause diseases that shorten lives. To address what is going to be a growing problem, the Department of Health established this mobile unit able to go to any environmental event and test people who have been at risk. All those who are found to have internalised toxic substances and other contaminants are then referred to the newly created Toxex unit at New Harshon General Hospital where a range of treatments and decontamination medical technologies are available. The critical factor is for action to be taken as soon as possible after exposure.

'*Talking Place:* this is a community psychiatric drop-in centre particularly aimed at teenagers to twenty-somethings. It is fronted by a coffee and milkshake bar, with a whole series of back-of-shop booths, small and large meeting rooms. A team of qualified mental health professionals, counsellors and volunteers staff it. Two modes of engagement are offered: **Chat and Rap** – this is just a casual drop-in service, as in "I would like to have an anonymous chat about a problem". The people who use it are those who don't feel able to talk to a person close to them, especially somebody likely to be judgmental. This exchange can be conducted in person or by phone. **Face to face** is a more formal service. Within it an individual can talk to a health professional by appointment. Usually this happens after a *Chat and Rap* consultation with anonymity, if wanted. So often these sessions are for people who do not feel they are in control of what they do, or have a profound sense of shame for an action done, while some are just very shy. The direct conversation with the health professional is usually on a specific problem. In all cases if any indicators of potential suicide are suspected or directly discussed, the staff member is obliged to make an urgent appointment with our resident clinical psychologist, indicating to the person that "you are strongly advised to attend this meeting". Over eighty percent do so. The other thing that *Face to Face* does is to provide an open group invitation: the times of meeting of three groups are listed on a chalkboard. The groups are: "I have a relationship problem" with six key words under it: parents, partner, boss, teacher, friend, other; "I have a substance abuse problem"; and "my problem is me". Everyone who comes to the shop is given a slip with a tick box for each of the options. On returning it they get a coffee or another drink and a call number which a volunteer will respond to with instructions. If the slip option is not accepted, the drink, and whatever else is ordered, is paid for. This description sounds very formal, but it works. The most significant thing about the project is that it is a place where people make friends, it's a gathering place, and the dividing line between its formal function and its informal character is very blurred.'

'Gerda, that was really useful. (*Applause*) You have given me a better understanding of what we are up against, and the three projects you outlined certainly show an affirmative response to the situation. What I especially found positive, after hearing earlier about the youth suicide crisis, is action on the ground that makes a really practical contribution. Some of what you have to say is familiar to me, but *Talking Place* is new. What I want to ask you is, what sort of picture are you forming of how things will go in the future?'

'Well, Carlos, it's good and bad news. Certainly stress in families that centred on the conduct of young adults has declined as the new city is taking shape. It's giving them hope. But countering that is how they feel about the world in general, which is bleak. So many of the young think there is not much of a future beyond the next few decades. Many girls don't want to have children. At best, almost all have a low level of depression, some more serious, and a few are chronic. They, and we, by degree, feel helpless. All you can say is that the future is uncertain and the only chance of having a positive future is to be committed to its creation in the recognition that millions of people are working to this end globally. We point out that despair is the ally of the negative. So the more successful projects like ours there are around the world the greater the possibility of a positive future. As far as I am concerned, if we want a future, we have to fight for it, and this is what we are doing now, and this is what we are learning to do better. So the message to young people from me is, be a part of making the future happen. The only weapon we have against despair is action.' (*Extended applause*)

'Gee, Gerda, it's hard. I realise this is something we all have to work at. Now we have more of a sense that while we have a city with a future, another project has arrived: the creation of a culture with a future built on action with the truth of possibility, affirmative stories, rejecting idealism, and, above all, refusing to be passive. Gerda, your contribution is not only appreciated, it has motivated me and, I am sure, others.' (*Applause*)

'Thank you, Carlos, we are trying.'

Money was once everything, but we have forgotten what it looked like. Now we have touch-pay but it cannot buy the things we need the most.

6. Gordon Chow (economist) – Localising the economic at the end of global capitalism

We economists are not alone in recognising that capitalism, as an economic system, is now dead. The market relation between supply and demand has broken, but local fiscal and non-fiscal modes of exchange are still created and live on.

'Gordon Chow was professor and chair of economics at Harshon University. He has an international reputation and has advised national and international governments over the past thirty years. Over breakfast this morning I reflected upon how many times I have interviewed Gordon, which I discovered was seventeen times! Gordon is another speaker I am honoured to count as a friend. But before handing him over to you, I have a little story about him I would like to share. I interviewed him last year, and after we finished we had a beer. During our conversation he told me he was trying to lead a life without money and was developing a system of comparative value based on trading in skills and knowledge. I was sceptical and said so. Gordon then told me he trades his knowledge with the result that his fiscal income is reduced by sixty-four percent but his standard of living remains the same. So when you hear what he has to say, remember that Gordon practises what he preaches. I commend him to you.' (*Applause*)

'Carlos, I hope I can live up to the expectations you have created, and likewise I am honoured to count you as a friend.'

'I want to start by posing and answering the question: how can we think of economics now? The glib answer would be that which is post post-capitalism. What this actually means is that capitalism, as it was known and understood, is over, yet not completely. Nothing in terms of a system has replaced it. In fact what remains, after the breakdown of the immaterialisation of money and much of the international currency exchange system, is the fragments of an older and more basic form of exchange centred on the buying and selling of life-sustaining goods, which means things, commodities, products and so on, that are goods in every respect of the world.

'As you know the economic situation that now pertains was caused by the collision of two catastrophic conditions that, in summary, were:

1   The environmental impact of a compound crisis of terrestrial, oceanic and atmospheric problems causing the loss of many major cities and smaller settlements, around twenty percent of the planet being too hot for human habitation, the collapse of the food system in around thirty countries, a crisis of biodiversity that is rending numerous ecological systems unstable, and, as you all experience, life lived in a hostile environment. The tragedy has been absolutely massive. Over the past fifty years one-and-a-half billion people have died. Billions of native animals and vast numbers of plants and trees have become extinct. So although we now live in a carbon neutral world and are told the situation will stabilise in two hundred to three hundred years what we don't know is what this condition will actually be. Informed opinion has it that our species will certainly survive, but not everywhere. It is thought our species will do this in two contexts: in relatively benign environments and with the help of a supportive technosphere.

2   The economic cost of the compound crisis of this scale has been incalculable and beyond the means of all states. But this was not the environmental apocalypse that was the stuff of dystopic films and fiction for decades – there were and are still cities, industries, farms, and so on, with operative capability albeit on a damaged planet. However, such was the scale of the impacts upon all systems of value that national and international exchange imploded. Now, as

you are so keenly aware, there was a decade of chaos and a super depression, together with the revalorisation of what became known as "futural essentials", which basically meant all those essentials that supported "utility life". Along with this, a huge "social system of swop and barter" was created. The other key factor that enabled us to reach the condition of semi-functionality we now enjoy was the lessons learnt from the informal economy of our own and other parts of the world that led to an economy of reciprocal need. This is called "mutuality" wherein knowledge, skills and help are exchanged in a credit system. As you all have experienced, this has been a major factor in establishing the likes of community health aid centres, housing construction collectives, and early childhood community centres. Added to this has been the annual citizen-service two-week options contracts we all are required to sign up for, whether it be "farm force", civil defence, "urban repair force", or "age and disabilities support teams". As you are well aware this is not utopia. Life is hard, resources are scarce, 'exploiters' and poverty are still widespread, and the social fabric of the city has totally changed. Yet life goes on. Everyone understands the lived relation between economic exchange and social ecology that manifests itself in friendship acquiring a whole new meaning.

'While there were moments of overt crisis it was mostly a normalised process over time. What remained, and has developed, as you know well, has been a money structure based on a system called "basics indexed against a basket of futural essentials", under the management of Bank One, an organisation formed out of the ruins of the World Bank. Thus, there exists a partial trade of commodities between what we now know as "shell nations", nations without an operative state.

'Before going further, I need to remind you of the economic reconfiguration of the relation between national, regional and local. As you know, this nation no longer has a representative parliament or a comprehensive public service structure. Rather, what now exists is a council of regional chief ministers who represent a democratically elected council of rural and urban mayors, who are also the chief ministers of elected local councils. The regional council receives no taxes but levies regions for an annually agreed amount which covers communications and inter-city infrastructure, a partial power grid, the regional law council, and land and sea transport standards council plus the national relocation department, central exchange bank and trade council, and the departments of agriculture and health. Organisationally it is small and essential to coordinate common policy between regions with its workforce distributed to regional centres. What will not be as familiar to you, and what I now want to talk in a little more detail about, is the emergence of our hybrid economy as it reflects an approach that is now happening, although with circumstantial variations, around the world.

'Let's start with how "resource revalorisation" is understood. While there are still extractive industries, they are a fraction of their past scale. At its most basic, the economic means to move and process mass extractions no longer exists. For example, while iron ore is still mined it is done on a small scale. There are no huge mining corporations; no vast open cut mines, bulk ore-carrying ships, massive iron works or steel mills – the energy industry to support such operations just does not exist any longer. What now exists are mini-iron works and foundries, plus solar-power arc furnaces producing steel from pelleted iron and recycled steel. Materials are transported by sea by the owners of mostly small fleets of solar-thermal powered cargo ships. All past resources, as you know from our own experience in moving Harshon, have gained a new value and have spawned a contemporary economy of material recovery, reprocessing and recyclables, reuse-structures and equipment repair, remanufacture and retrofit. This includes recovering and multi-cycling materials and engineered components. What resulted from all these changes was a huge growth in recyclers, a really big reduction in heavy industry, and the construction of large steel-framed buildings, plus a new arms industry based in a military enclave. There is still some light engineering production; component manufacture, assembly and fabrication; and electronics manufacture/remanufacture and repair, with a massive expansion of repair and retrofit workshops for the motor, domestic and office technologies industries. Building construction, materials recovery and manufacture are also substantial. Our modest development of industries reflects these trends. It also indicates the need to consider a micro-retrofit of the old port or the creation of a new small one.

'The other areas of post-development economics to comment on are the local urban and extended peri-urban economies of primary needs, which subject to local conditions includes food and agriculture, plantation forestry for construction timber, renew-energy generation and public transport, city security and regional defence, telecommunications, education, health care and more. The Regional Department of Trade (RDT) administers much of this, together with other elements of the hybrid economy. It is also responsible for the large amount of inter-regional and the small amount of export trade, all conducted with a commonly agreed currency. A trans-regional economy was created after the bankruptcy and complete breakdown of the national banking system and debt write-off of the nation. This centred on establishing local currency and banking, and materials exchange in an inter-cities trading system. The transition period was, as everyone recognises, enormously hard. There was violence, death and suffering, the breakdown of law, and a lot of material damage, but somehow, from the organisation of disparate activities of small groups, a new order started to emerge. Life was and remains lean. There was and is no material excess of anything. Our ingenuity is tested every day. Things are not going to change. In fact, environmental challenges continue to arrive. But even so we are making a future, we are learning. There will be no return to the material sacrificial destruction of the future perpetrated by our industrial ancestors.

'Now before I started Carlos told me I must end by talking about the new cultural economy, so I asked him, why? He had what I thought was a very good answer. Carlos, would you please tell everyone what it was?'

'Well, Gordon, as you will remember it was short and I think sweet: it is our major path to making a quality of life.'

'I totally agreed with him. But what does this economy look like? Well, Angela has sketched a significant part of the picture by talking about what could bring a mimetic city into being. What I will to try to do is map the concept onto our current economy and lives. The starting place is just to point out that the economy depends on exchange, and in our context cultural economy implies an exchange of culture. This does not reflect how it was understood in the past which was as a cultural commodity exchanged for money. So what does exchange of culture look like? Let's view this question through two frames: pleasure and knowledge. The point of doing this is not to specify a list of actions, although some examples will be given, but to jog or seed your imagination so that you become active generators of a cultural economy, which I will conflate with its cognate: creative economy.

'Pleasure so framed means *the discovery of cultural production* be it drawing and painting, sewing and knitting, composing or making music by voice or a made instrument, cooking or pot-making, writing or reading and so on, and the *gifting of the produced*. The giving of the made is an exchange for: a meal, an invitation to perform, listening to a reading, or another cultural artefact. Pleasure is the currency, the object of exchange: a bridge across cultures. The banality of the everydayness of so many of these activities puts art in its place, not as the owner and keeper of the discourse of culture.

'Education is fundamentally cultural exchange and acquisition across generations and generative of culture, which is one definition of the German concept of *bildung*. This notion of education has to be extended from the earliest and most basic to the highest levels of formal education. What needs to be remembered is predominantly learning how to be and function informally in the world. To bring such thinking to consideration of a cultural economy in the context we are in, which is a new world formation, a three-part question needs asking: what do we need to learn, what has our experience already taught us, and how do we exchange this knowledge pleasurably and, in so doing, improve the quality of our lives? Imagine a cultural exchange market with home-made candy, coffee and cake, and gingerbread animal stalls, where boards placed around the room display pinned template notices, that have been prompted by the notification of the event. On each notice an offer and a request are made. For example: I speak Mandarin and I can teach it, but I want to learn French from a French speaker who wants Mandarin; I am a piano teacher, and you are a quilt maker I can learn from who wants to learn piano. I am a home brewer who wants to find a guitar maker I can learn from who wants to learn to brew good beer. What is going on with such activity is a voicing of unspoken small dreams, informal opportunities of learning with formal possibilities that increase sociality and social networks. All this costs almost nothing but time. It is serious and fun. Maybe some of you have better ideas. So that's it.' (*Extended applause*)

'Gordon, that was great! I think you have completely blown out of the water most people's ideas of what an economist is. I have one question for you, and so does Angela. Who will go first?'

'Great to meet you Gordon, can you come and visit us? Sorry, that's not my question. I want to ask if you have a response to this problem: we want a whole series of events like the one you have just outlined, but there is an issue of language and perception that is distant from content and intent. For example, the word "festival" characterises the content as entertainment, and it displaces the idea of the event as serious. Our group wants to create events that are serious entertainment that give pleasure. We feel that the language of the cultural economy is tired and clichéd. If you agree, do you have any suggestions?'

'Angela, I do agree, and misperception is always a problem. In these situations there are really only two choices: you give old words new meaning, or you invent new words that people can't make sense of. In your case I would go with new meaning and create an event called "the event without a name" in order to brainstorm – another tired word – an invented name. Here is a word that's a bit of both: "a taval"; here is an invented example, "a sparker". So invite folks to "rebirth of the blues taval" (a kind of journey), a pleasure biased event; or "creative writing for the future sparker" (the spark that causes the blaze).' (*Applause*)

'Gordon, you've hit it! I'm inspired. Thanks a trillion.' (*Applause*)

'After that, my question is going to sound a bit flat, Gordon. Anyway this is it. At the moment an economy exists that does not produce wealth but does deliver a basic condition of social function: can it take us to the future?'

'Carlos, over a century ago an organisation called the Club of Rome commissioned Donna and Dennis Meadows, Jorgen Randers and William Behrens, who were supported by seventeen researchers, to write a report on "The Limits to Growth" in an age of rampant capitalist consumerist expansion. The report was criticised and mostly ignored. Expansion continued globally and is one of the key factors that brought us to our current juncture. Why am I telling you this? Well, it's because we now live in a condition where "the limits to growth" are structural and imposed upon us as a constant pressure. Our situation, as we all realise, is not stable. Environmentally, the situation is still getting worse from processes created in the past. This means the economic propensity is for the limits to continually increase. This is an entropic trajectory that we work against every day. The objective has to be to maintain this situation in ever better ways if we are to have a future. This is what the Meadows told us, and what we have learnt for ourselves. At the same time, living in this utility world requires us to improve the quality of our lives, which is exactly what we have been talking about doing. It's not that we need an economy of modesty; it's the only one available to us.'

'A last and very general question Gordon. Having heard the presentation by Gerda, and in the context of what you have said, how do you feel about the future?'

'Well, we can't ignore the world we live in. But in terms of action none is available to us. For me what this means is addressing what is available to be acted upon, with the hope that it becomes influential as a form of the future, and protecting what we have to the best of our ability.'

'Are you implying doing this with military means?'

'Yes I am, but only with defence intent, and in saying this I realise it opens a whole host of hard questions.'

'That was all challenging and excellent, Gordon. Thank you.' (*Extended applause*)

We face many choices of direction, but there is really only one to follow. Hallelujah! Being futural.

7. Carla Boas (redirective practitioner) – New thinking, new action

New thinking and action are not a matter of choice but a necessity equal to the food that nourishes, the water we drink, the air we breathe. What I'm saying is that without new thinking and action we humans will not survive.

'I met Carla for the first time yesterday. She is a newbie. Carla has just been hired by Kase, Pheun and Curvitz, the urban design company who we know well as a partner organisation in the city move project. She has come today highly recommended by Lilly Kase. I suspect, like me, you are not exactly clear what "redirective practice" is, so, Carla, tell us all a little about yourself and what redirective practice is.' (*Applause*)

'Thank you, Carlos. I will be happy to do that. Like you I was born in Brazil. My father worked for the H-gen-electric car company, Volkswagen, and we moved to Germany in 2041 when I was two. At university I studied engineering and on graduation I went to Finland to do a PhD in Redirective Design Practice at Aalto University. This was in 2062. I gained the PhD in 2066 and scored a position in the Berlin office of Group Arup. I was especially excited by this appointment as I wrote my undergraduate honours dissertation on Ove Arup and his contribution to the design of steel structures. He formed his first company Arup and Arup with his cousin in 1938, and he was an interesting man. Born in England, his father was Danish and his mother Norwegian. Ove was educated in Denmark, with his first degree in philosophy, and then he enrolled in engineering. I tell you this because his spirit and intellect have always permeated the company. What he established was a kind of reflective instrumentalism that I have brought to redirective practice. I did this when working on the "Crisis Europe" metrofitting projects out of the Berlin office where I was a senior redirective practitioner until I accepted my position here in New Harshon. I was hired by Kase, Pheun and Curvitz, this to specifically form a small team to develop redirective practice within the company. So now to define what redirective practice is.

'The first thing is the activity is about remaking a practice by redirecting it. The aim of doing this is to take it beyond its existing limits of knowledge and practical applications. In simple terms this means transcending the box your education and professional history placed you in. While I have engineering, design and philosophical knowledge, what I know and do is a synthesis. My thinking, even my identity, can no longer be assigned to a disciplinary regime. I have redirected what I know. And what I know is used to redirect the knowledge of others, no matter the disciplines, towards synthetic relational knowledge. Why? Because nothing in the world in which we live functions in conditions just based on the separation of knowledge into specialisms. Rather it needs to function more like the inter-connectedness of an ecology. The schism between how our species has mostly thought and acted, and how "things are/were in the natural world" is deeply embedded in the mess we are in. Redirective practice therefore aims not to discard existing thought and practice but redirect and transform them to break down the divisions that disconnect knowledge from activities that continue to be unsustainable. We should remember for all the impacts of climate change we are familiar with there are still many technologies with defuturing consequences. With redirective practice it becomes possible to redirect these technologies so they can contribute to creating *sustainment futures*. This means futures in which we all live within the means that renewable resources afford. The age of the materiality of un-sustainment that governments, corporations and institutions did in the past, often unwittingly but in many instances knowingly, is over. Action in the past was undertaken in the name of development, but the reality was the creation of the worldly conditions of the mess that we are now in. As you know as well as I do, now we have to advance and support all those processes that sustain the conditions of life for us and all other species. This is the intellectual and material challenge to be faced, and to which all redirective practice actions are directed.

'I now want to draw out four implications of adopting redirective practice. The first goes to how it makes a demand on thinking, which can be summed up as: unmaking the received way of thinking that arrived with the divisions of knowledge and exercise of practical reason that formed and occupy so much taken-for-granted thinking and work habits. What gets unthought is "how to" knowledge, whether that be making, reviewing, reporting, writing, repairing, discussing, evaluating, judging and so on, *while not asking why and with what consequence*. This denotes a culture of "going along with" – as centred forms of compliance and conformity that structurally positions hundreds of millions of people to perform their jobs automatically in accordance with the rules and requirements of a system. Without ill intent, often in a state of resignation, they exchanged their labour for a wage and a consumerist way of life, and, in so doing, sacrificed freedom of agency. Here is a way of being formed in the factories of the early twentieth century that became completely naturalised. It established an inter-generational condition of conformity that didn't, and doesn't, suddenly disappear once the working day is over. It becomes habitual, and so established taken-for-granted ways of thinking and acting. Unmaking such a world view is a huge task and requires a change in circumstances, which is exactly what we have experienced, and instituting another way of making, which is what redirective practice opens up. Currently we are in a situation where the remaking of thought is becoming possible, but for this to happen new knowledge has to be created, and then become concretised. In part, moving the city affords this opportunity, but it can only be realised by a great deal of effort.

'In context, the intellectual dimension of everyday life, as you all are aware, does not function in an abstract domain. This is where redirective practice comes in as a process, and central to it is working across specialisms, restrictive practices, and disciplines, and against habitual thought. For this to happen unfamiliar projects are needed, which is exactly what moving a city is. Moreover, a city move is a project that spans decades. So from a redirective practice perspective it is ideal: that's why I'm here.

'As I have said, such a remaking of thinking does not reject all past modes of thought, philosophical traditions and their epistemologies. Rather it redirects them and passes them through a complex matrix of imperatives as a selection filter that is not universal or definitive but created in specific situations. It is these imperatives that force a thinking otherwise and for the altered thinking to be appropriated by new imaginaries directed at unmaking and remaking practices – new circumstances, imperatives, problems and responsive actions that unmake old thinking and practice. They are not available, and as with the old city, there is no choice but to remake differently, and this means constantly thinking and acting another way.

'Next, it's very clear that what essentially unmaking is doing is removing those defuturing practices and their outputs. At the same time remaking puts in place that which futures. Again, a basic example is to hand: like a vast number of other cities, Harshon over its functional life contributed to the impact with negative effects that created the future that sealed its fate. In contrast, New Harshon, remade from the old, has provided the conditions that enable another kind of future to be made. To know this is to experience, in spite of all the hardship, a life force.

'What I hope is becoming clear is that unmaking the city is an undoing of mind as well as matter. As an event the city is not just where we are but, in large part, what we are. We become subjects of the city. So in remaking the city we are also within an event of remaking ourselves to be futural. Both the recreated city and self are essential, but can never easily or quickly be done. I know most of you will feel what I have said to be challenging or radical, but it's not an idealistic dream. It is a task, one you all have already started. All I am here to do is to help add momentum to what is already under way.

'Obviously I am still getting to grips with being here. I have lots to learn about the history, place, people and problems, but especially about the move process. So being at this event has been a wonderful experience for me, not just because so much of what has been said has been interesting and informative, and not just because I have met some fantastic people, but because I got to feel the spirit of the place, which is strong and grounded. I am sure you will understand I am reluctant to say much more until I know more. I am excited to be here! Thank you.' (*Extended applause*)

'Carla, thank you! I think I can speak for all of us in saying we are very pleased to have you here. (*Applause*) Yes, the ideas you have talked about are challenging. We have spent many years overcoming the massive practical task we gave ourselves. What I, and I hope others, take away from what you said is that we have to reflect upon, consolidate and develop the knowledge we have gained to take us to a viable future, because in moving a city we have been immersed in a redirective practice. Your knowledge and experience are so welcome. As you might know, you are the first "outsider" to be hired for a long time. So from today onward please consider that you crossed a threshold here. You are now an insider and part of our change community.' (*Applause*)

We create our built environment from the gifts of the desert and a broken past, and from the imagination of inspired people.

8. Chris Glover (construction team leader and instructor) – Construction from the future to the present

Friends, not only is a new city being built largely out of the rubble of the old but we are also totally remaking the world in which we work and live.

'I met Chris at the start of the "move day", which was June 20, 2066. He was a member of the project's first disassembly team, and one of many skilled workers I interviewed that day. After the interview I asked him if he would have a beer and chat the following week. I wanted to get more of a perspective on the guys and gals dealing with the physical reality of the massive task of disassembling the old city and using much of the material to build the new. We have been meeting for a beer most weeks ever since. What I heard – the highs and lows of everyday work experience on the ground of the men and women dedicated to the task over the years – was a great corrective to the continuous flow of media releases. So I first want to publicly acknowledge my debt to Chris and to say that I truly value his honesty and friendship, which has gone well beyond its initial practical dimension. From his humble beginnings, Chris has risen to become one of the most important and valued persons at the sharp end of the move. It is with pride and pleasure that I introduce him.' (*Applause*)

'Carlos, you know no matter the situation I've always got a quick word, but today I just don't know what to say. When you asked me to talk about my job and my experience and to come in my work wear it didn't make much sense to me. But I now think I've got it! I really appreciate what you have said about me. Thank you Carlos I have to say I'm proud to stand here before you all as a representative of the workforce, the human backbone of the project, the working men and women who have done, and still do, all the hard graft of moving Harshon and building New Harshon. The simple fact is that nothing would have happened without us. (*Extended applause and stamping of feet from the back of the room*)

'I want to pick up on something Carla had to say. She made it clear that the circumstance that we are now in, with most of New Harshon now built, has changed what and how we build as well as us workers. Central to this is improvisation – what and how we build is based on improvisation. Long gone are the days when building construction was based on fixed regulations and national building standards. This does not mean that health and safety, and construction quality have been forgotten. Rather it means we have had to learn how to adapt and improvise. About eighty percent of what we build is from salvaged materials; the remaining twenty percent is locally acquired. One building is never the same as the next, even when they look similar. In the past, specifications were precise and tolerance very tight. While we do calculate stress and load-bearing factors and the like, we can only build with what is to hand. This means we do what was done in the distant past: we over-specify; we never cut it fine; we never take a risk. As you know and can see, we can no longer build large buildings or very high load-bearing structures. We do not have the fixings of the building technology of the past. Neither do we have the mastics or bonding agents of the past, all of which require a chemical industry we don't have. The industry we now have is very basic. We do have many power tools but we don't have as many generators and compressors as we need. Many that we do have are old and have been converted to site solar electric from diesel engine power. What this means is that a lot more work is done by hand. We are more like workers of the mid-twentieth century than the late twenty-first. More than this, to innovate in construction means you need to have ideas and be good at solving problems. And, by goodness, we are! One last "human factor" for all the reasons I have just outlined. Teamwork was always important in construction, but now it has become massively so. The other thing is that everyone has to be multi-skilled. What was so interesting for me listening to Carla was that much of what she was talking about and had theorised we were already doing. All of us are redirective practitioners. None of us work in the ways we used to, think like we used to or behave like we used to. We take so much more care over what we construct and each other. We really trust each other and build buildings that you can trust.

'One of the really important things related to trust that needs to be understood goes to how the design team – a cooperative group drawn from all the architecture, planning and civil and services engineering companies in Harshon – designed the urban form, buildings, infrastructure and services of New Harshon. Supporting this activity was a "futural needs analysis" conducted by a team of economists and sociologists recruited from the university and the business community. The entire approach was based on creating everything by applying the design principle of "designing back from the future" to the present. Based on risk and impact studies and demographic growth projection for a century, the city has been designed to be able to be expanded by twenty percent, and to withstand increased climatic-environmental impacts at an average rate of 0.4 percent per year. The risks of violent attacks on the city were also addressed, but responsive measures were classified. The three most discernible outcomes of taking this action are evident in: land allocation, urban farming planning policy, and building and infrastructure design and specification. All of these measures were incorporated in the city "Population, Environment and Economy Action Plan 2075–2175" and ten-year review processes. For building construction, beyond building design and specification, the approach meant great care was taken in site selection, and the full utilisation of available site material: already situated, reclaimed and renewable. As you no doubt know, all of this was directly connected to the care taken in the mining of Harshon for its reusable building components, materials and recyclables.

'None of this happened by magic. It all took a lot of planning and training. From my perspective it meant transforming workers who had been inculcated into an industry based on prefabrication, high-volume use of huge amounts of timber and plywood formwork, and concrete supplied from a large ready-mix industry, plus major usage of steel framing and fabrication. All of this equates to a particular skill base. In contrast, our mode of construction now uses very little prefabrication, and a dramatically smaller volume of concrete, not just because we are constructing smaller buildings but because there is no longer a large national cement industry, only small-scale local plants. We have plenty of steel, but are not building large steel-framed buildings. When steel is used there is more cutting and welding as our supply is from large structures with large unit sizes. For example, most of the stockpiled steel beams we have, in profile and dimensions, are much larger than we need, as well as being massively over-length. I have very many examples of the adaptive challenges we have learnt to deal with. But I recognise if I continue to give them, I may well end up talking to an empty room! What I do want everyone to really understand is that all this has meant a lot of training to develop new skills and reconfigurations in the skill mix. For instance, we needed a much higher ratio of carpenters and bricklayers than in the past. One of our first jobs was to build a brick works.

'As for training we developed a very sophisticated training programme with a team of on-site trainers. A specific training programme for each person was drawn up, based on their performance in a skill assessment test set by the trainer and myself as head of training. What this means is that the length of training is customised. One person might take three months, another six. Remember that all these people being retrained were already time-served and certificated trades men and women. Trainers were working with trades people who, in the past, could run training sessions, give demonstrations and be assigned a training partner. However, before working as an independent trades person in their retained area in New Harshon, a trade test had to be passed. All unskilled young people we sign up acquire their trade via an indentured apprenticeship, which means they are paired with an experienced qualified trades person to teach them their trade. Again, capability is tested by trade tests. Effectively what has been done is to revert to methods that were used in the early twentieth century, not for ideological or romantic reasons, but because pragmatically this is what works in the circumstances we are in.

'So the better we understand the city as a built structure, the more able we are to cope with what comes at it in the future. Oh, almost forgot. I need to say more about the nature of the buildings. Carlos, is that okay? I know this might not be gripping stuff for everyone, but I feel that understanding how the city works and its structure and how buildings are designed to function under stress is a significant contribution to having a sense of security.' (*Applause*)

'Chris, I think everybody is with you. Some of us may not fully understand every term you have used, like I thought formwork was what public servants did, but that doesn't matter. The point is you're painting a picture that changes how most of us see the city.' (*Applause*)

'Okay, Carlos, that's good. I will just plough on.'

'As you have discovered, the New Harshon buildings are basic: they are utility. We don't have any plasterboard to line walls, our supply of plaster is limited, as is paint, although we do have a good deal of locally made lime-wash. What you don't see is how they have been designed and built to deal with the future. All buildings are ground anchored and can withstand very high wind speeds and object impacts. Likewise, all roofs are cyclone secured and have the ability to retain high volumes of rainwater via pipework to above and below ground storage. This can be patched to the water supply via a micro-charcoal filter system, a building sprinkler system, or the city fire wetworks. Every floor has storm shutters for all windows. Every commercial building has: a basic uninterrupted power supply (UPS); BatSet emergency telecom local area network protected connection; and emergency food storeroom. Effectively every building can become an emergency shelter. All domestic buildings, while not being of the same specification, are still storm and cyclone protected. This includes the bathroom box-frame construction making it an in-house shelter. They won't win a bathroom design competition, but one day they could save the life of a family. Last of all, a quick word about infrastructure: all services are underground in a common trench. The high volume use of a huge amount of timber and ply formwork for remote telecom, trans-net and sensor-net boxes is sub-surface with multiple concealed building-mounted micro aerials. That's about as brief a rundown as I can manage. Glad to see you are all still awake! (*Laughter*) But seriously, while what I have said may not be very sexy, it is important to understand how the joint works and how different it is from the old city beyond mere appearances.' (*Extended applause*)

'Chris, I have something to say to you, but first Angela has a question.'

'Chris, I actually have two. The first relates to a comment you made. You said that paint was in short supply. Does that mean our building colour painting project will run out of paint?'

'Angela, short term I can promise that we will be able to find you enough paint for a significant number of walls of CBD buildings. I know I can get support from the city engineer and architect on this. They think you are doing a great job in giving the city a distinctive look, and rate your project highly in general. We have discovered it is possible to buy paint from several other regions, but it is extremely expensive and in terms of the amount we need unaffordable. So in the longer term we have plans to create a small local paint industry. Through talking to the chemists at the university we will be looking to develop a plant-based oil paint, again going back to the past to go forward. We cannot, and do not want, to manufacture a polymer-based synthetic paint. We don't have the material, knowledge, plant or money to do so. It would also be an environmental nightmare. But the project is going to take a year or so.'

'That's all really helpful and interesting, Chris. My second question relates to an idea a group of artists have been talking about over the past few weeks. It is to build a giant solid structure billboard on the eastern foreshore at something like forty-five degrees so a ship coming into port would see it, as would anyone travelling down the Port Road. The artists have been looking at images of Harshon, and selected one they think would make a great mural. Sign-written on the reverse side would be the words "In memory of the city that made New Harshon". I should say that these guys and gals are really good. If they do it, it will be spectacular. I have a proposal with me that I would like to give you. Will you accept it and pass it on?'

'Wow, Angela, what a gas! I think if it's done well it's a great idea, and I will pass it on. Thank you.' (*Applause*)

'Chris, Angela, an idea of sadness and joy: what a fitting ending to the day. Finally, Chris, I think I can speak for everyone in this room: you and every single person who has made a practical contribution to moving Harshon and building New Harshon has done, and are still doing, an incredible job. It's taken many years and there are still a few to go. For this, for the city of New Harshon, we owe you and every construction worker a huge debt. (*Cheers and applause*)

'Now, for some, these remarks, linked to others made today, might be taken as an exercise just devoted to patting ourselves on the back. But we all know of arguments, of thankfully small disasters, of an odd failure or three, but we came through. So on behalf of this event of thinking and seeing a way forward, I ask that you find a way to communicate to every construction worker our sincere thanks for their labour, from all the speakers and the audience of this gathering.'

'Carlos, I can't remember who, but someone said that your introduction to them was gracious. I hear the words you have just spoken in the same way, they are truly appreciated. Cities are not just built by visionaries, but by anonymous hands. I will do what you ask with pride.' (*Applause*)

'Well, thank you all for coming to what for me, and I hope for you, has been an amazing day that has given us so much to think about. Above all what has arrived more powerfully than anything else is a sense of a future to look forward to. I hope you agree. Finally, I would like to thank my team for the work they put into making the day run smoothly. Above all, I must thank Grace, Lena, Kendrick, Angela, Gerda, Gordon, Carla, and Chris for their wonderful presentations. Please show your appreciation.' (*Cheers and standing ovation*)

A postscript to the event – the day of attack

It was almost exactly four months after the Harshon moving cities event that the city was attacked. I was woken at around 5.15am by the sound of loud explosions. I have written an account of this and subsequent events here as a postscript to this publication, which was just about to go to press.

Less than a week after the moving city event public reports started to arrive saying that there had been a series of armed attacks on communities in the region. While the possibility was voiced in various ways at the event by Eric Fontenille and four other speakers, and therefore was something I feared, I was nonetheless surprised. Intellectually I knew it was likely, yet I did not feel the prospect emotionally.

Before I start to give an account of what happened, I need to provide a brief background. The news of a series of raids on communities in the region generated considerable concern. Three days after the news arrived an emergency Council meeting was held to discuss a course of action, followed the next day by a public meeting to report what had been decided. At that time all that existed to defend the city were two small lightly-armed police force SWAT teams. Obviously this was totally insufficient. At the Council there was a contention over whose responsibility the defence of the city was. While legally it was the state, in its condition of dysfunction all responsibility had been abrogated. Effectively, by default, defence was taken over by the military enclave under the direction of a military council that already had troops deployed in serious outbreaks of violence in the region. Clearly, the chance of getting any military support from anywhere was zero. The non-violent position was argued for well over an hour and, while touching nerve endings, it went nowhere. In the end the pragmatists tabled a motion to create a rapid response local defence force. The motion was passed with ease.

At the subsequent public meeting it was clear that the majority of the city's population were frightened, wanted protection and supported the Council. A small number of dissenters spoke, but they were shouted down. At the end of the meeting a delegation was formed to convey its overwhelming view to Council. They visited the Mayor's office the following morning and, as a result, were invited to make a short statement at the Council meeting, which their spokesperson did.

The decision to form a local defence force prompted issuing two calls to arms: first, to ex-service men and women to volunteer, and secondly to men and women between the ages of twenty and thirty. Some one hundred and twenty ex-service volunteers came forward: seventy-two were selected on the basis of age, fitness, skills and experience. Among them were eight formerly commissioned, and twenty-six non-commissioned officers: twenty were placed in a reserve group. There were eight hundred and nine untrained volunteers: two hundred and fifty were selected and four hundred and twenty placed on the reserve list along with thirty-six ex-service members. The local defence force (LDF) was formally established, contracts were issued and a public ceremony of collectively swearing allegiance to protect the city was held.

On the same day an arms procurement committee met. It had been established with membership from the LDF, the Mayor and members of the finance committee and finance officers. The immediate task was to arm the LDF so it had some fighting capability recognising it would take longer to fully equip. A police armed rapid response group (PARR) was formed with the twenty SWAT team members at its core and an additional twelve policemen and four policewomen who all had small arms training. Two ex-infantry NCOs were attached to assist with further training. PARR was to be an independent better-armed and equipped unit, but under general LDF tactical command. At the same time, PARR retained its police function. In addition, the police were to provide and equip a telecommunication control centre at which the LDF command group would be based. All of these arrangements took place within a month of the decision to form the LDF.

In the following six weeks an initial basic training was delivered to all volunteers, with a two-week refresher course for all ex-service people of all ranks. Ranks were reordered in a simplified system. Three defence companies were formed, each with five platoons. Additional support companies were also created. An initial cordon was designed established, and construction work got under way. Almost forty percent of the arms purchased arrived within five weeks. What was lacking were refurbished armoured personnel carriers, heavier weapons, and short-range and anti-tank rocket launchers. A fleet of trucks and utility vehicles was established – some donated, others loaned as a stopgap. The eight officers met and selected a commanding officer – Jay Comora, a former infantry captain and company commander with combat experience of just a few years ago. A command structure was established. A fully equipped and combat-effective defence force was several months away, but the city was no longer defenceless. Now back to the dawn attack.

The attack

The small rogue militia launched the attack on the eastern industrial area of New Harshon. This area contained two medical equipment warehouses; the regional seed bank office; climate controlled storage for produce prior to distribution; a refurbished machine tool workshop; a warehouse full of computers, office machines, audio-visual equipment and telecom equipment; a vehicle retrofit workshop; a large used parts warehouse spanning numerous technologies; an industrial chemicals store and chemical recycling plant; a helicopter service workshop and parts store; and lastly, the yard and office of a scaffolding hire company. Obviously, some of these assets were seen as more strategic than others. The assault's specific objective was not clear, and it was unsuccessful as a result of the arrival of a SWAT team and ten police men and women armed with just their side-arms and a few pump-action shotguns. There were fatalities and a number of injuries. One policewoman and three civilians were killed, with one SWAT team member and two policemen wounded, one seriously. There was damage to five buildings, the most serious being to holding tanks in the yard of RID Chemicals hit by rocket-grenades. As a result, a large area in and around the yard required environmental remediation.

Our intelligence identified the attackers as Group 75, a collection of disaffected discharged soldiers and redundant copper miners who are apparently often hired by a consortium of black-market dealers to plunder whatever goods they can find that are easy to resell. They gained notoriety two years ago by raiding a guarded mothballed army reserve depot, killing twelve security guards, and stealing twenty-eight vehicles, including armoured fighting vehicles, plus a large stash of weapons, ammunition and clothing. The attack was seen as serious for it increased the group's aggressive capability and firepower, and thus significantly increased the risk level for many cities.

Additionally, at the time of the attack, an intelligence report was provided by a small remote surveillance detachment incorporated into the military enclave from the former national army. The enclave flies a fleet of always-airborne solar-electric sensor and imaging auto-report drones. This was the first time a code-red report was ever received by the city. It identified a rec-probe raid by four light vehicles and one heavy truck: two trucks armed with medium machine guns, two with 80mm rocket launchers, accompanied by a lightly-armed twelve-person attack team. Three hits were recorded, one being possibly fatal. Material was extracted from three buildings. The raid lasted thirty-six minutes, fourteen seconds, with an armed response start time of fourteen minutes, eight seconds. This was rated at minus ten minutes of a target strategic-set response time. Perimeter defence was rated as zero.

Later surveillance data from the same source revealed the attack team travelled one hundred and eighty kilometres north-east (grid reference withheld) to re-join a major Group 75 attack group of six AFVs armed with light cannons, heavy and medium machine guns, plus twelve light trucks, armed with 80mm rocket launchers. It noted each AFV can carry up to eight fully equipped assault troops. In total this represented a fighting force of approximately one hundred and eight combatants, plus ten all-terrain trucks with drivers and co-drivers. Threat rating of this attack group was designated major level three.

This report was initially restricted to security cleared Council members and selected staff. However, a general statement was released to the media. A later report by the LDF provided the Council with a detailed evaluation of the response action, a review of risk assessment, and a list of recommended measures to defend the city in the future, both immediate and long-term.

A day after the attack the Council announced the casualty list. A damage assessment was completed nine days later with provisional costing, but its details were withheld. What was made public was that the security sensors all functioned well. However, the fact that no appropriate timely, sizable and well-armed response could be made prompted acknowledgement and serious comment on four counts. First, lives were lost. Second, the delay in response and its limited firepower gave exactly the wrong 'soft-target' message to the attackers and increased the chance of a later, more serious incursion. Third, it did a lot of damage and was very costly for the building owners and to those who had stock stolen and damaged. It should be noted here that the days of being able to insure against such events have long gone. Fourth, and also critical, was the consequences of the attack in creating fear and insecurity in the community. The decisions of Council went to all these issues, especially action to address community insecurity. There was a general consensus that the Council acted as quickly as possible.

A second emergency Council meeting was held three days later. It formally commended the actions of the members of the SWAT team, and other members of the police force who responded to the attack. They were not on standby, so were unprepared when it started. In these circumstances it was acknowledged that they attended very quickly. A motion of condolences was passed for those who had lost their lives and the date of an official memorial service was announced. It was reported that all the injured were recovering well, although one will not be returning to service. It was stated that the Mayor had already visited the injured in hospital and had met their families.

Strategically it was crucial to show a force able to deter potential aggressors and communicate that any attack would cost them dearly, while at the same time not revealing the full defence capability. The local defence force command established a defence action plan and terms of engagement, some of which was publicly released to boost a community sense of security. The first action would be to slow, and if possible, halt the aggressors' advance; next was to hold our ground, and then counter attack. A defence perimeter was established with automated observation towers and a sensored warning system that would automatically arm (or disarm) mines. All forces, beyond the immediate movement arrest period, would be deployed to defensive positions with missile batteries behind them. The last line of defence would be provided by a mobile missile armed reserve force.

The Council debate

At each Council meeting the LDC reported, in camera, on progress in terms of equipment acquisition, training and defence capability to the defence committee. A redacted report was presented at the full Council meeting attended by the public, and released to the media. A summary of regional intelligence reports was presented at each Council meeting. Five months after the attack the presented summary indicated a worsening situation and advised that action be taken to go to a higher level of preparedness. An emergency Council meeting was held to discuss this situation.

The meeting was opened by Councillor Jong Li, chair of the city defence committee, who presented a motion stating that the existing capability was already based upon having the means to respond to a major attack, and this was supported by the ability to mobilise reserve forces equipped within the means already held in storage. The only action proposed in his motion was that reservists be required to attend a one-week training course and thereafter eight days of training per month. Councillor Li then requested that the defence commander, Captain Jay Comora, be invited to respond before the motion was opened for debate. This was agreed. Captain Comora said that he and other members of the defence committee were at one with Councillor Li's view and recommendation. The only suggestion that he would make, if Council wanted go beyond what was already a capability to deal with existing and projected threats, would be to put a second remote missile battery into the old port area. This would entail adding water force capability by converting small, very fast, locally owned boats into an armed patrol boats to deal with Superzodo rubber raiding craft used to land troops for projection into positions behind the defence line. There is no evidence that this capability exists but it is a possibility he thought open for consideration.

Councillor May Na objected, in opposition to the motion and the Defence Command Report, stating that the existing defence arrangements were inadequate to deal with a major attack. Councillor Li replied stating that Councillor Na had either not read the Report, or had done so but failed to understand it. Councillor Na stated she had read it and the inference that as a woman she was incapable of understanding it was offensive. At this point the chamber became very noisy. A 'point of order' was then called for by the Speaker; within a few moments the meeting calmed down. Councillor Jarra stated that she opposed the position adopted by Councillor Na, saying she rejected the idea of turning the city into an armed camp. Councillor Kay added his voice to the position. At that point Councillor Tiro gained the floor stating that the voices who resisted strengthening the city's defences were in a fairyland and clearly had not the slightest idea about the scale of dangers the city faced, and they obviously must have slept through the defence briefing given. These remarks were met with boos and cheers. Again the Speaker called order, but it was clear that the chamber was polarised and getting more edgy. Councillor Murdon was then called. He asserted that the real issue, the safety of the citizens of New Harshon, was being put at risk by the warmongering brigade of the Council who were inviting the city to be attacked. Councillor Jong Li, angrily asked Councillor Murdon: 'what the bloody hell are you talking about?' Jong Li said his committee was all about the safety of the city, and the better it was defended, the safer it would be. Did Murdon not understand defence is not aggression? Fighting to getting himself heard above the ensuing din, the Speaker said that unless order in the chamber was maintained he would suspend the meeting. Councillor Na returned to the floor to say that there was a group of men present who were of the view that the more military hardware peppered around the city the better, and they were like a bunch of little boys with big toy guns. At this point the chamber erupted. It took the Speaker all of five minutes to declare the meeting suspended, with the instruction to reconvene at 9.00am in an orderly and civil manner.

The Mayor by this time was standing by the exit door. As Councillors Li, Na, Tiro and the Speaker left, he touched each of them on the shoulder telling them he wanted to see them immediately in his office. As the Mayor told me later, when the quartet arrived, even before they were seated, he said how appalled he was at the conduct of the Council at such a moment of crisis. It was the conduct of a kindergarten! He then said he wanted the situation resolved in the morning, stating that since it was clear a consensus had no chance of being reached, vote would decide the issue. At this point the Mayor said he become more directive. He reported the following exchange:

'Councillor Na, would you be willing to propose an amendment to the motion "there will be no changes in the city's defences", except on the basis of review whenever the threat level significantly changes?'

'Yes, Mr Mayor, I am willing to do so.'

'Councillor Li, would you accept the amendment?'

'Yes, Mr Mayor, I will do that.'

'Councillor Tiro, would you be willing to move for an immediate vote in recognition that the actions taken to defend the city reflect the will of its population, and that they understand that defending the city is not an act of aggression?'

'Mr Mayor, you are correct. My own views were intended to curtail debate, but I understand the imperative of not presenting an illusory impression to the public that this Council is seriously divided on this issue.'

'Now Mr Speaker, after making whatever opening remarks you deem appropriate to opening the day, are you willing to open with a call for amendments for the motion on the floor?'

'Yes, I am Mr Mayor.'

'Lady and gentlemen: I have not enjoyed doing this intervention but we cannot give way to chaos. This remark concludes my business. Thus I bid you good evening and look forward to your return to the chamber in the morning.'

The meeting was duly held the following morning, and a large majority passed the amended motion. The Mayor then stated that a media conference would be held at 2.00pm. The meeting was closed. The media event was a non-event. The Mayor announced that City defences would be maintained at the present level and then would remain under constant review.

Thinking back over the move and recent events, we have been lucky. The politics of moving the city were very challenging. There are still some unresolved problems, but there is now a mood of positive resigned realism. What this actually means is the acceptance of the conditions of limitation in which we now live as being relatively stable and secure. We, and the city, have a future, but it will never exceed a condition of modesty. It is viewed without false hopes and in recognition that the quality of life can still be improved. Strangely the risk of another attack had a big impact on giving greater value to what people are willing to defend. If their hopes are entertained, they are almost certainly that a condition of climate stability would arrive, and that our young people would start to see a future for themselves.

The conclusion: an interview with the Mayor

Mayor Kumar Rarge Singe, known by all as KRS, came to Harshon with his family from India when he was eight years old. His father was a doctor, his mother a piano teacher; he had one sibling, Anna, who, at the time, was three. KRS studied and gained a law degree at Harshon University, but never practised. Instead, he became a journalist, specialising in economic affairs. I have known him for thirty years; we have a friendly relationship but have never actually been friends. He became the first Mayor of New Harshon at the Council's founding elections of 2076. We met for a prearranged interview in his office the day after the increase of the city's defence capability was passed.

'KRS, how do you feel about the outcome of the Council meeting yesterday in the context of the future risks?'

'I feel the risks over time are much higher than even the defence committee recognises, and I am totally bemused by that small faction who thinks increasing defence is a provocation. I also think the destructive power of aggression by attackers will exhaust itself as settlements consolidate and more adequately defend themselves so that the cost in lives in attacking them will be too great. My view has been influenced by the conversations I have had with the defence commander who is a smart and thoughtful young man. The fact that he is worried worries me, and what he fears is that some of the rogue militia may combine and acquire even more powerful weapons. However, both of us think this is unlikely because they then become a target for the powerful military enclave forces.'

'With the qualification you have just made, are you sanguine about the future of New Harshon?'

'Well, there are short-term concerns beyond security. Establishing a viable economy is a big challenge, the climate remains unstable, and living through a dystopic age is really hard for the young who, even if getting on with their lives, still see the past as golden and the future as a bleak and dark struggle.'

'But how about you, how do you feel?'

'Personally, I feel lucky. There was a time when I thought we all were doomed. Now I feel like a growing number of people do: if we can get through the next couple of decades, the long-term prospects could be quite good, especially if enviro-climatic stability starts to arrive. Having said this, I am concerned we may have a mid-life crisis.'

'Can you expand on what you understand a mid-life crisis to be?'

'There are still a lot of people who think that while at a material level their world has gone backwards, the conditions that have now been established will allow a return to going forward to something like how things once were, which means that their standard of living will continually improve. But you and I know that's not going to happen, as, to be frank, all thinking people and most of the young realise. There has been too much environmental damage, too much destruction, too many conditions of breakdown, and the collapse of the economic foundations, state structures, and world order upon which the late modern world mostly functioned. Utility and modesty have to remain the material norm, with developmental efforts directed at social, political and cultural advances, as was recognised by the speakers of your excellent event. So the mid-life crisis turns on the general shift from the large, but not total, disgruntled backward-looking older order who already show signs of coming up against a new forward-looking mass of people of mixed age. What I mean by a mid-life crisis is a cultural clash between the progressive realists' ideas and the disabling and thwarted utopianism of the anti-realists. The latter would not win, but the clash could be costly to what I call the spirit of affirmation for a short period.'

'KRS, that's an analysis I can relate to and share. But I have one concern that you have not mentioned – the old people, especially those left stranded in old Harshon.'

'Carlos, I think my concerns are the same as yours. These old people are a tragic and, it seems, an intractable problem, except, in the end, it is sadly a self-resolving problem. They just have refused to make the move. Their families, if they have them, social services, religious leaders, and myself – we have all tried. We only had two choices: to bring them here under duress, or to make them as comfortable as possible in the ruin of the city. So there it is. Both we, and they, have to live with this situation. What we have done is to make sure they are not forgotten. They get a weekly social worker visit, home nurse support if needed and a weekly "bus and shop" trip with volunteer carrying support and a free lunch on the way home. They also get the same concessions, such as library readers, as the old people living here. Having said this, it is clear that the older people who came to New Harshon have done the best. Many have grandchildren here, they have places to socialise, and the fitter ones get involved in the life of the city in many ways. While most miss Harshon, they still get enjoyment out of life. In truth we always knew we could never win this problem.'

'A lot of people at the event, speakers and the public, talked about the issue of young people. You have said a few things in passing, but what do you actually have to say on them as an issue of concern?'

'The young are a major challenge for us. The youth suicide problem is a constant heartbreak, but I see the arrival of a perceptual shift away from a view of an empty future with nothing to offer to the realisation that they have to be the makers of a future for themselves, even amongst those who have yet to find a way. I believe they will. What this means is working with them to create a desired and realisable future out of the circumstances we are in. The commodity culture of youth has gone. What they, and we, have to do is focus on cultural production in and beyond the arts and music. I am seeing positive signs of progress, but I am still very worried and I know it will take years to resolve.'

'I have heard you use the term "politics of utility" a number of times, but I have never heard you actually spell out what it means?'

'Well, Carlos, I see utility as a concrete example, practice and condition of sustainment: a politics of utility is action toward that end. I should say I don't see utility as boring, or plain or unattractive. I view it as elegance without excess. I see it all over this city. As for sustainment, as you have heard me say before, I see it as a continual project of creating and maintaining the ecological, social, cultural and economic conditions that sustain the environment that we and all other creatures depend upon, while living an affirmative life that advances a just and equitable existence for all.'

'KRS, I have really enjoyed your insightful answers. I have one last question. Over the years I have been impressed by the organisations that have designed and managed the city move. The level of cooperation and the competence of the technical staff and the workforce have been outstanding. Not, however, politically. Some of the Councils have been better than others, as have Councillors. Mostly the right decisions have somehow been made, as with the decision yesterday. But it seems to me, to put it bluntly, that more astute members of Council are needed, and that all Councillors need some form of professional development: do you agree?'

'Carlos, you have been very circumspect. My answer will be more direct. We have more than our share of Councillors not intellectually equipped for the job. They would have been fine in the old days for problems like garbage collection, parking and dog poo on pavements, but moving and creating a new city is of a totally different order. What this has meant is that the Councillors as much as the Council have to be managed. And, to be frank, I am sick of it! I spend half my life putting out fires as a result other people's stuff-ups. I'm not sure if you remember, but when there was an elected national government, new MPs did a week's orientation course before being able to sit in parliament. Now, while the Council system cannot determine who is selected to stand and who should, or should not, be voted for, the system should, in the circumstances of civic life, have the right to test the competence of those who wish to serve the city. They have to be widely informed people and have decision-making ability. To this end, again prompted by the events of the past few days, I am going to begin a campaign for an assessment process that requires prospective Councillors to be more rigorously interviewed and endorsed, in order to be eligible to stand for election and for their performance to be reviewable. I am not suggesting in any way that all of this is ideological. It's not about screening out political difference. Rather, I am suggesting an intellectual benchmark needs to be set.'

'Mr Mayor, that idea certainly begs some thought. Once more I want to extend my thanks.'

'Carlos, it has been my pleasure.'

[... FICTION ENDS]

3

The Observation of Observation: A Review

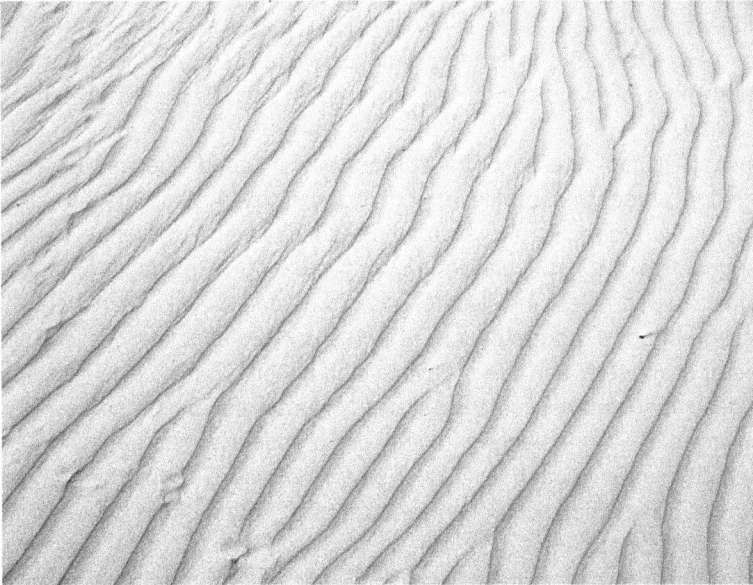

The conceptual essence of second order design fiction is the observation of observation. The fiction of moving the city is a product and object of observation that has been created to illustrate and exemplify this concept. It was based on fictional elaborations of a variety of city-move-related experience and observations. With the qualification that the concept of 'system' is being used judiciously, the approach to observation is guided by what Niklas Luhmann had to say on an observing system: it '… can discover that the environment observed is not constituted by boundaries at all, but, perhaps, by constraints' (1989: 23). The fiction is underscored by these constraints, but they are not immediately visible, but can be made so by critical observations. Once present they thereafter can become subject to critical interrogation (via the second order of observation).

Now in this review process the fiction itself will be subject to review. The form of this review will arrive as comments directly related to the fiction, and others beyond it, relevant absences and the gift of the 'unthought' accompanying its creation (Heidegger 1968: 76).

Putting the review in place

The scale, scope and quality of the fiction invites being taken seriously, and not merely treated as a device in the service of design. A novella-length work is deemed the appropriate form of writing a second order design fiction as the moving cities story strives to show. It follows that the narrative of the fiction invites review based on its being a developable craft and the basis for the establishment of evaluative criteria to assess credibility, evocativeness and readability.

Such a fiction needs to be contextually situated. Hence the moving city fiction presents a profile of the fictional city against the backdrop of changing world conditions over multiple decades. The challenge here is to be suggestive and speculative without creating a distracting tangential narrative that completely dislocates it from its contextual circumstance. The establishment of a 'future present' is perhaps more effectively done with the voices of characters, and their activities and history. This is certainly favoured over describing futuristic techno-scientific fantasies. Certainly, any kind of escapism is likely to disengage actual or potential design agency. What the moving city narrative does is to steer a path between idealism of utopianism and the nihilism that accompanies dystopias. Doing so is perhaps worth adopting as a principle.

The path that had to be navigated, against the backdrop of a particular time and place of worldly crisis, was between developing characters and while not digressing from their narrative function in the story of the move as a discernable design process. Yet at the same time they needed to be different and interesting. The narrator's voice and persona needed not only to become familiar but also the means to direct dialogue, and over time. Key to the realism of the fiction is it does not present the resolution of every problem. Thus it ends with an event that clearly indicates that crisis is ongoing for the city. This approach links to one of the fundamental design propositions of second order design fictions: designing in time. What this means is correctively designing back from a projected future. Thus the moving city narrative does not design how to move a city but it establishes issues and a basis of correction, modification, addition that advances such a design task

Two particular readings of the fiction are important to emphasize. The first is the already-mentioned review exercise of 'corrective' (with a focus on an interrogation of the fiction, how well design challenges are identified and characterized and what can be reworked in the writing of a city move brief). The second is a critical reading of the text to expose not only what is present *but equally* what is absent (be it the unsaid, unthought, unknown). This void is always going to be present, this as it exists between production of the text and the situated context and sense of a reader. By implication a brief should be informed by what the fiction makes present and lacks.

The fiction presented was based on existing knowledge and observations from two historical experiences. The first involves exposure to and research related to the sea level rises in southern Florida, USA, in the Nile Delta, Egypt and in Australia. The second draws on work on a number of design projects that have addressed the environmental circumstances of climate change, prompting the need to move a city and the means to do so.

Rising sea levels are already impacting upon coastal settlements. This is a situation that is going to get worse, and for a long period of time. No matter what mitigation measures are taken to reduce global warming, sea levels will continue to rise. This is because warmed ocean surface and deep-water temperatures (which act as the planet's thermostat), along with ice melts, are expanding the volume of water of the oceans. Even with a stable or cooler climate these temperatures will still take two hundred years or more to adjust. Consequently over the rest of this century and beyond, many settlements will be abandoned or moved, resulting in several hundreds of millions of people being displaced. The cost of dealing with this situation will be astronomically high.

The moving city narrative was also based on retrospective reflections of direct observations of communities facing the prospect of losing their land and settlement. For example I co-led a workshop in Fort Lauderdale in 2013 which was created to consider the impact of rising sea levels on the high-risk area of southern Florida. Since then the prospect has worsened, with the City of Miami increasing coastal defences, building pumping stations and raising road levels. Likewise, in 2014 I led a group looking at related issues in the Nile Delta where, again, sea levels are a major, extant and future problem. More agricultural land is becoming seriously salinated, inundation is increasing and the prospect of relocation of communities is growing. But in a nation without the economic means to begin to respond, the prospects are bleak. If the problem is as bad as the United Nations' Intergovernmental Panel on Climate Change (IPCC) has projected (and each projection is worse than the previous) many thousands of coastal cities will be impacted, including major ones. It is therefore unlikely that even wealthy nations will have the financial means to act to prevent and adequately deal with the problem. Attempts to do so could well bankrupt a nation.

The second experience drawn on comes from an actual city move project in which I participated as a member of a design team. These and other projects are detailed in the Appendix at the end of this book. Lastly, over the past two and a half decades I have worked on many urban design projects from a metrofit perspective, which is a complementary practice to moving a city (Fry 2017).

The aim of the review

As indicated, the imperative to move large and complex cities will increase. The instrumental and technical means to undertake such projects are challenging but not beyond existing technological capabilities. The same cannot be said of the political, economic, psycho-social, design and environmental dimensions of such an exercise. The city move fiction is an impressionistic view of the process to evoke its complexity. What will now be done is to engage in a range of observations on the fiction that widens the frame by which moving a city can be viewed. This has two objectives: to contribute to the development and critical use of design fiction; and to contribute to building the knowledge needed to move cities in non-violent ways so that they are adaptive to changing worldly circumstances. This review goes beyond the content of the fiction and addresses issues that were absent.

Moving cities registers far more than a response to the impacts of rapid environmental change. These impacts are significant markers, among others, of the world our species inhabits as it for 'us' is fundamentally changing. Post the ice age, the degree of this change has no equal. So positioned, reviewing the changes that have been presented in the fiction are of a contextual process without any clear indication of what will happen or when. Thus its placement in time is notional. In this setting what the fiction denotes is life in a world of crisis, where the assumed ground of certainty of knowing and acting has been unsettled. People (already) feel and act with a sense of this unsettlement. They try to find a stable ground of thought and action while being uncertain: effectively they are groundless. The notion of an emergent future, with functioning operational systems and continuous technological advancement, has been thrown into doubt. The very idea of living in a world in which things develop has been shattered. It becomes clear that regression can happen – things can go backward. The very concept of what we are has also increasingly been brought into question, especially as changes between 'us', the privileged and the abandoned globally increase. The design fiction indicates that not only will 'the nature' of cities start to radically change but, in a world of very challenging crises, knowledge itself is changing. What is yet to be recognized is that this means that very new kinds of social organization will be needed. By implication this means new kinds of politics have to be created out of a new political imagination.

Put more concretely, the fiction is not claimed as how the future will be, but it allows corrective ways of thinking action in the present. This is exactly how moving the city is to be considered. The aim of such a fiction is the creation of a brief informed by a possible future, as Part 4 will show. The coda for this way of approaching a brief is the 'designing back from the future' of designing in time. What this effectively means is the creation of a trajectory of possible events, the response to which is brought back to the present. To do this requires knowing where you came from and where you are. What this enables is a situated present able to be reflected on from a notional future. Such a fiction is a projection of a future based on futural trends that have been critically examined. The present thus becomes redefined as between a future and the past in order to acquire a triangulated corrective view of the future.

The setting, or 'how did "we" get here'?

Beyond climate change, the city move fiction really does not deal with the larger and more fundamental crisis in which it is situated was created. It can be argued that a longer view of its causality is appropriate to develop for a truly prefigurative exercise of designing in time. To this end it is worth registering that in differences of time and place, the most general observations of the current planetary moment is the arrival of the fate of our plural worldly existence. Forced by a long-spanning intergenerational mistreatment of the environments of the planet, especially by the industrialized and industrializing peoples of our species, it has been discovered that a sixth planetary extinction event has commenced. The speed of this situation is directly indexed to the impacts of the actions of those populations and nations that retain a commitment to development that conceals its inherent truth: it is named defuturing. The duration of our species-being may itself be fated, but the time 'we' have is, to a large degree, of our own making (of the environments in which we come to be and thus also of ourselves).

The impacts of ecological destruction are not contained within the realm of biological effects. Once the impacts produce social and economic dysfunction they will destabilize an already fragile world order, increase geopolitical tensions and thereafter precipitate conflict especially over who commands diminishing life-sustaining resources. Of this unfolding situation this is why the question 'how did we get here' needs to be asked.

While there are immediate instrumental answers, including the failure of the international order to act with urgency to dramatically reduce greenhouse gas emissions, there is a far more deeply embedded cause. This goes beyond an instrumental understanding of the problems to be faced. It actually connects to the primordial being of 'our being' and to a non-theological eschatological issue (Stambaugh 1992: 122). At the very moment of the coming into being of the human species 'it' occupied a cosmology that travelled toward 'enacted choice', a turning away from the being of being itself toward becoming the maker of a world of artifice in being. Simply characterized, a split occurred between our animality and it's culturally constructed Other – the human becoming its named dominant form. However, there were other hominoids who created and occupied cosmologies that positioned themselves as an animal among animals. But these Indigenous others were subjected to almost total erasure by human imposition, most overtly through the global colonizing actions of Western nations whereby 'the human' imposed itself upon its Others who were not seen as the same, but as animals to either be eliminated or forced to become the same as the history of genocidal colonialism and its subjection of native peoples affirms.

It is important to acknowledge a continuum of the dehumanization of the colonized peoples, ethnocide and the persisting failure to allow them autonomy. Colonialism is not of the past but is continually reinvented in the present. The remaining Indigenous peoples of the world are so often the oppressed survivors of this violence. Their cosmological difference still mostly goes unrecognized by the universalization of hegemonic humanity. It is this human being in its 'development' beyond its animality that totally exceeded its condition of animal constraint and in doing so created conditions of un-ecologically absorbable excess that destines the condition of defuturing (Fry 2020). It is this trajectory that leads toward 'our' extinction.

The human, as it is, is an unsustainable being. Contra to this historicity is the residual evidence of difference that resides in the histories, cosmologies, epistemologies and ontologies of Indigenous peoples whose numbers and modes of being in the world could be ecologically accommodated. It is not suggested that modern beings can revert to a pre-human naturalism. But it is to suggest that there is much to learn from those Indigenous people who managed to survive. The potentiality of such learning in a borderland of epistemological transition changes the relation of the human to its repressed animality and engenders the material modesty upon which being futural depends. What is being intimated here is a condition of constrained cosmotechnical futural hybridity that is other than a posthuman techno-centrality (within the process of our species' fragmentation that, it is argued, is already under way within debates on plural forms of the human).

As an overview, one can now say that 'we' humans, as the inheritors of this untellable account of the historicity of our/their coming into being, need to confront the destined negation of an unrealized modern being (Latour 1993). This means confronting the fact that the dominant world-shaping agent that 'we' are has never actually been modern (Latour) nor fully 'human(e)' (Heidegger 1968: 76). To confront 'ourselves' is to stand before our defuturing nemesis. 'Our' past and current actions, coming toward us from the future over coming decades, will determine if extinction travels ever faster to a looming present or recedes into the distance. At the most distant 'our' fate (whatever we become) is sealed. At the extreme, what is certain is that life on Earth will not survive that 'solar catastrophe' which Lyotard contemplated happening in 4.6 billion years (1991: 8–12).

Although there is no absolute knowledge of the duration of the future, what can be understood is that at present, through our life-negating actions, the time of life as we know it is being expended. The more the same is sought to be re(sus)tained, the faster the expenditure. The more futuring actions are taken to counter the defuturing processes of human unmaking, and the more we adapt to change and advance conditions of sustainment, the more time our fragmenting species will have. The stage upon which this action will predominantly take place is the city – the city in its futural forms, the city as event.

This basic statement can be taken as the primary ethico-political imperative of counter-human construction in an asserted age of the Anthropocene displacing the Holocene. This means recognizing that human agency, constituted as productivism, is the foundational causal base to the problem of structural unsustainability. Unless this changes, nothing affirmatively futural arrives. All other imperatives are subordinate to what the Anthropocene strives to name in its arrival as a condition of a globally hegemonic anthropos (a consequence of monstrous denaturalization flowering in Euromodernity and Western colonialism). As indicated, the propensity to unsustainability was prefigured in a mode of making and early manufacture that long predated the Industrial Revolution – a moment that prefigured the origination of the *Anthropo*cene. Yet it, the imperative, still goes fundamentally unrecognized, by the power of *the same* (conserved and reformed, economically and geo-politically) remaining absolutely dominant.

Yet breakdowns will arrive, such as loss of settlements to the sea, perhaps sooner rather than later. They have the potential to rupture the order of 'the same'. In doing so they may starkly make apparent that 'our' future, our Earthly duration, is in our own hands. Thus what most threatens may be the 'saving power' that enables a realignment of our actions to sustain what is needed to sustain us. In such a context, the moving and remaking of cities can be considered part of a transformative ontological condition of being human.

Revisiting contingency: remembering 'contingency is always contingent upon something', the moving of a city is contingent upon the city being abandoned before it is overwhelmed by natural forces. But what underscores moving cities is a shift in the much larger commanding contingency of the imperative of hominoid 'world (re)making'. A future with a future that includes the continuation of our species-being's ability to be, along with all we depend upon (organic and inorganic life), requires understanding the indivisible relation between creation and destruction. Life now depends on knowing what to destroy. In these end times the eternal truth is that there is no natural right to be. Like it, and admit it, or not, the end looms as fully present. Our future is now a fiction to be elaborated and turned to fact. In the everlasting quest to give life meaning – the quest of mythology, religion and philosophy – and in recognizing, as Darwin did, that life (as a biological process) is meaningless, this truth has become unavoidable. The quest to find meaning is over. The post-natural nature of life now will only be sustained if life becomes a posited transcendent value: hereafter life becomes a *created* contingent meaning.

Breakdown: Harshon was assumed to have reached a point of breakdown that made moving the city essential. This point would have arrived well before total collapse and on the basis of a critical judgment rather than being self-evident. As an unfolding condition, and in a time of criticality, the issue of how breakdown is seen and defined is problematic as a naming and moment of action. So acknowledged, breakdown is a critical condition existing somewhere between recognition, observation and understanding that needs to be discovered. As such it brings something to presence by the absence of its available utility and the arrival of dysfunction; this in three ways: the conspicuous (unuseability), obtrusiveness (a lack of function because something is missing) and obstinacy (the presence of an obstruction that prevents function) (Heidegger 1962: 103, §74 and 109, §78).

The commanding ideas (world(s), ground, system and technology, development, the human and inhuman and politics) that knowingly and unknowingly form a city, that direct its moving, and ordering, are going to shortly be addressed. All are understood as being situationally framed by the contingent factors of place, the political and resistance. *All* are inflected by conditions of breakdown and limitation. Reflecting on the epistemological basis of the commanding ideas informs the fiction of moving a city, and any other second order design fiction. They all require development in the context of an understanding of the critical condition out of which a design strategy, redirective practice and project can be formed. To this end the framing of moving the city comes from the breakdowns that expose critical conditions.

Obviously moving a city depends on confronting the imminent threat it faces, be it general, local, long or short term. An imminent threat can itself obviously materialize as an actual threat. The certain knowledge of sea level rise is a good example: property values collapse, businesses close, people who leave with ease do so, bankruptcy and suicides are common, then some systems start to become less efficient and fail, more people cut their losses and leave and a sense of panic already present as an undercurrent starts to break out. There is looting and civil disorder, not just in one location but in many. The number of people on the move becomes large. They arrive in cities near and far, which in turn causes problems, including crime and civil unrest. Many of the world's cities under threat from the sea are in delta regions: these are ports with many millions of inhabitants, often with major industries and with key locations in supply chains supported by container handling facilities. Thus the combination of several million people on the move and the breakdown of the operational functions of the city soon produce a national crisis.

As breakdown escalates, it relationally spreads as inter-related systems fail. Partial faults become temporary malfunctions that are not repaired; they in turn lead to complete breakdown. Thereafter, total dysfunction becomes the normative condition. Moving a city exists against such a background. The cost, legal problems and material challenges are huge, but the implications of not doing so are greater. The actuality of moving a city, as the design fiction indicates, exposes much of this complexity. It shows moving is not just about moving 'things'. It takes time and has substantial economic, social, cultural and political impacts. It begs a massive project of planning, communication, design, investment, logistics, social change and support over many years. Globally, this is a project and process that should have already started in numerous cities. It has not because the few attempts that are being made by government, local authorities and capital are general and misguided in seeking to protect the status quo and short-term interests. Likewise professions, like civil engineering, architecture, planning, law and sociology, are failing to develop the expertise needed to respond to the challenges of moving cities. A deeply embedded false sense of permanence exists, but in conditions of fluidity.

Cities are obviously not uniform. They are constituted as different worlds within a world over time. Sometimes their life is short, often it is long – this substantially adds to the difficulty of moving them. Moving a city, as a world (lived and symbolic) within a world (refracted through a cosmology), cannot just be approached instrumentally. This understanding goes to thinking about what needs to be moved. The fiction exemplifies a struggle to articulate and answer this question. It is certainly beyond the identity of a city in its representational forms, which increasingly has become a fiction of tourist and commercial projection centred mostly on iconic physical and cultural features. Cities are always fragments that in their projected identity are never captured, but there is always an identification with a fragment standing for the whole. The fragment is more than the now clichéd term 'a sense of place'. Such identification is not reducible to the character of the locus, ambience and 'the community': rather it is where belonging is posited in passing, in permanent presence or in memory. These thoughts take us to the issue of 'the construction of the identification of where to move to' – this overrides the question of how to move. As was seen in the fiction this is not a universal question but a circumstantial and an inter-generational one.

Revisiting commanding ideas

As Part 1 made clear, ideas are present, both consciously and unconsciously, in directing the form and content of the moving of a city. They are key influences in forming the second order design fiction narrative. Abstracted from a fiction they expose *constraints* that can provide clues to how ideas that direct an actual planned city move are expressed and communicated.

Observations on seven commanding ideas are drawn from the fiction as they register the start of what will be a growing trend for coastal cities around the world. These observations will address: the presence of worldly influences; the rising condition of groundlessness of so much that was once grounded and seemingly certain; the fate of the technosphere; the move from development to postdevelopment; the changing 'nature' of our very species; a shift of knowledge from place to event; and a shift in notions of the political and political imagination.

1. Opening worlds

The moving city narrative places the city in the world, and reflects a response to worldly events, both environmental and geopolitical, since such events are shown to encroach upon it. Equally significant is the presence of a perceived 'state of the world' as it occupies the thoughts, imaginations and fears of especially young people. World events in general have a designing, varied and invisible influence on the conception of moved, new and existing cities.

As recognized, our species lives on the same planet but in different worlds divided by cosmologies, cultures and associated values and beliefs, and economic conditions, all carried in language. Geo-culturally, cities are situated in this plurality of worlds, as well as within varied biophysical environments.

As such, cities constitute complex material and socio-cultural worlds within the world. Cities break down divisions between the natural and the artificial within the serviced environment from which they are formed and within the microclimates they create (from heat radiated from thermal mass and exhausted heat of polluted/polluting emissions). The waste and contaminants that accompany the production of these emissions also impact on the environment. Such consequences produce a pressing need for the reduction of urban environmental impacts while rapid urbanization continues apace.

In moving a city, worlds are also moved, but in fragments, and when reassembled they are unlikely to ever be in the same order as they were in the past. Likewise, moving a city, by the process of identification of what materially and immaterially needs to be moved, exposes the world from which it is constituted. This is a world where settlements are not only being destroyed by the likes of drought, fire and coastal erosion, flooding from rising sea levels and, as ever, war, but also by a culture corroded by living in a geopolitical and socio-cultural world of crisis.

Living in a world of crisis: Crisis has always been implicit for 'a being' *in the being of being*: everything dies but being continues. Now the conditions of criticality have changed. The relational confluence of the unfolding risks of climate impacts, associated conditions of biological extinction, geopolitical conflict and technological mutation, has placed 'our' being, as we are and exist in difference, in a deep crisis. The feeling that the continuity of our species-being is fated, in the mid and long term, and that life is lived amid serious threats unsettles vast numbers of people. Yet, as indicated, our species-being's choices in this situation are present. While many are unaware and many knowingly or by default opt for nihilism, a minority search for a form of action that will make a difference with a difference. This attainment, if possible, can have a profound impact on many others, instead of knowingly and unknowingly maintaining the status quo (with its token reforms). It is possible to begin to rethink, remake and resettle the world of unsettlement, but different ways of habitation demand other imaginaries. As will be shown this means becoming ungrounded from the ground that holds us in the grip of our defuturing propensity. Affirmatively 'we' have a future with a future if we learn how to make it and act on this knowledge. New knowledge is generative of new imaginaries.

Gaining new knowledge and imaginaries requires a series of abandonments of thought, values and action formed out of transformed ontological conditions. Imagination is not formed independently from worldly encounter and engagement, neither is new knowledge. The process and consequence of moving a city can be seen as one of the ways in which such ontological transformation of our being could/can be undertaken and occur. While not completely sufficient, and certainly not posing as a utopian condition, it does provide 'an opening' (with metrofitting as another example; Fry 2017). To support the argument for abandonment (a substantial project in its own right), three examples will be given:

(i) The saving power of technology: there can be no technological fix of the condition that the Anthropocene seeks to name, that unsustainability defines and that acts of defuturing deliver as process. This is because 'we', in the myopic anthropocentrism of our mode of 'being-in-the-world', are the foundational locus of the problem. As previously said, for fundamental change to occur we have to change, by *remaking what makes us (as we are)* so that thereafter the efficacy of our material interactions and actions result in our becoming futural. This elevation of ontological design to a 'condition of worlding' is not a matter of general will or transformation of consciousness (a failed agenda even for elites) but, as indicated, a massive, differential and protracted remaking of much of the material world. What makes this seemingly impossible transformation possible is an unstoppable momentum of material adaptation forced on us by a significantly changing climate in the company of related crises and breakdowns. Unevenly, this implies un-chosen sacrifices that create conditions of material modesty countered by an enhancement of conditions of sociality. Such aims and ambitions would, in part, gain their specificity in the social development of the city move process. There can be no independent appeal to technology in this process, *for as technological beings* we are already a technology as enacted via our colonizing instrumentalization. One can say technology does not deliver a saving power as an external agent of appeal, but it does have transformative agency as it is turned against itself as instrumentalism redirected in the instrumental futural agency of the material conditions of 'our' ontological auto-designing. Here is an opening into technology to be further qualified later.

(ii) The nihilism of material fatalism arrives in various forms but essentially what it means is giving way to the idea that the only way the human can survive is in a form of life after the destruction of organic life (Barrat 2013; Kurzwell 2005; Thorne, 2014). The notion that the mind can constitute life independent of the body and the senses invites criticism on multiple levels, but the most dangerous aspect of the proposition is that it embraces an abandonment of being itself and any attempt to secure its conditions of continuity. Rather it is a giving over of absolute reduction of existence to a mind supported by self-replicating machines. The proposition also comes with the horror of a techno-racist unnatural selection of those minds deemed worth saving. But the most extraordinary thing of all is that there are intelligent people and powerful organizations actually taking such a *mindless* idea seriously and investing in such an artificial intelligence (AI) nightmare.

(iii) The attachment to linear disciplinary thought, and the naive faith in the saving power of technology, including the misplaced belief that the retention of the mind in an organically lifeless world is survival, all expose the insufficiency of reason. This condition of limitation is more generally structurally present in the very institutions upholding the divisions of knowledge disciplines. In doing so they negate the relationality of complexity, and partition causality and abstract understanding from an ecology of mind that enables distributed intelligence. This is not an argument against reason, but one that exposes its insufficiencies (this based on the construction of conditions of containment that allows unreason to be the over-determining agent). War is a clear example of this limitation. In war, reason is applied to constitute the means to conduct actions that by any measure by which life is judged are irrational. Reason instrumentalized has enabled nuclear arms to proliferate, tactical nuclear weapons to arrive and fully autonomous weapons to multiply, all at a time when geopolitical tensions are increasing and the world order is fragmenting. War remains ever imminent and this is non-sense.

2. Ground and groundlessness: acting now on the basis of laying a ground

The circumstances within which the action of moving a city are now placed goes to unfolding conditions of major change for which there is no currently adequate descriptive narrative to express the process of being ungrounded. The following address to ground and groundlessness is set in this context.

Ground is taken to be the foundational condition that 'things', material and immaterial, rest upon. From this perspective the multiple levels of the ground of a city can broadly be approached as:

- the material foundation it rests upon
- the conceptual forms of its origination and development
- the material fabric from which it is constituted
- the infrastructure that enables it to function
- the knowledge that allowed its initial construction, expansion and operation
- the cultures that gave it its social form

- the economy that maintains its continuity
- the institutions that animate it, and
- the populations that occupy it.

Underscoring all these dimensions of the city are the epistemologies that inform actions taken and, more fundamentally, the very idea of the city, urban life and a condition of permanence itself. The circumstances that make it necessary to move cities bring these very assumptions that underscore 'the city' into question. It follows that the moved city, de facto a new city, is a re-laying of ground. The moved city is an urban foundation predicated upon futuring and operational performativity as a result of its (re)creation being based on an epistemology that recognizes the ground of the city as impermanent, thus groundless.

At the most basic is the question of settlement. For well over 150,000 years Homo sapiens, like their hominoid ancestors, were transitory. Movement was determined by environmental change and availability of food. The global distribution of human population and the subsequent establishment of settlement (initially a place to depart from or return to according to the seasonal availability of food) transitioned from transitoriness around ten thousand years ago. Climate change is already making it clear that many long-standing settlements will not survive impending change. For instance many delta cities will be inundated as sea levels rise. Other cities will lose their water supply, some will be too hot to live and work in. A foreseeable scenario that is not too hard to imagine is cities in low-impact areas adapting to change, with other cities in higher impact areas either being abandoned or moved to safer locations. New cities may be conceptualized to be moveable. All the instrumental implications of these changes, while presenting challenges, would be resolvable. Harder to think about are the ontologies, subject positions and social formations of such a world and the processes of destabilization that will be experienced. History informs us that if 'normality' can be retained it will be. But in so many ways, and in so many places it will not. Change and mobility will become a general norm. National and local economies will fail; large elements of the legal order, like land tenure, will become redundant; the social order in many places will be disrupted and civil unrest (or worse) will be common; and many old industries will not survive, but new ones will arrive. The same can be said of institutions. What will become even harder to contemplate are changed social and cultural transformations. Realistically the expectation is of a significant period of instability before relative stability is re-established which, if it does arrive, may take many centuries to materialize. All of these certain coming conditions of change make it important to start to think of the nature of ground more thoughtfully.

At the most fundamental level, our individual being-in-the-world is transient (Heidegger [1967] 1998: 110). Thus our individual mortality derives from the possibility of a posited groundedness, a situation that is also true of our species, which is equally finite. Likewise our world(s) (and planet) are transient, yet are contingently posited as grounded, and taken to be origin (127). In letting our worlds 'prevail' the ground becomes a projection 'casting it over us is freedom' (127). This is to say that while our being has no absolute ground, in letting the world prevail as transcendence, grounding occurs whereby 'freedom *gives* and *takes* ground' (127). Freedom to act in making a world is thus contingent on a taking of ground as *given* (the projection). Hereafter, grounding establishes and sets forth possibilities of existence in its projection of world (130). We can now say 'ground has no essence' – it is without substance while having agency and delivering support. What is abstractly described here is translated in difference across cultures in their taking of a ground upon which they freely act. This freedom determines that humanity itself has no common ground, and so cannot be collectively gathered. Hence, and notwithstanding the rhetoric of humanism, the projection of the human as universal is an imposition on the differences of our being found at the union of modernity and colonialism and their afterlife.

What has been projected from the mid-twentieth century and embraced in recent decades is a repositioning of ground, by it being linked to form and technology wherein the sphere of the mind (the noosphere), via the mediation of technology, becomes unified with the biosphere. This thinking extends to the notion of the organic and has been posited as the third stage of the planet's development after the geosphere and biosphere. As such it sits problematically within the information ecology of the Anthropocene as a moment and condition that negates the possibility of planetary biophysical evolution. The idea of the noosphere was first mooted by the Russian scientist, Vladimir Vernadsky (1863–1945), in a lecture at the Sorbonne in Paris in 1922 and published in French in 1924 (reprinted 2005). By 1927 the concept had been adopted by Pierre Teilhard de Chardin (1881–1955), a French idealist philosopher and Jesuit priest, who wrote a series of essays centred on the evolution of consciousness and the noosphere between 1920 and 1952 (Teilhard de Chardin ([1959] 1976). His dissemination of the concept of the noosphere was elemental in the formation of the contemporary ecology of the mind where technology, in its nexus with the environment, is thought to have prefigured the coming of concepts like the technosphere, superorganism, technological universalism, Gaia and the fantasy of singularity (Hui 2019).

Hegemonic technology as a constructive force of reality, the full realization of metaphysics, constituted as a cosmology and posited as 'unifying humanity', is now given the status of ground (Hui 2019: 250). Certainly technologies are not purely 'elements' of our reality but are part of its 'primary causes' (222). The counter view that is fracturing humanity (as evidenced in proliferating debate on the nature and relation of the human, non-human, posthuman, inhuman and inter-species) is equally part of a complex technical system (Roden 2015: 165). The very idea of ground as support has been destabilized as the certainty of being has become more insecure: groundlessness arrives as the void into which futural being opens. Displacement and unsettlement, of ideas, minds, bodies, cultures, futures and cities, all arrive and immediately concretize.

The proposition of the technical object as having 'the ground of their own movement' actually 'obscures the cosmic reality' and in doing so conceals the assertion that 'technological acceleration becomes the value of all values' (Hui 2019: 226). This needs to be contested and resisted, but not with idealism based on the attempt to conceive 'different cosmotechnics in which technology is reconnected with the cosmos and the moral' (226). This reifies technology as an independent entity that can be engaged by another force (cosmotechnics) to reconnect it with the 'cosmos and the moral' that it was never fundamentally connected with. The actuality is that all 'human beings', by degree, are technological as they occupy varied cosmologies – there is difference, but no outside. Intrinsic to our hominoid coming into being (Fry 2012) technology has an ontological appropriative and appropriating status: the latter with an ambiguous and culturally relative moral status. The counter view, one that brings us back to reflecting on the moving city narrative, is that the focus of action has to be on ourselves based on a position recognizing that 'we' are anthropocentric technological beings. Knowing how we ontologically became such does not liberate us from being so. But it does put those who do know this in a position to redirect/recreate/newly create ontological conditions able to (re)make us otherwise.

Moving a city is one such opportunity – one that totally reframes how one would think, approach and undertake such an activity. The city so positioned needs to be understood as a designing event and a domain of the organicity of the naturalized artificial.

The meaning of ground is contested in different discourses. It can be said that while our being has no absolute (biological or metaphysical) 'ground' (change cannot be reduced to a fixed moment or point), a contingent sense and appearance of ground can arrive (as support) if the world, as projection, is allowed to prevail. But to be free to act otherwise, the illusion of ground has to be confronted and our groundlessness acknowledged. What this means is sacrificing an illusion, which in turn implies abandoning all that holds us in a condition of dependence, namely, giving up attachment to the notional ground (Haar 1993: 141).

Registering the problematic notion of ground upon which a city rests is also to acknowledge that this ground can no longer appear as secure. Enviro-climatic and other disruptions have commenced, and a process of abandonment has started to which no end can be forecast. Place, as certain and fixed, will ever become dis-placed. Likewise, every epistemology is at risk of being displaced, because 'after every dead-end there is a new epistemology, a new ground; even if this ground is groundless' (Hui 2019: 38).

In such a setting, existence moves from a sense of being grounded to one of groundlessness. In the normative groundlessness there is a falling back to establish 'definite divisions and demarcations' projected onto the ground (Mander 2010: 16), as an idea, that *can be taken as* denoting certainty. Carl Schmitt 'conjured up these firm lines of *nomos* in protest to the modern predicament of rootlessness and displacement' ([1919] 1996: 16). For Schmitt these lines were the *nomos* of the earth and, as such, marks of the political that enveloped the earth as with the global political community united by common rules (Ulmen 2006: 19–25). Now characterized as 'the world order' they are breaking up as geopolitical divisions fracture and the relation between global power blocs change and enter, amplify and fold into the general conditions of crisis. Neither place nor world have ground.

What has been briefly sketched is a historical shift where the ratio between settlement and unsettlement has started, and increasingly is going to dramatically change the relation of nations and people. This understanding will very significantly influence how moving a city will be thought of and approached. The most significant question is: is the new location simply a point on a line of a transient city? If so, how should it be constructed, where does the line lead and what do you need to learn and know to make such a futural decision? Here it can be remembered that drawing a line is one of the first acts in the claiming of ground: its transposition from paper to site creates a rupture of smooth space and the arrival of the striated.

As said earlier, these questions cannot be considered or answered, independently from the instability of contemporary global conditions wherein omnipotent crisis comes in and out of focus according to the severity of the impacts and duration of the planetary crises delivered by climate change, pandemics and geopolitical tensions. The speed of these events is now such that commentary is always 'out of time', with responsive action even more tardy. One very clear example is the numerous global delta cities whose fate is sealed by sea level rises. IPCC reports indicate that sea levels will rise by almost a metre by 2100 and by this time some 400 million people will be displaced.[1] Notwithstanding this knowledge, planning action to move a city as a social and economic entity has not started. As is evident from reflection upon the Harshon design fiction, and from the actual example of moving cities, such a process takes decades.[2] Where action is taken, and the funds can be raised to do so, the trend is to try to save the city. For example, Miami, an at-risk coastal city, spent $500 million building pumping stations while also raising roads by 60cm, an action that leaves businesses and homes stranded (Ruggeri 2017). Such a strategy has to be understood as an attempt to prevent the flight of capital as much as holding inundation at bay. For cities at risk, the reality will be that as soon as it is clear that the city is going to be lost, capital will take flight and property values will crash.

Rising sea levels are obviously not the only threat cities face. Heat, drought, fire and other extreme weather events are equally substantial dangers. The combination of temperatures exceeding 50 degrees Celsius and drought is more than just putting many towns and cities, and their populations, at risk. It is creating conditions where whole regions will become uninhabitable. Likewise, the number of towns and cities in proximity to forests at risk of destruction by fire is also continually increasing. No matter the cause, the destruction of a city, and the displacement of its population, unless addressed, can create a very dangerous situation, as tens of thousands of people descend upon other cities looking for food, shelter and work. Moving a city is thus one clear way to avoid this problem.

These very obvious destructive impacts are not the only threats cities face. Breakdown in water supply and energy, the collapse of an agricultural system and food security and the decimation of a population by disease are all real risks. The comprehensive mapping of risk and community participation in this activity, as ways to build knowledge, understanding and organic systems of communication, are just not being recognized. Yet recent global events and data have made it clear that there will be no return to a past order of stability. Climate change, COVID-19 and ongoing consequences of the reconfiguration of global powers portend continued instability with a terminal moment in sight.

3. Futures, systems and the technosphere

Returning to, and going beyond what has been said so far, technology is uncanny. It is so familiar yet so strange, so present yet so absent. Of technology so much is known, but even more of it is unknown as it acts and becomes even more integral to the being of a large percentage of the human population. As the substrate of 'our' world within the world environment, it arrives as an increasingly unnatural agent in our posthuman mutation (as opposed to contributing to the evolution of Homo sapiens). To give meaning to technology is to 'give it rationality' (Hui 2019: 35) but it is beyond reason. Technology is plural: its past is always present in the present and its future, notwithstanding a projected telos that colonizes its image.

Thinking of technology in the context of moving cities, as part of a future and advanced climate crisis, generates a series of challenging questions. To try to identify these requires considering what the consequences of major climate impacts on technology are likely to be. This recognizes that a historical failure to comprehend that anthropogenic amplified climate change is one of the results of the defuturing consequences of many technologies from the moment of introduction and over their life.

Several trends already are starting to become clear. First, the condition of breakdown that climate impacts will create will produce corresponding breakdowns of many technological systems, not just because of direct damage (which will occur in some cases) but also because of economic collapse and conflict. The costs of addressing massive environmental impacts, the loss of major cities, the failure of entire agricultural systems, hundreds of millions of displaced people, major public health crises and more, are not only going to be absolutely enormous but also, to reiterate, beyond the means of most, if not all, nations. Against this backdrop there will be a technological response, but it will be inadequate by any global measure. A contraction of technology and its advancement into spaces of privilege are predictable (the rise of mega-regions has already established the conditions that make this contraction politically and economically possible; Fry 2017: 82–4). At the same time there will be a resurgence of utility, which for economic and practical reasons will mark the character of moved cities (as the design fiction suggests). This invites exploration.

Moving large cities as a proliferating practice in conditions of deep and deepening crisis will present enormous financial challenges to even the wealthy nations. As the fiction communicates, it will take a huge amount of creative effort and improvization. The technological means will be dominantly basic and centred on those common to essential industries, like construction, energy, health, materials extraction, transport, agriculture and food. The demand for practical skills and live labour will be high, as will the ability to innovate and adapt existing machines. Their functioning in activities of materials recovery, recycling and reprocessing will be extensive – crushers, electric arc furnaces, metal detection and nail extraction, large angle grinders and other cutting equipment, small and medium-size lifting equipment, wood machining and welding equipment. These are just some of the kinds of technologies that will be needed in volume. New cities will likely, as the fiction suggests, be marked by a far more organic and utilitarian relation between materials, technologies and structures. Complex facades and cladding, as well as sophisticated heating, cooling and ventilation systems with vast amounts of ducting controlled by computerized building management systems, will just not happen. Overall, the systems created would be, by necessity, smaller and cheaper than would be required to build a current new city. Again, as the fiction indicates this process would be staged and there would be no expectation of the total population of the old city moving to the new – significant numbers could be expected to move to other locations. The fact of who does and does not move to the new city, and the labour involved in its construction, the built form of the city and its economy and culture, as the fiction suggests, would mean that the new would have a very different form and character from the old city. Not only should the planning and conceptualization have already started but site selection and the evaluation of logistical needs should also be under way.

Worldwide, a process of re-globalization (a smaller trend) and de-globalization (the larger trend) can be expected – the former occurring as some industrial production is relocated, supply chains are reconfigured and consumer markets shrink and change. The latter arises as failing and failed economies delink from conditions of exchange and localize resource protection. All this is seen against a backdrop of increasing clamour for command of the prime sources of global natural capital, already under way.

Obviously what has been outlined is a very brief and impressionistic account of what will be a very complex situation. Actual changes will be more diverse and complex. So while the specific forms that trends will take remain vague, the overall pattern suggests it is certain to be massive and inevitable. All remarks made now about technology need to be considered against this backdrop of crisis, because the crisis is indivisible from its coming and the forms of its future negotiation. This negotiation begs a better understanding of technology, and this is what the following review seeks to contribute. What is now needed, and is beginning to be recognized, is that technology is not fully under 'our' control. It is now an environment as much as an object, system and tool. Perceptions are out of step with its *reality*. In sum, the demand to think of the future strategically, comprehensively and in diverse and complex ways, which are neither full of utopian techno-bubbles nor endless dystopias, is enormous and is neglected by governments, thinkers, research institutes of universities and industries that act in their own self-interests.

Reiterating the being of technology

The technological construction of reality has been a slow and uneven geo-cultural process that was destined by our species being born into a world of tools.[3] The skills developed, the use of those things made with tools, the mental challenges of imagination and technique and the biomechanical and cognitive changes resulting from thinking with and using tools have had significant and continuous ontological designing consequences, transforming our being over time. Tools and technologies made a huge contribution to our becoming what we are and the world we occupy (Fry 2012). By mind, skills and technology our species made a world of creation and destruction as a 'world within the world' where, in large part, we exist in a condition of dependence and negation. In doing this 'we' determined a future by the accumulative effects/affect of our collective actions. The problem now is that the future we have made has been discovered to be an unmaking of the essential conditions of the being of biological life. It is this that is now named as an extinction event. The crisis of the crisis constituted by the form of 'world within the world' that our species-being created as the agent of the unmaking of our biological conditions of dependence is that its materiality is just not being confronted.

There is no way to deal with this situation without making crisis unavoidably present and by our overcoming, by an affirmative ontological redesigning, what predominantly designs us via the externalization of will. This occurs by establishing an intergenerational ontologically designing counter force of recreated futural life-worlds. This does not imply a universal transformation of consciousness, an act of choice or political enlightenment. Rather it requires the liberation of transformative forces and sufficient imagination to bring enough futural redirective designing and cosmotechnical change into being to create organically reconfiguring ontic conditions of being otherwise. Put at its most basic this means the initiation of a process that changes the ontological agency of the world into which future generations are born. The realization of this transformation depends on breakdown/crisis/unmaking and remaking in difference as a project of making time directed against extinction's presence by foreclosing its imminence. Thereby, the material emplacement of conditions of reversal via an ontological designing action counters the worldly negating world in which our being became. It is contingent action in response to the imperative of futuring. What is being identified here can be 'grounded' in the example of the ontological futural performative character of a moved city on the basis of understanding that the city is already an ontologically designing event by default.

The ontological nature of the moved city as event is hereafter conceived with futuring intent: it is redirectively designed to sustain being futurally in place. This does not imply determinism but rather the determination of individuated conditions of difference. The action should not be one of 'materially' trying to create 'a new world' but redirectively remaking what already exists (again, this is how moving a city and metrofitting an existing city are both understood). Rather than a mega construction project arriving in a city, the move invites being seen and created out of a pluriverse of difference formed by expanding pragmatic autonomous designing and action from within the resources of a community. Poor 'informal communities' already demonstrate this capability; and what is being proposed is the amplification and advancement of this capability. The conditions of design limitation for such action are very simple: excess can only be tolerated if it can be ecologically accommodated without harm; all other actions are directed at the constraint of excess and a reformation of the meaning and form of utility. What this recognizes is the unlearnt dialectical nature of 'our' world making – we cannot create without destruction. In a pluriversal moved city there is no limitation to what can be made except the limitation of an ethos of constrained destruction. Working within this condition of constraint implies considerable learning and an acquired judgment that in time results in a sensibility inscribed in a habitus that is generationally transferred. What is being described is an ontological designing process. While the context in which this action is set is new, the process is not. It has been, as is, intrinsic to many Indigenous cultures. Hunting in conditions of abundance without exceeding need in conditions of restrained accumulation is a clear example.

There is no prospect of a reality that is not technical; there is no possibility of saying yes or no to technology: it is and will remain omnipresent in our being and worlds. But, out of crisis, there is the possibility of breaking the grip of the ontologically designing determinism of a great deal of 'our' extant being with technologies. In order for this to happen requires making its designing present in conditions of anticipated and actual breakdown. Again, a moved city creates the potential for technology to be assessed differently in the context of contingent futural actions and ontologically designing imperatives.

Comment so far has been on technology in general. We are now going to look at four areas of concern that shed light on the contemporary character (rather than nature) of technology.

The machine/organic relation

Central to this relation is an understanding of the connections between life and technology. This understanding arises from the mediation of organology, it breaks the hold of 'a common sense' that separates the machine and the organism. This becomes all the more important in a world of technological inequity where, for a minority, technological development will continue to take two forms: regress to more basic industrial technologies (as characterized by the moving city fiction), and a technological bricolage spanning elites and the poor that will reflect greater structural disadvantage. This will be nowhere more evident than in weapons, whereby poor nations are armed with rich nations' hand-me-downs while the rich ones will move toward fully autonomous warfighting machines. The prospect of men and women fighting with self-directed machines is a looming possibility. This disparity equally transposes to industrial production.

By examining the structure and function of the organism it becomes possible to make the construction of the machine more understandable. Georges Canguilhem argued that this relation now needs to be understood, in part, by a critical rereading of Descartes' view of the body as machine (Canguilhem [1952] 1992: 45–69). Going beyond a biomechanical view of bodily functions, and anticipating contemporary biotechnology, Canguilhem, drawing on the ideas of Raymond Ruyer from a prior decade (67n28) set out to justify the view that *machines can be considered as organs of human species*. A tool or a machine is an organ, and 'organs are tools and machines' (55). Canguilhem further points out that all organisms display autoconstruction, automaintenance, autoregulation and autorepair capability (56). Machines have advanced by striving to attain these same capabilities and thereby acquiring the means to enable the self-organization and autonomy that Yak Hui assigns to recursivity (2019: 42). Obviously crucial to the articulation between the organism and the machine has been the function and exchange of code. Underscoring this impetus of bio-technical advancement has been what Jacques Ellul described in 1964 as 'technical progress' being 'no longer conditioned by anything other than its own calculus of efficiency' (1964: 74).

Clearly the relation between the organism and the machine directly connects to the nature and question of life. The question of life was of central concern to Gilbert Simondon's entire project. In particular he was interested in the relation and distinction between life, non-life and machines. His views are a clear expression of the character of his radical empiricism and expose the strength and weakness of this position that centres on his Eurocentrically formed universalism that excludes the cosmologies of others and how they objectified other realities. In doing so a different regime of truth is constituted, one that can register 'the same, as the same but different'.[4]

The presence of life in non-life is a good example of the relation of sameness as difference. For Simondon non-life has a presence in life, and emerges out of it; likewise this understanding has been common in many Indigenous cosmologies past and present. Thus a commonly asserted truth is concluded from totally different epistemologies. While Simondon argued that there was a passage and process of non-life toward living, other cosmologies posited the relation as circular.

What Simondon recognized was that the transformative dynamic of life was not constrained within the biological but had become linked to the technological. This view, echoing the thinking of his teacher, Georges Canguilhem, has now become much clearer with the arrival of biotechnologies/genetic engineering/ medical genetics and the ability to modify and manufacture living matter and produce nanotechnology machines to work within it. One of main issues is the disjuncture between: the actuality of encountered technology, perceptions of it and its invisibility. It is not just what we see. As the history of chemical and electrical engineering affirm this disjuncture is not entirely new. But the arrival of advanced electronic and digital technologies, genetic engineering and nanotechnology has dramatically added to a state of invisibility. Added to this is the gap between the everyday and increasing pervasiveness and complexity of technology and diminishing critical concern. The point about reflecting on technology and moving cities is that, as indicated, this allows consideration of futuring ontological designing possibilities, including the impact of urban built as itself an organic relation between designing and constructing the built environment, and the conditions in which the ontologies of the citizenry will be formed.

Systems and cybernetics

Norbert Weiner is credited as the originator of cybernetics, which he defined in his 1948 book, *Cybernetics: Or Control and Communication in Animals and Machines*. The influence of cybernetics has been huge in the rise and application of artificial intelligence. Its notion of feedback and information has been viewed as constituting 'a new cognitive schema' (Hui 2019). Cybernetics is also seen as one of the contributing ideas in the development of General Systems Theory attributed to Ludwig von Bertalanffy (Bertalanffy 1969). Systems theory can be broadly understood as a structure of control across multiple domains including being operative as a 'powerful thinking of governance and social regulation' (Hui 2019: 241). Open 'allopoietic' systems theory was supplemented and contrasted with a third influential theoretical concept of systems: autopoiesis. This concept, created by the Chilean biologists Humberto Maturana and Francisco Varela, describes a self-organizing homeostatic system that reproduces itself in conditions of material inflows and outflows, similar to a cell in an organism (Maturana and Varela 1973). All of this thinking influenced how systems were/are understood by the sciences (especially biology), technology and the social, cultural and political domains. Equally, this thinking has been exposed to a considerable amount of criticism.

Cybernetics is turned back on itself via second order cybernetics' exposure of the problematic of there being no external position of observation, thus requiring the corrective position of the observation of observation that self-reflectively adopts a critical view via various lenses including epistemology and ethics (Luhmann 1989: 22–7). The autonomy given to systems boundaries is challenged by relational thought and by the disruption of contingency. The integrity of a system is continually unsettled by breakdowns of environmental function and inter-system interfaces. This has been especially evident as the climate system, from an anthropocentric perspective, increasingly produces ecological damage, dysfunction and extreme weather events from droughts and floods that damage and disrupt agriculture, urban infrastructure, the life of coastal communities, the order of governance and the stability of civil society.

More specifically, the general conditions of unsettlement and breakdown of the urban metabolism have the ability to interrupt the recursive feedback of many cybernetic systems, whereby the greater the dependence of a system the greater its risk. The major bush fires in Australia during early and mid-century provides clear examples. Not only did they destroy homes, towns and millions of hectares of forest, as well as over two billion native animals, but they also rendered the energy and telecommunications delivery systems' infrastructure dysfunctional. This meant communities lost power for many weeks and those stranded and surrounded by a ring of fire had no means to communicate with potential rescuers. In the past older technology, like sirens, flares and distress rockets, at a basic level, would have served this function.

The ascent of immaterial information systems-based technology continues to have profound impacts and implications for the nature of technology itself, cultures, psycho-social life and economies. As such systems have made a significant contribution to ungrounding becoming a predominant feature of existential everydayness, wherein emotional investment is made in categories and activities without substantial meaning (friends who are not in any real sense friends, commitment to causes without any real commitment, community membership without any actual community, presence without being present and so on). To make the expansiveness of this 'technoscape of affect' clearer three of its features will be registered.

The first is **psychotechnology.** The mind that this technology inhabits is not being approached as vested in a psychological, anthropological, phenomenal or in any familiar characterization, but via the particular focus of what Simondon (1980) defined as 'psychic-individualism'. He understood this as the non-physical emergent means by which 'we' deal with our individuation in a world of challenges, problems and opportunities, and in relation to the implications of our actions and associated tensions.[5] For Simondon, what makes psycho-social life possible is the artefact as the carrier of 'the being that produced it' (Barthélémy 2008: 110–11). The artefact can also be understood via an ontological designing that collectivizes social engagement or disaggregates it. In the case of social media it does this via inauthentic sociality, and the fragmentary character and attention-seeking 'noise' of information content, as well as the reduction of communicative engagement to entertainment, all of which diminishes a user's capacity to sustain any form of prolonged attention to serious and 'rich' informational content.

Feature two goes to the issue of **attention**. Stiegler emphasizes this as 'the reality of individuation in Gilbert Simondon's sense of the term' (2018: n.p.). He goes on to qualify his understanding of attention as 'the mental faculty of concentration on an object, that is, of giving oneself to an object, is also the social faculty of taking care of this object'. For Simondon, the destruction of attention is: 'both the destruction of the psychical apparatus and a destruction of the social apparatus (formed by collective individuation) to the extent that the latter constitutes a system of care, given that to pay attention is also to take care' (Stiegler 2012: 104–20).[6]

Number three is **memory**. Loss of attention is directly connected to an inability to remember, thus futurally structuring a loss of memory. This loss is technologically 'offset' because 'many aspects of our lives are gathered and retained in databases' (Kinsley 2014). However, this gathering is dominantly not by us, and is not available for us to access. Memory is being made malleable. Additionally, the information that we do deposit in computer memory lacks the responsive materiality of the written and printed word and the other associated prompts of recall that are intrinsic to situated memory: the sound of a voice or a piece of music, a recognized face, place or gesture, a date in a diary, the hint of a scent from a once familiar perfume, a photograph that returns the forgotten.

The context of this psychotechnological situation has become paradoxical. Subjects of modern life are exposed to a rapid and continuous flow of information and images. Consequently, forgetting has become a coping mechanism, while attempts to remember have become ever more selective and narrowly guided by 'matters of concern' and self-interested 'interests'. Thereafter, the 'what wants to be remembered' is often channelled into systems of data storage, where it continually accumulates, eventually getting electronically archived and mostly forgotten. More substantially, the contemporary technology of the exteriorization of the memory of thought, word, image and experience constitutes what Stiegler calls epiphylogenetic (tertiary) memory that is created and exists outside us (1998).[7] It is held in encounters with artefacts, and this has always been so (specifically Stiegler names the tool as being 'before anything else, memory' [254]). As Stiegler realized, the ability to reassemble the content of tertiary memory is de facto the ability to reconfigure events in time.

Memory should not be understood as universally uniform. In particular, in Indigenous cultures, their lineage of oral culture, cultural practices that 'transmit' traditional narratives, totems that de-subjectify the remembered and carry it in time, artefacts that function abstractly to prompt a collective recall of major (village) events[8] and 'sacred objects' that hold memory only to be articulated by their keeper(s) – in a contemporary context – exist in lieu of visual and written records. All such activities and objects are examples of a recursive relation between action, world/object and mind/memory.

Making decisions about the relation of technology to the form of a moved city in a changing world will become directionally critical for the future of the population of that city. The implication is that decisions have to be made from a well-informed position in the context of just how complex this task is. Cosmotechnology arrives in this setting as one significant and possibly viable alternative choice to the technological hegemony of the restricted pragmatic instrumentalism present in the global status quo.

Cosmotechnologies

The anthropologist Tim Ingold argued that humans in Western thought are essentially ambiguous (2013). They are seen as an animal among animals but also as a moral being above animals. This begs two qualifications: humans are animals whose moral being represses their animal immorality (most evidently, but again ambiguously, in sexual conduct). As acknowledged elsewhere, this notion of the human became a universal imposition delivered by modernity and its interlocutor, colonialism. In so doing other constructions of our species-being as 'animal' among animals, and as a being that embraced its animality, were sought out to be destroyed or displaced. However, this was never totally realized. The human has never been totally universal.

By degree, all cultures configure a view of their world via a particular cosmology, and thereafter are informed by it, creating an artefactual and semiospheric world of occupation (life and work). To do this every modality of Homo sapiens (the 'knowing animal') constituted a particular epistemology and technology. As colonializing Euromodernity aimed and acted to erase 'being in difference' so likewise did it disregard, dismiss and displace the existence of Indigenous knowledge and technologies. In contemporary worlds of difference only traces of these technologies remain. Many of these technologies did not announce themselves in ways colonies were able to recognize. For example, the traditional dyeing of fabrics by Indigenous women in Timor was part of the technology of the manufacture of woven garments. It required what is now seen as botanical and chemical knowledge. Some plants were collected and crushed to extract their juice; others were placed at the centre of a ball of clay and placed on the bed of a stream for several months to undergo chemical change. Pounding kernel nuts and roots with a stone was yet another technique to extract a dye. These activities extended across seasons and required a substantial amount of knowledge that passed from generation to generation for a great expanse of time, but until exposed by anthropological inquiry the complexity of this activity went unseen.

Futurally, difference is destined to return out of displacement. Thus, techno-fracturing of both inequity and privilege, from abandonment and breakdown in a climate change impacted world of territorial and resource scarcity, will create a great deal of conflict. In such a situation it is not impossible to imagine a confluence between emergent cosmologies of other worldly habitations in a de-naturalized environment, situated technological improvization and socio-cultural reordering. Counter to universal technological modernity, this situation will create multiple cosmotechnologies, albeit inflected by degree by the afterlife of the hegemony of the universal.

The scenario outlined prompts a particular way of understanding cosmotechnics as: a regime of time and futural technical means and activities coming out of resisting particular defuturing conjunctures; exploiting material circumstances of improvization; and utilizing available resources. But understood as within a cosmology that makes the actuality and potentiality of this lifeworld meaningful. This view of cosmotechnics is influenced by Yak Hui's definition of cosmotechnics, but presents a different construction in response to a world of ongoing climate disasters and breakdowns. For Hui, cosmotechnics means: 'the unification between the cosmic order and moral order through technical activities' (2016: 19–20), that he claims overcomes the opposition between technology and nature. Such an understanding could be said to lack a posited specificity of 'cosmic and the notion of a moral order', but more problematic is the nature/technology binary it adheres to in an age where the distinction between the natural and the artificial has been dissolved (as genetic engineering affirms). Likewise, while recognizing the non-universality of technology (264), the futuring and defuturing ambiguities of technology go unacknowledged. Moreover, in worlds of naturalized artificiality there is no clear line of distinction between technological agency, or its impacts and 'nature'. More appropriately, and nearer to Simondon's disposition, technology invites being viewed as an environment in its own right that is organically articulated to the natural environment. The instabilities of such inter-related environments render ungrounded technology an issue of critical concern linked to understanding it's ground as:

Technology – the instrumentalization of skill and knowledge to constitute a material or immaterial independent agency that a human may employ as a simple or complex tool; or an autonomous functioning entity that has reified a human/animal attribute (making, destroying, calculating, transporting, sheltering, flying, feeding, picturing, communication and so on). The first characterization is developmentally unbounded and enfolds conscious and unconscious action. The second recognizes that some technologies are gaining/have gained conditions of independence beyond human control.

Technologies of colonialism – stone tools, and those of wood and bone, mark the inception of technology (*tekhnologia*[9]). Their arrival was a key moment of hominoid existence and development that predated the arrival of our species by millennia. Tools set a pattern of being colonized and colonizing in so far as they became articulated to instruments of power. The specific use of technology as an instrument of colonization has been recognized (Adas 1989; Harding 2011), but remains underdeveloped. Technology as an ontological mechanism of colonization is even less recognized.

4. Development and the 'end times' postdevelopment

Geopolitically 'development' in the modern era is a Hegelian-inspired concept of progress taking 'the world' to the end of history. This notion was recast in the post-Cold War moment (now completely discredited) by the declaration by Francis Fukuyama of the 'end of history' being reached, essentially by the 'victory' of capital and democracy delivering the 'end state'.

Modernization theory moved modernity beyond its historically enacted philosophically underscored ideological and economic practice of a universal imposition of the modern, this as to an ideal to materialize, and thereby create, a world of and in its own image. European colonizing nations sought to realize this ambition for centuries, with 1492 (the 'discovery' of the New World) notionally designated as a founding moment. Modernization theory revitalized this ambition in the conditions post World War Two. Two seemingly different world-shaping forces overlapped: the reconstruction of a ravaged Europe and the beginning of a withdrawal of European colonial powers from the colonies with 'encouragement' from independence movements. Modernization theory, posed as a theoretically informed transnational institutional policy aimed at economic, social and political development, was presented as a humanitarian path to modernity by the world's wealthier nations. In actuality it was de facto a means through which most of these nations could resituate their power and extractive capability over their former colonies and poorer nations, at the same time as the United States expanded its global sphere of influence. Modernity simply became pursued by other means. To do this a number of structural and conceptual devices were employed that recoded how 'the world' was perceived and what it was that development set out to develop.

In contrast to a picture of the world constituted by sovereign and colonized nations, imperial powers and empires, the world became divided into three divisions: the First (the wealthy and industrially developed); the Second (the communist bloc); the Third (the poor and to be developed). A Fourth (the abject and dysfunctional) was a designation that arrived later. This model of division is credited to the French demographer, Alfred Sauvy, who published the concept in 1952 (Sauvy 1952: 14). The concept immediately resonated with the United Nations (established in 1945) and its financial arm, the World Bank. The Bank had already made its first loan to a designated 'underdeveloped' nation (Colombia) in 1948 (Escobar 1995: 86). This was the year the US-funded Marshall Plan to reconstruct Europe commenced. In association with the hierarchical division of nations was the classification of the 'developed' who were to be the developers of the 'underdeveloped'. It is in this distinction that the violence of development becomes evident. Many of those underdeveloped nations were actually undeveloped, with an Indigenous population with a sense of their future formed in and by other cosmologies. In this context development was an imposition with the assistance of an epistemological colonization enabled by the afterlife of the social infrastructure of colonialism and/or a political ideology that equated modernization with emancipation. In this setting there were communities who were poor, but also many self-sustaining subsistence communities whose economy was de-valorized and thereafter the people became classified as impoverished. While development and its theory continued to be elaborated and gain support and global momentum it also started to attract criticism which has eventually led to the current critique presented by postdevelopment thinkers. A brief account that makes development theory and criticism of it clearer now follows.

Walt Rostow, an American economist and sociologist, represents one of the most influential authors and promoters of modernization theory. He asserted that all countries should pass through five stages of economic development: the traditional society, the preconditions for takeoff, the takeoff, the drive to maturity and the age of high mass-consumption (Rostow 1960: 191). Another American, the political scientist Samuel Huntington, places modernization in a political context by arguing that modernization requires and includes political development. This view has equated with 'the mission' to globalize democracy (Huntington 1965: 386–430). In both cases, the timing and content of these positions place modernization theory in the Cold War and the ideological resistance to communism. Undevelopment was a condition that modernization theory redesignated as underdevelopment, this to legitimise the imposition of modernization as a means of induction into power and function of the global economy. The proposition was that these economies would be made to catch up with those already developed. But, of course, developed economies did not remain static waiting to catch up with – they went on developing. The arrival of an age of neo-liberalism (effectively a reversion to a laissez-faire colonial mode of trade) meant that any pretence of development having a United Nations'-inflected humanist idealism was abandoned. The economic market determinism of globalization and universal consumerism became the rule.

The critiques of development as an ideology of modernization and of equality (that never arrived) are extensive, complex, accumulative and long-standing. The idea of underdeveloped as an imposed model of development that was destructive of undevelopment – i.e. the development of Indigenous peoples – was recognized decades ago (Cockcroft, Frank and Johnson 1972), but failed to be sufficiently acknowledged. The futural social and environmental values of the knowledge of many Indigenous cultures went unrecognized, while the consequences of the long-term effects of dependence continued. Likewise, the unequal conditions of exchange between developed and 'underdeveloped' became established and endured (Amin 1976). The relation of third world markets for technology and arms is an evident example of the inversion of the benefits of development, as is the continued exploitation of the once third world's cheap labour. The structural corruption of development and its 'deal making' in so many ways have facilitated the creation of what is now endemic local corruption. Globalization stripped the illusion of humanization from development, with continuing extractive injustice undercutting the very possibility of fair trade. All of the flaws of development fold into the arrival of the critique of postdevelopment in the 1980s. As an ethically informed mode of thought and practice it rejected the notion of a Western-led path to progress and engages the ongoing negation of the Global South by the Global North.

Alongside the longer-established and direct critical confrontation with development, postdevelopment confronts the implications of neo-colonialism, recognizing that postcolonialism does not actually define a condition without colonization. Instead it is mostly the physical absence of a colonial power. It is into this context that the project of decoloniality has arrived as an imperative of epistemological delinking. But what has still to gain equal force is a clearer recognition of the forms and agency of re-colonization in which technology is deeply implicated. This is very evident in the 'development' (as becoming modern) of an ontology of techno-colonization, especially in the young people of industrializing populations, and diaspora of the Global South in the North. Here is the destructive force of defuturing as a desire to conform to a technocentric hyper-consumerism that turns against the industrializing population's own future and the future in general. The actual logic of such development now must be contested as the agency of the Anthropocene negates organic life itself (Hui 2019: 254). No vision of a mutually desirable sustainable future currently exists. The issue is no longer one of the South catching up with the North but rather freeing, prompting, assisting nations to redirect themselves futurally to sustain their population in time.

Rather than being a better life realized by a higher standard of living, 'consumption' is being exposed not merely as an economic activity, but as a pathology. Consumption was formerly the non-medical characterization of tuberculosis, a disease whereby the body eats itself. Effectively this is exactly what economic hyper-consumption does – it consumes the renewable resources upon which life depends, generates toxic conditions and eliminates the ability of living beings to sustain themselves. Unchecked bio-economical, non-regenerative consumption (that is non-ecological) is a killer.

Postdevelopment has to become a discourse able to create non-utopian imaginary and practices able to materialize conditions that sustain viable futures under conditions of limitations. The coming global breakdowns will make this clear. Thinking about moving cities, especially from the uneven environments of newly industrializing nations, enables this objective to be brought into view as elemental to a much larger demand for new forms of thought, epistemologies, imaginaries and action. For this to happen investments in the creation of new educational, redirective and political practices and spaces have to be made, and not just by a general appeal to enlightened action. By predominantly exposing the material forms and processes of defuturing, and thereafter structurally emplacing operative modes in resistance to it, the objective will ensue. A project like moving a city not only situates such action but also constitutes conditions of observation from which other actions can be derived.

In our epoch there is no universal state of being to arrive at, no evolutionary trajectory to travel along, no stage of development to achieve, be it in the fully modern, a socialist world order, eternal life or the noosphere – these prospects are all evaporated dreams. What actually exists are forms of action that secure the means to sustain our being in difference, together with all we fundamentally depend upon. The problem is that our being itself is fragmenting, epitomized by the divide between the other, that is an Indigenous lifeworld or the abandoned, and those of relative degrees of privilege, with conditions of instrumentalized posthumanity at the extreme. Effectively our fragmented being is becoming beings in fundamental difference.

5. A coming geometry of humans' and inhumans' relationality

A moved city can be seen as a redirective space in which a reconstruction of relations between non, extant and post humans could become possible. Cities are designing events (Fry 2017: 35–48). To move a city is not to replicate the event of the city from which it came but rather to enable 'futural urban being in a changed world' to arrive as ontologically re-formed, wherein humans are able to sustain themselves, their others and the environments of the inter-connected inter-dependency. To understand this relational condition, the un-natural nature and relationality of our 'human and posthuman' being need critical reconsideration.

The language of the human, posthuman and inhuman presumes a totality that simply does not exist. 'Humanity' was fractured long before posthumanism and techno-postmodernity started presenting its variants of denaturalized and enhanced being(s). The first instrument of division was not technological innovation but racial division. Race, as recognized by W.E.B. Du Bois in his paper, 'The Conservation of Races' (1897), had no biological substance. Science has subsequently confirmed this. But race had been made into a key social category in the classification of humans in the context of global colonialism, dividing the constructed and homogenized fully human from the no less constructed and homogenized subhuman, as analysed by, among others, Aníbal Quijano (2007). He writes, 'Unlike in any other previous experience of colonialism, the old ideas of superiority of the dominant, and the inferiority of the dominated under European colonialism were mutated in a relationship of biologically and structurally superior and inferior' (Quijano 2007: 171). In the early modern era race became a Eurocentric grading system of differential of life value. It fluctuated over time and ranged from classifications of the non-human to the cultivated human (for example: Kant's well-known observation concerning the inability of women, children, working classes and 'savages' to appreciate the sublime). To realize this structuring, as we shall see, recasts how the arrival of the Anthropocene and global unsustainability are understood. To be able to see this, the relations between technology, its creators and their worlds need elaboration.

Technology is, as indicated, a powerful ontologically designing agent. As was argued earlier, our species-being has always been technological. Thus the tools by which we incrementally made our world equally contributed to making us – specifically our biomechanical and cognitive qualities and abilities. This interaction has never stopped, but as the complexity and variations of technologies increased so did differences in the ontologically designing consequences: change proliferated. Although dominantly discussed in a totalized way, the global diversity of technology is now enormous, which means it also contributes to the large differences among and between people: for instance, a carpenter in Bangladesh working exclusively with hand tools is different, and not just economically and culturally, but ontologically from one in Berlin working almost completely with power tools. Both are even more different than an electronics engineer making light sensors in Tokyo. There is no universal ontologically designed technical subject/user. All language that presents a linear account of technological development is flawed. Technology does not exist independently from contexts, or from other ontologically determining agents. Technological beings are not uniform. The lack of relational complexity in the entire technology/posthuman discourse totally undercuts its critical capability and reach.

As has been recognized by many anthropologists, many Indigenous people's cosmologies inform cultures that function without dualisms dividing people and nature, or hominoids and animals. However, technology has been/ is being introduced into many Indigenous communities without any sense of the consequences, especially in relation to cosmology/world connectivity (this includes the impact of social media on their social fabric). A whole cluster of dilemmas and problems now gather around this issue – none with easy answers. Indigenous communities have adopted, for instance, communication technologies and used them in culturally innovatory ways, but these and other technologies have also led to young people rejecting traditional practices and values, and embracing commodity culture (arriving via corporation tailoring products to them as just another market). Even worse is when drug culture becomes introduced into such communities. Interestingly the values of their own culture are often the most successful means of dealing with this problem.

Industrial technology cannot now be divided from its establishment of the historical conditions of defuturing. However, the collateral destructiveness of so much of this technology went unseen and un-thought, from its conception to current use. As such it made a major contribution toward the defuturing of ourselves and much else besides. There has been a constant process of extending capability to create technologies, but without any sense of consequences. The telos of unrestrained technological development is in error, and rather than this being widely recognized, many people still believe it to be a means of progress and salvation. The consideration of risk associated with technology has become 'uncool' in the intellectual hothouse of what can be called a socio-cultural nihilist condition of denial. It seems that as the sophistication and proliferation of technologies has increased, the ability of critical inquiry to engage them has diminished, partly because of the speed of the rate of change and also because of their seductive power, reducing the size and agency of a critical community as universities become ever more instrumentalized and subordinate to the economic status quo.

More pointedly, in the now instrumental culture of the academy, having a critical position toward the technologies of the contemporary economy is not a good career move. It is not a position from which to win research grants. Yet as technological beings, in an unevenly globalized technically constructed reality, a critical discourse of technological redirection is urgently needed if 'we' are to survive its psycho-social and environmental impacts. So said, the breakdown, as it has been addressed, presents an agenda that invites action to be posed against the unthinking of thinking technology and a diminishing use value of posthumanism – in fact, the emergence of breakdown will evacuate a great deal of the noise of its theoriasphere. We are technological beings. Technology is here to stay, but 'our' (as a plurality) relation to it cannot be divided from how it is positioned toward the extent of our (multi) species' duration.

As will become apparent in the next few decades, (the coming) breakdown(s) of enviro-climatic systems, infrastructure and the social/cultural spheres will require not only an expanded condition of repair to redirect the broken but also the use of fragments of the broken to contribute to creating new naturalized artificial ecologies. The plural character that these ecologies would need to have would centre on their being an environmentally generative counter-weight to a technocratic and technocentric response to breakdown. At the same time, they would need to be totally other than a dystopic utopianism of techno-posthumanism.

The essence of these ecologies (their ontological agency – or what Heidegger called 'thinging') is an undoing of an anthropocentric propensity by ontologically designing structural means (seen via a retrospective view of the means that are intrinsic to Indigenous cultures). Such an approach to anthropocentrism is in direct opposition to the unrealizable call to consciously transcend being anthropocentric by an act of will to meet a moral imperative. Obviously thinking of such ecologies begs to be brought to the thinking of moved and new cities as designing events.

There is something else about breakdown that needs comment. It names variable conditions of malfunction, temporary inoperability, or total dysfunction that cannot be universalized. Breakdown can only be engaged in a situated conjuncture: it has no stock solution. There is no way of it being understood without a diagnostic analysis of its particularity. Against such a backdrop, the ontological designing of technological romanticism, which underscores much of the discourse of posthumanism re-breaks the already broken fiction of the human (the one that was never one but was always two: the (biological) animal and the 'human' (of imposed and repressed animality). Over the course of modernity, human has been the colonializing of being of Indigenous other but its agency long predates this and is embedded in the historicity of 'our' species-being. In this context if the pluriverse is taken seriously and informed by the human as broken, Homo sapiens is perhaps now more appropriately understood as Homo pluralis (the being that evidences the technological breakdown of natural evolution).

If the inhuman is viewed as the negation of what is human (Hui 2019: 32) it follows that the notion of Homo pluralis also renders the inhuman problematic. But it was actually always so, this because the negation of the being of the Indigenous other (now designated as dehumanization) cannot not remove that which they never had – 'humanity'. There is also another dimension to this issue: 'we' are born an animal and are made 'human' (McDowell 1994), the agency of transformation being education, of which Lyotard says, 'All education is inhuman' and is 'without constraint and terror' (Lyotard 1988: 4). Ontological design disrupts this claim in that it prefigures, and is, the 'thinging' essence of pre-school and early education. Technology comes into this picture (at least for all societies where arrival into the world is in a techno-medical environment) as ontological design commencing from the very moment it (technology) monitors and manages the life of the animal in transition to 'human' incorporation (the animal in (the) human).

There is something other 'in' the Eurocentrically formed human being, colonized by reason, and lived as an instrumental sensibility, that Hui, following Lyotard, calls the unknown 'positive inhuman' (Hui 2019: 266). What needs to be grasped here is an alternative he named as 'intuitive resistance to the sufficiency of reason' (266), a deemed positive in (as a relation within) the human. As such it could also be taken as a residual link to an internal other – animal intelligence – which perhaps could be thought of as a developable and not totally inactive node of inter-species relations, as well as being an external link to a trace of the pre-human being (and, as such, a potentiality of trans-Homo pluralis connectivity). These remarks take us to a reconsideration of the human and inter-species relations.

As the hybrid formed from our being biologically an animal, a socially and culturally constructed other, and a bio-cognitive constructed technological being, the plural that we are exists as an infra-species in inter-species worldly relations. The view of Dominique Lestel and his colleagues at the Laboratory of Eco-Anthropology and Enthnobiology in Paris (cited by Tim Ingold 2013: 19–20) reiterates that every human society is a society made up of animals, stressing: 'becoming is always becoming with'. He qualifies that 'we' join with, and learn from, the human and animal becoming, which in turn can be further qualified by the being (thinging) of our infra-relationality. Ingold's thinking echoes Dona Haraway's notion of inter-species 'entanglements' (Haraway 2003), as elaborated by expositions of non-human exceptionalism and 'companion species' and 'inter-species kinship' (Haraway 2007).

While all these potentialities and speculations are the stuff of academic inquiry, they afford another possibility offered by the event of the moved and remade city understood as a space of reconstituted becoming other than human, or even the ethical superhuman of moral posthumanism. Remaking from the broken, a new utility and material modesty can be seen as complemented with an enriched condition of being created upon a provisional ground of being-with-others in the wide sense indicated. Clearly this would be no utopia, no easy life. But it could be made a rich and rewarding futural life countering defuturing conditions prior to, and diminished by, breakdown. Central to the realization of this possibility is the creation of an epistemology of unlearning an education of learning in error able to: displace the divisions of knowledge and disciplinary structures that obstruct relational understanding and identify the productivist drive inherent in the unreflective instrumentalism integral to the habitus of so many practices that replicate the status quo. Unless this unknowing is present there will be a general tendency to repair or recreate the broken rather than employ it as a contingent and then negated ground of change

6. Questions of epistemology, cities and movement

In thinking the city, what is there to know, and what is the relation between this knowledge and moving a city?

Approaching city as event

We, in our plurality cannot change at the fundamental level unless 'the event of our (continual coming into) being' changes. For more than half of the global population a key event of this event is that it constitutes the urban. To understand the urban as such calls upon a relational cartography of epistemologies, even though so much of its complexity would still go by unmapped. Partly this is because the generic forms of the city, like buildings, roads, infrastructure, people, economies and so on reveal very little of the specific ontology of place. To gain knowledge of the specificity requires understanding the determinate epistemologies of located physical and social geography, ecology, demography, class structure, cultures and cultural dynamics, aesthetic ambience, operational and political economy, history, built form, political landscape, power structures and zones of conflict, dark side and a sense of its destiny. In large cities, the complexity of what could be known overwhelms. Much can be learned, but the possibility of it being fully understood folds into the impossible. Even in small cities, knowledge will always be partial. In all cases so much of what would like to be known is vested in 'the informal' and carried by popular memory. Inevitably, whatever becomes reified as data, and used to direct action, rests upon abstraction and concealment. All cities remain visibly invisible, unevenly known and unknowable, with megacities amplifying the scale of difference. The mystery of the city that travels with its familiarity begs comment.

We can never actually see the city. To completely rise above it, so as to embrace its totality, all of its qualities, features (save major geographic ones), details and populations disappear into an abstracted pattern. Views from the street reveal much specific detail, but nothing of the whole. The knowledge we think we have is always incomplete: the larger the city the less that is known. In the case of a megacity, like greater Tokyo with its population of thirty-nine million, gaining knowledge of the whole is totally impossible.

Cities are not static: they are dynamic, animated by commerce and trade, culture and social life, movement and noise and, above all, by the occupations and lives of people. The sum of this activity is what constitutes the city as a diffused, designed and designing event. As designing events, cities are designed by a vast range of professions, from sign writers and street furniture manufacturers to architects, planners and civil engineers; informal designing is done by occupants in the form of gardens, graffiti, busking, shop displays, street stalls and more. None of these activities are passive, as they all have designing effects.

Cities as events constitute a nexus between habitation and habitus – 'we' inhabit them but they inhabit(us) as a designing event that 'we' design – whether we are aware of this or not. As such cities infuse the political, economic, psycho-social and cultural environments of our life as a terrain of knowledge and conduct. We read the urban environment with a knowledge of its context and act on the feedback of our interpretations: genres of industrial, commercial and domestic buildings are recognized, as are welcoming, safe or dangerous places; distinctions are made between the familiar and the strange; the urban environment in which we grew up, work, live, walk or drive is a variable 'field of memory'; we discern wealth and poverty; the soundscapes and olfactory atmosphere of the city are objects of continuous information that informs our action. All of this and much more feeds the taken-for-granted knowledge of our habitus. Life in the city is always a mix of the certain and uncertain, the familiar and unfamiliar: we know what to expect but are often surprised. Thus drama is elemental to the event of the city, often as a trivial incident and sometimes as a major one, welcomed or unwelcomed (like a carnival, fire or bombing).

Staying with the known and unknown of the city, the first observation goes to the disjuncture between it as a condition of dependence and a consciousness of this situation – for instance, it is structured in the designing of the 'eventing' of the city as lived. Here then is the designing of the relation of all facilities and services as a lifeworld of the development of a city as place. As directive of city-dwelling, and self-placement in an environment, these facilities enable lives to function in a relational matrix of utilities and public services, health and education, employment, sport and leisure, entertainment, housing, nutrition, and the economic infrastructure and more. These conditions of dependence are partial, and the whole is known only in a fragmentary ways by the system of governance and by the public and private institutions, that administer constituent elements of the city. This because the city also functions by dint of informal structures, with the well-being and livelihood of many also equally depending on knowing how to negotiate these as much as the formal. All of this is to say that the city functions organically as an open system of natural and artificial component parts. Entered into the event is the notion of 'the smart city' (a sensor-monitored and partial AI systems-directed infrastructure, based on technology of multiple modes of environmental surveillance, from the weather and traffic to the conduct of people on the street). Here is an example of information and systems masquerading as intelligence. The smart city rhetoric is unhelpful and exemplifies the covering over of knowledge of the ever-growing complexity of the city that underscores a host of epistemological inquiries from urban sociology, social ecology and social psychology to environmental mental health and biophysical ecology that recognize part of the dynamic of the city as a process of accelerated change and continuous learning. This is all the more so in an age of increasing enviro-climatic impacts pending breakdowns. So framed, understanding the city as event arrests its reification as disarticulated spaces, economies and relations.

Yet in moving a city the picture changes because it can be an act of review of the 'to be moved', and of the learning selection and assemblage that will inform and form of the city to be brought into being. While this does not mean an absolute disclosure of knowledge it does provide the opportunity to consider the form or/and character of the city as a designing event. In many ways the constraints that come with having to decide what is to be transferred from the old, albeit in a retained, modified or remade form, can be seen as more critically reflective than the idealism that always accompanies the creation of a new city in the dominant design-form of the master plan.

Thinking the event now

Certainly there is no consensual philosophical understanding of exactly what 'the event' actually is. Difference proliferates as the discursive contexts within which the way 'it' is viewed change. 'The event' alters according the particular epistemological prism through which it is seen. Such thinking goes right back to the birth of classical thought and fundamental questions of what exists, and how and why. Thus the 'event' has remained an enduring eternal object of critical philosophical inquiry. But our concern is not with retracing the philosophical concept's intellectual history but rather in bringing a contemporary understanding of 'event' to the city. To this end specific examples of how it is now thought will be outlined. In doing so the essence of the city will be seen ontologically, as an ongoing process.

Thinking of the event in our conditions of being and becoming exposes it as something not contained in time or place but cosmic: the world and the cosmos flow into and out of the city. Every city on the planet is touched by and contributes to the atmospheric conditions of a changing climate. The scent of smoke from the fires of 2019/20 in Australia was evident in cities globally; information connects cities around the world via satellites in space. These are but a few examples of many.

Over modern times 'the event' has been thought of from the level of the cosmic to the sub-particle's becoming and being. Thus the concerns and conjuncture brought to the thinking of event will direct what ideas and thoughts will be assembled to constitute one's object of inquiry.

To assist with this task, comments from four (of many) thinkers of 'the event' will be considered: Alfred North Whitehead, Gilles Deleuze, Alain Badiou and Martin Heidegger.

Whitehead substitutes occasion for event and observes that the world is made up of 'actual occasions'. He then explains the ontological principle that whatever 'things there are' they are 'derived by abstraction from actual occasions'. The nexus of these actual occasions is gathered in 'one extensive quantum' he named as 'event' – this process being common from the molecule to the world itself (each constituted by molecular assemblages that themselves are 'a historic route of actual occasion' and as such are an 'event'. Whitehead 1978: 72–73). Thus, for example, one can see the cellular structure of any animal body as an event of continual cellular generation, death and regeneration in the larger event of a life. There is no stasis.

Whitehead, who Deleuze acknowledges as the last great Anglo-American philosopher, produced an echo carrying the question 'what is an event?' from Western thought while bringing a contemporary thinking of event to presence (Deleuze 1993: 77–82). Although there is a degree of overlap between how Whitehead and Deleuze understood event, Deleuze more specifically sees relations as events, and events as relations which, in both cases, exist in time (52). However, beyond their common concern with epistemological problems of corporeality, Deleuze occupies a more visceral perspective on the 'passions' and on the 'living presence of bodies', while Whitehead, at a foundational level, posits the 'individual as creativity' (52). Deleuze's most developed exposition of 'event' is found in his *The Logic of Sense*, of which Badiou provides an excellent summary and exegesis, done in the form of four axioms (2007: 37–44). In brief, the event is 'the ontological realisation of the eternal truth of one, the infinite power [*puissance*] of life'. Centrally, this defines the event as 'becoming'. Axiom two situates the event as that which 'has just happened and that which is about to happen', asserting it is never that which is 'just happening now'. As such the event is deemed to be a synthesis of past and future – a view influenced by Deleuze's work on Bergson. The third axiom places event outside 'the actions and passions of the body, even if it results from them'. And axiom four states that 'a life is composed of a single event', and, as this, is 'composed' of a complete gathering that draws all its variety together into the one. There is no last word made on 'the event': there is no line drawn under it, no absolutely resolved position to proclaim. As Badiou says of Deleuze, he 'strongly marked the nature of the philosophical combat in which the destiny of the word "event" is played out' (40–4).

Lastly we come to Heidegger, who positioned the event at the centre of his concern with the question of being (understood as 'the event', as an occurrence (time)). Being so evoked implies the active relation intrinsic to the difference between the ontic and the ontological, and between being and/ of being(s). Heidegger's most substantial exploration of 'The Event' (2013) was undertaken in his *Beiträge zur Philosophy* (1936–7) and in *Das Ereignis* (1941–2).[10] Our focus here will draw upon the latter work acknowledging, of 'the event' that 'Being begins, and does so essentially: the appropriating beginning' (127). But first the term appropriation needs clarification. To do this comment will be made on the translators' foreword of *Beiträge zur Philosophy* – Parvis Emad and Kenneth May reject 'event' and 'appropriation' (as the event of appropriation) as adequate translations of Heidegger's key term *Ereignis*. Event is quickly dismissed as 'totally alien'. They do this on three counts. The first is that it is more static than the German *Ereignis*. But appropriation has been used by other translators so one can assume their judgment is contested. Second is the claim that appropriation 'brings to mind the act of seizing', and this misconstrues how *Ereignis* is, or needs to be, understood. Their third objection is that appropriation lacks a prefix, whereas *Ereignis* can be hyphenated. What is assumed here is that language usage is fixed, when it is actually fluid.

These remarks serve to qualify how 'appropriation' will be used here in recognition that it is a rich and complex term, able to be *appropriately* linked to *The Event* as a demonstrable acceptable translation of *Das Ereignis* as 'the appropriating event', evidenced in Richard Rojcewicz's translation (Heidegger 2013: 153). As Heidegger states:

> We must learn to experience the event as the appropriating event ... The appropriating event is essentially inceptual; what is not yet past, what goes down to the beginning. The beginning is older than anything established by historiology. The event can never, in the manner of an idea, be established and represented.

Thus, essentially the event is that which is gathered and animated through appropriation, and as such is the beginning of what exists and is experienced prior to intent and narrativization. Heidegger extends this view such that 'The event is the appropriation of the human being to humanity' (162). The sentiment carried by this position directly counters the reduction of moving a city to a technical exercise, for the move is appropriation of a city in its totality as event.

Events of consideration and new epistemological horizons

As indicated, the moment of the act of moving a city is epistemologically and politically prefigured by 'the to be moved', and with profound ontologically designing implications. This means knowledge going ahead of observed crisis. The horizon of this knowledge has to exceed the empirical situation of emergent risk so as to comprehend the consequences of relational impacts. The degree to which there is a consensual understanding of the becoming of the complete event of the loss of the city – the disaster as knowledge ahead of it as experience – determines the amount of time available for the move. To recognize this is to grasp the centrality of the relation between how political power is mobilized and the nature of the collective within which a consensus is formed, as well as the efficacy of the conceptual representation of the political and move processes together with the projected form and character of the new city. So contextualized, how the political decision to move is made, and what results in in terms of support or resistance, and how this is responded to, constitutes the determinate event of the event of the move. As such, the becoming of the moved city, as event, will significantly shape the 'organic nature' of the city itself as event.

Breakdown vs collapse – in a global system context, breakdown, as has been indicated, takes the form of three levels of lost utility and dysfunction: unusability, the missing and obstruction. Whereas collapse is not graduated, and it can be an end point of breakdown. Moving a city can be triggered by breakdown, while collapse creates a condition where there is unlikely to be much of use to move. The ability to understand the characteristics and process of both conditions requires study in the specificity of place. Knowledge needs to be acquired prior to, during and after the act of moving. Again, this knowledge should not be viewed as purely instrumental: moving a city is not just a question of matter but equally one of mind (as is breakdown).

Destruction and creation – the process of organic life is an indivisible relation between destruction and creation. What comes from the earth returns to the earth, even if the earth has been polluted and contaminated. Whenever 'we' make we also destroy – this is the dominant story of our relation to natural resources. The more unsustainable our species has become, the faster the rate of the planet's destruction and the less its ability to repair the renewable resources upon which life depends. Defuturing has become the normative condition, and extinction a likely fate of almost, or all, species. In current global circumstances what, at the very least, has to be learnt is how to slow this process, and if possible, reverse it. Moving a city, in the ways described, provides an opportunity to contribute to advancing such knowledge, albeit in unfavourable conditions.

Loss, displacement and unsettlement – this is painful, but it is also a clearing and beginning if the spirit and the means can be found. There has been much created out of the ashes! Displacement is something different. One no longer stands on the ashes, they are out of sight. They, and what was before, are now mere memory. Unsettlement is the lived condition and psychology of displacement, and witness to it triggers loss. Increasingly it will become the existential reality of 10 per cent of the global population and the state of mind of everyone. Moving a city, while not overcoming loss and displacement, for many people can provide a beginning whereby unsettlement can be lived with. More than this, there can be a certain unburdening and freedom of material loss if the potentiality of a desired and attainable new is in sight. This is exactly the promise of the new city to be moved to.

Abandonment and the unknown – abandonment does not always mean the abandoned has been lost to the world, but only to s/he who was forced to abandon, which means what is lost is lost to them. For the lost and displaced, the unknown is the future, and together with memory, such unsettlement is a complete entrapment. There is no way out but the work of the making of a future (once more moving a city illustrates such making). Making here brings the reconstruction of a self and the construction of a new world together.

Metrofitting the leftover city after the city – the assembly of fragments (the new as difference). In some cases there are islands of stranded viable structures that will withstand the coming forces of natural destruction. But on their own they have no future (other than as un-serviced shelter for the dispossessed). What metrofitting provides (the project of retrofitting cities impacted by climate change but not under threat of destruction) is a means to connect/bridge these fragments and thereby creates conditions of functionality. In the context of the fiction, this can be seen as a way that mostly old people, who would rather die in the city than move, could stay in a condition that provided a quality of life. What begs to be understood is that in old age much of one's world has already died – people, environments, relationships, capabilities are all gone. Thus what remains accrues a value that cannot be perceived by others. It, and memories, are all one has.

Movement and arrival in time – the uneven unfolding moment (beings and things in time). Globally the event of breakdown is already under way. It is arriving at a different speed and time worldwide. Increased temperatures, sea level rises and floods, drought, fire, cyclonic weather, climate change related conflict, rates of reducing biodiversity and all related impacts do not conform to the projection of averages. This means reactive and adaptive actions are occurring unevenly in time and intensity. Yet what is clear is that action everywhere is tardy, and prefigurative planning, especially mid and longer term, is insufficient. The concept of 'acting in time' (the medium of time with a sense of urgency) is under-engaged. Knowledge of time *as change* has to be increased! For this to happen alienation and resistance to the speed of technological change need to be created.

Resettlement and a new order – change in place (the non-universal telos). There is no model for a new world order in the unfolding disorder of a world moving toward breakdown. Order has to be a consequence of situated action (most likely local and regional). Resettlement, as with moved cities, cannot and should not be based on re-establishing the old 'normality'. It has to be predicated on the future-now. The implication is to design and create from the future back to the present and thereafter examine the past as it arrives from the future (which means the norms of past settlement are left in the past). The idea of the permanence of settlement can no longer be retained.

Futuring and being futural – making time (action in the face of defuturing). The imperative of all action can now be stated as being futural. This needs to be understood as the basis of an ontology of individual and collective action, and the ontological designing of what those actions bring into being. Again this can only happen if the knowledge to do it can be generalized and materialized in a futural-grounded culture.

The event of the sign – the contest of what's coming (truth over concealment). This contest maps onto the relations between futuring and defuturing thinking, knowledge and practice. The demand is to make the content of this contestation present, interrogated, understood and re-communicated. A major problem is the lack of presence of the reality of defuturing; making it visible is an absolute necessity for futuring – this has to become an event in its own right. For this to happen the 'crisis of the crisis' (the concealment of the extent and seriousness of the global crisis in play) has to be the priority, and for this to happen the concealment of the 'truth' of crisis has to be at the core of the event (as it constitutes a new semiotics).

7. Politics and the political imagination and the shift

There has been a general societal failure to distinguish between the political and politics, in large part because, as Claude Lefort has pointed out, the latter acts to conceal the nature of the former. What this situation produces is a political misplacement of the materiality of the political, and it has serious consequences, including an elite who strand 'politics' within a text. This language of the 'critical' is dislocated from grasping criticality and a passage to critical action. To give substance to these judgments, the relation between theory, the political, breakdown and praxis will be identified in the context of the city move. After doing so the problems of the political dislocation and problematic of the Anthropocene are to be examined.

The political

Between the actuality of politics and the political is a rhetorical space of 'textual politics' that exposes specific and wider problems of the political, particularly its claims of having transformative agency. Climate change is an evident example of this problem.

Climate change is a registration of the climate of injustice based on the long history of the desires and impetus of developed nations to become ever more wealthy and powerful by the creation of technologies, industries and desirous populations that unwittingly engender a polluting toxic atmosphere, along with terrestrial impacts that, in association with other anthropogenic forces of negation, are diminishing the viability of 'life on earth'. This is being done without the knowledge or consent of the vast majority of the 'human population', who were, and still are, inducted into the reality of a nightmare masked by the promise of the dream. This 'dream' was imposed by modernity and projected by globalization – both of which rest upon structural injustice. Those projected as having entry into the promised dream are actually the inheritors of the aspirations of the perpetrators of the forces that destroyed the present life and expected future of the people of the nations that were colonized. Here the (dishonest) promise of justice came with the means that negated the very conditions of its possibility. Moreover, from the position of the historically dispossessed the very notion of justice was not their 'justice' but the Eurocentrically constituted modality of the colonizers. There can be no appeal to universal justice for there is no universal foundation of ethics or morality in the age of climate change (Colebrook in Cohen, Colebrook and Miller 2016: 105). Thereafter, any theoretical discussion of justice and the possibility of its future realization fold into the voice of re-colonization and its institutions. There is no voice that speaks for the universal 'we' or 'human thinking'. Contrary to the claim or hope, there is no politics that promises *us* (situated or globalized) anything.

A text cannot be political if its 'politicization' is deemed as a 'political effect' upon subjects that have no means to exercise a political effect. An ideologically inflected text and reading does not produce political action independent of a conjuncture in which the associated object of political engagement exists. There is no politics without a worldly political act. There is no politics without change even if the reading of the text produces a 'critical subject'. There is sadness in the discovery of a political aspiration and intent disabled by erudition that recoils against any possible applied reading of the text as instrumental or programmatic. The political cannot avoid the double bind of instrumental action and the rejection of the sufficiency of instrumentalism, or the intervention of politicized theory in this context to enable the possibility of praxis.

In the critical conditions of now – of which the Anthropocene is an inadequate and partial characterization[11] – that lacks a grasp of the dialectic relation of creation and destruction that arrives with designating the generalized concept of industrialization as prime cause. Likewise, as suggested earlier, and as will be re-emphasized, the characterization of action in response to the crisis it names (the worldly transformation versus the transformation of 'the human') is equally inadequate, especially when placed in the differences of time, place and conditions of what is an increasingly becoming a condition of 'our' fragmenting species. There is no prospect of salvation, all loss will be unjust, the fear of extinction will not mobilize the 'global masses', and even if it did there are no foreseeable leaders able to lead them. Certainly the form of appropriate political action is unclear. In such a context, and recognizing the cultural diversity of such a mass, appeals to any kind of un-situated universalized aesthetics have nowhere to go.

Colebrook, in alignment with Paul de Man, shuns a politics of sustaining 'the polity, or the political' (116) because 'It would then be possible to look at technologies – primarily inscriptive and aesthetic – that generate the beautiful soul of critical reading, and the equally beautiful ecology and polity that is its natural other' (116–17). Here is a textbook example of what Carl Schmitt called Political Romanticism (Schmitt [1919] 1986) as it constitutes a subjective political reality.

How does design fiction in general sit alongside a literary theory inflected with a configuration of the political? As literature it would be dismissed as outside literary discourse, and designated as a genre of little significance. Politically it would be exactly what de Man recoils against in his literary politics of the counter-political. Being bracketed by texts that overtly frame its reading, it subverts any notion of the sufficiency of the text, or of the text as itself being political. It could be expected that the (act of) reading and the reader produced (vis-à-vis a structuralist theory) would be seen as purely instrumental. This, at first glance, may be true, but in the way that the reader is equally reading this text it may be false. The intent of this text is to enable a critical review/reading prefigurative of the practice of moving a city, but not at the level of instruction. Instead it is a learning of issues toward the ontological designing of a sensibility, while recasting theoretically informed instrumentalism as a means to conceptualize/operationalize ontological designing of an action (like moving a city) as political practice (the politicization of practice being the counter-politics to the ideologically bound institutionalized politics of the status quo). The critical judgment of design fiction is not based on an assessment of its literary merit (although the narrative is created with the aim of creating an engaged reading) but on the basis of it being elemental in the constitution of political efficacy.

Such political efficacy is based on understanding both the political and ethics as a materiality. The political, to have efficacy, has to have a material effect/affect of affirmative futural change; anything other than this is passive or regressive. Likewise, ethics ungrounded from idealism and Eurocentric universalism has to be seen as the material validation of discernible affirmative change. In both cases they are grounded by critical practice being completely articulated within the criticality of crisis, as it names conditions of existence and the divisions of negation and creation in which being, itself, is becoming determined. So positioned critical practices are what is to be learnt, made, continually evaluated and refined. But for this to happen institutional spaces of unlearning and new learning have to be created – clearly a project in its own right (Fry 2020).

The **Anthropocene** appears to totalize the threat to 'life on Earth', but it is more complex than the designation suggests. Likewise it is presented as overriding differences and the divisions of our being, by suggesting the continuity of the species acting as an overarching imperative (Colebrook 2016: 82). But it will not do this. The concept and concerns are Euro-America centrically bound; as such it cannot be delivered and accepted as a universal master narrative. Billions of people have no knowledge of it at all, and vast numbers who have encountered the concept have little or no critical understanding of it. Others have an onto-theological epistemology that would oppose it with other than a human narrative. The familiar objection is that it lacks a political perspective (83). While having some substance, it substitutes for a wider political critique that acknowledges there is no political discourse or project that is globally confronting the recursive forces of negation in which we all, know it or not, are implicated. The reductive propensity of political actors to alight on, or search for, a specific cause (capital, modernity, consumerism, the essence of the species and so on) gets no way near grasping the complexity of the complexity that our species, mostly unknowingly, has created. Unrelentingly, 'things' are brought into being without the slightest understanding of their futuring or defuturing consequences.

This situation is long past being able to be approached and understood at an individual object or system level; it is now an environment that has merged into the ontic. Equally, there can be no appeal to humanity: as indicated, the species is fragmenting and the actuality of this situation is in advance of the rhetoric and theory on the transformations of the human. Dominantly, the exclusivity of this rhetoric lacks recognition of the human as an imposition of modernity upon Indigenous others (with their very different sense of being). There is now no singular; 'our' being is not unified. 'Man', mankind, humanity, the human, humankind – these are now non-inclusive terms. Humanism, socialism, capitalism, all theologies, and all ideologies, are epistemologically bereft in the face of the complexity of complexity of 'the world in being now'. Yet the de-worlding of the worlds in difference 'we' occupy has yet to be engaged, and this engagement begs to be understood as the essence of the political now, deemed as 'process learning' (this positions actions like moving a city as contingent, rather than a lasting a solution).

The condition that the Anthropocene claims to name, is not of the moment of the arrival of industrialization. It is far older and was destined even before our species arrived. As soon as hominoids started to make a world for themselves in the world, the process of planetary degradation started. For millennia, damage done was small and ecologically accommodated, but the ontology of worldmaking was set and powered by the tool, which transitioned into technologies that amplified creative and destructive powers. Epistemologically, the failure to grasp that crucial dialectical relation between creation and destruction is at the core of the defuturing essence of the plurality of our being. Dominantly, destruction goes by as disconnected from creation.

Creativity is a preoccupation of education at absolutely every level: it is at the core of the economy (as innovation); it is integral to the development and activities of the arts, humanities and science. In every endeavour destruction is overlooked. Yet terrestrially, environments, commodities, industries and products are created by the destruction of environments. Atmospherically, industrial processes are massively destructive as the complex inter-related effects of climate change, along with other sources of pollution. Destruction is of the immaterial as much as the material: new ideas, theories, beliefs and values can and do destroy old ones.

Clearly destruction cannot be avoided, but unless what is happening is understood, and with what consequences, 'we are flying blind'. 'We' simply do not know what 'we' are doing, and so have no possibility of acting ethically in a worldly sense. Even more elusive is the recognition of the destroyed that is covered over by the created. This has been the destruction of the time of being (the essence of defuturing). While the move from the imperceptible to the perceptible is impossible to know, what is clear is that the problem existed well before being named.

Thinking of the Anthropocene from a fatalistic view that sees it as a condition of impossibility is not only unhelpful but flawed. Notwithstanding evidence existing at the time, the impossible is not a certain. Rather it is epistemologically perspectival – it depends on what you know.

So many of the attainments of the present would have seemed impossible if viewed from the past, be it the body that defies where once it was assured death, matter seen at its most fundamental constituent level or the mind exposing secrets of the universe. The implication of a history of the attainment of the impossible is that action has to be taken with uncertainty and responsibility for consequences. These observations return us to the need for unlearning those epistemologies that obstruct the creation of and engagement of a new learning appropriated to our plurally becoming futural. This is not merely a pedagogic challenge, but one that is profoundly political.

The failing structures of politics

The broken breaks the institutional structures of politics. What does this mean? To answer is simple: extant political structures, ideologies and institutions are in a condition of epistemological and conceptual limitation that has constituted worldviews and practices that cannot 'grasp' (gather, hold and comprehend) the complexity (of the complexity) of the issues that demand address and the means to address them. The scale of the redundancy of politics prohibits the possibility of paradigmatic change. What this means is that the broken, in its gradations, goes unseen or ignored. This also means that the speed of the reduction of finitude delivered by compounding acts of defuturing is not recognized as occupying a future travelling increasingly faster toward the present. 'Our' being, and all else in being therefore exists in a diminishing expanse of finite time. The primary objective of politics now is the making of time. Without being able to comprehend, view and act in the recognition of breakdown, there is no way to avert collapse. Even when the prospect of collapse is acknowledged, it is discounted by being placed in a distant future and by an absolute preoccupation with the imperatives and instabilities of the status quo. Such a resistance to empirical events and knowledge exposes not only extreme myopia but also complete irresponsibility. Underscoring this situation are two factors that negate the political foundation of politics and its degeneration into administrative process:

- Technical theology as the displacement of politics: this is the belief in technology and technological systems as full automation delivering complete liberation (from work and capital) together with, in the last instance, faith in its ability as a saving power to solve those problems that threaten 'our' very being. Such beliefs have no substance, not least because the presence, distribution and sophistication of technology directly correlate to globally uneven economic conditions (Hui 2019: 264).

- Cybernetic governance is another expression of the faith in technology. This is based on an uncritical attachment to metrics and machine calculability linked to a feedback mechanism that provides data that objectifies and directs action. Such algorithmic systems can 'feign' human presence, while at the same time actually removing it from the realm of decision. This kind of mechanized intelligence not only mobilizes understanding without understanding but also contributes to a technical construction of reality.

Both cases evidence the creation of politics as a simulacrum and thereby sever any relation to the political and thus constitute a truly post-political politics. The dislocation of such a 'politics' can but contribute to breakdown and world disorder by feeding political institutions with information and decisions that actually mis-inform (unhuman information lacking a being and vital information). Post-political politics also evidence a fusion that is occurring between technology and an ontotheological-epistemology that posits futural action in a non-transcendent secular agent of faith.

A review of questions of trans-political resistance

With varied degrees of efficacy, the politics of protest lives on. The problem with it is that even if it overthrows the organizations, regimes or institutions that rule, it would still be unable to implement fundamental change because of the structure, managerialism and political paradigm in which sustaining the unsustainable status quo is encased. Protest against and 'demand for' plural interests of competing agendas (for example, the Occupy Movement) do not provide 'a vision of an affirmative future, or the means of its attainment'. Resistance of itself is never enough.

In conclusion, consider the following: in the political condition of technical theology bonded to cybernetic governance, reason has to be recuperated and mobilized against reason. So positioned, the reason of 'the inert machine' is contested by 'speculative reason', as it goes beyond 'the sensible, given data, and calculation' (Hui 2019: 31–2). This in turn requires making public the history of the history of defuturing as it exposes the extent of the future destructive consequences of what capital/industry/political institutions have created. Added to this is the need to pit futurally operative technology against its defuturing technological other (a simple example is renewable energy overcoming fossil fuel generated energy). In a larger frame this implies a politics of resistance to the human (as hegemonically formed by colonial imposition) and what Lyotard (1988) called the 'inhuman', which now requires redefining as that imposed 'inert being' that displaces or destroys organic life itself.

In order for a futural politics to be possible, a new political imagination that does not accept extant politics as the end-point of political thought and a shift of political action to the domain of practices (creative/aesthetic/critical/instrumental) informed and directed by a materialist understanding of ontologically (designing) agency as 'care' are needed (Fry and Tlostanova 2020). What second order design fiction aims to do is to add to the efficacy of design increasingly becoming a political agent of care, manifested as an ontological effect of design as a materialized ethical political practice of world making and remaking.

4

Closing and Opening:
Toward the Brief

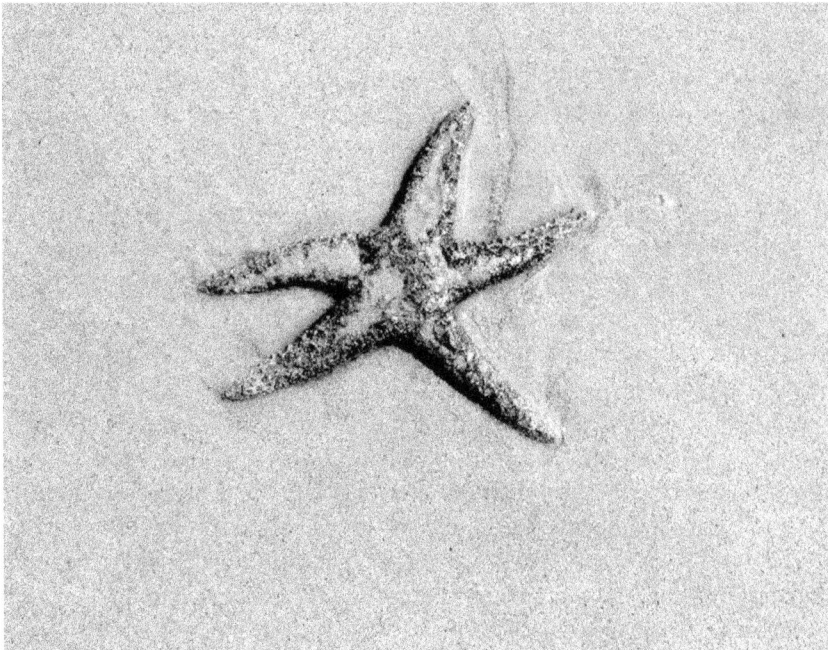

The metanarrative of this book, as it overarched its particular narratives, has sought to initiate a process of theorizing, fictioning, interrogation and futuring that methodologically can be transposed to other projects. So conceived, and linking to redirective practice, second order design fiction can be understood to be mobilizable in the service of a political agent of affirmative change. It should not be regarded as having a restricted use within design as it is dominantly understood and practised.

The curtain falls and another story begins

This final part places design fiction within a design process based on 'designing back from the future'. The fiction is not presented as providing a solution or projecting an end point. Rather it is intended as a means of production of conditions for exploration, and as an exercise of applied research and learning. The fiction brings a theorized mode of design fiction to the creation of a narrative, this informed by observational research on critical issues that are in turn subjected to observational analysis to identify those conditions that define problems able to be addressed by design as truly futural. Out of this process a brief can be produced, the content of which goes to the issues deduced from the fiction, after its strengths, weaknesses and possibilities have all been rigorously examined.

The process of 'designing back from the future' is predicated on designing in the medium of time wherein the designed is understood and engaged as 'event' (rather than object). The transformative agency of 'the designed' is brought to projected occurrences in time (the events of the event) as all of these occurrences are back-cast to the present as the moment of designing. The events elaborated in the fiction are not pure fantasy; they are selected on the basis of plausibility and imperatives informed by research. The review of the fiction would change, develop and refine the problems brought to the content of the brief, and thus to the direction of what is to be designed. There is no suggestion that the future characterized by such a process is certain, but it is a far more responsible, considered and appropriate way of designing than restrictive design practices of attending to performance standards and conditions based on the present and a posited design life centred on current materials and conditions, and market demands. The process of 'designing back from the future' is not claimed as applicable to everything designed, but rather to that which is exposed to changing critical circumstances over time. As a response to the impacts of environmental change (understanding environment in the broadest terms), the nature of what is designed in this way would not only have to endure but at the very least have minimal defuturing environmental impacts. What makes the approach viable is that it takes extant knowledge, conditions and practice as a basis of redirection: it starts from where 'we' are.

A schematic note toward a brief

Here is a minimal outline of the scale of a brief, arriving out of the review of **a second order design fiction**, that would overarch the entire project of moving a city. All the details given are indicative of, and aim to show, the scale of process and action of what in actuality would be an even more complex exercise.

The concept design of the newly moved city would require a process of identifying and elaborating needs. This needs assessment would be responsive to the situated context in which the external and internal needs of all sectors of the population of the city would be met and thereafter sustained over time. This would involve a comprehensive programme of circumstantial and futural research and consultation spanning extant political, economic, environmental, social and cultural determinant conditions requiring a rapid response. This process would not assume an unexamined transposition of any of the structural elements of the old city, but would seek to identify those essential to transfer, especially those that can contribute to the sustainment of the moved city socially, environmentally and economically. This necessitates producing specific instrumental briefs for functional elements of the city – its buildings and economic and operational infrastructure – while challenging what exists mostly within the domain of current knowledge and expertise. The same cannot be said for political, social and cultural institutions in an age of significant enviro-climatic, biophysical, technological, psycho-social and geopolitical change. This situation makes major demands on unlearning, relearning and new learning, which by implication means creating new epistemologies and modes of imagination that would create ontological changes in the entire city transformation team. This observation is an example of an absence in the design fiction, as implied in its review. One could expect this process to be intensive and take a year or more.

Phase One: Organization and project management

What follows is no more than an initial indication of where the organization and project management for moving a city could start to think about how to take action to commence the move process.

Transformation team induction

As suggested, moving a city so it is able to be futural and advance sustainment starts with the team that has been given the responsibility. Each member has to put themselves in a position whereby they understand the need for, and is willing to commence the process of, their own transformation. This is because, on a planet in increasingly unsustainable circumstances, cities of post-industrial, industrial and industrializing nations are all de facto machines of production and, overwhelmingly, destruction. Their hyper-consumptive metabolisms and cultures of desire are agents of unrestrained defuturing that are already heading into a state of dysfunction. Conversely, cities of the poor that function by informal means in conditions of structural dysfunction slide deeper into a morass where the impacts of a 'natural disaster', pandemic or war mean they further down-cycle, and are unlikely to have the means to fully recover. **In all circumstances, moving a city needs to be made an opportunity for futural and directional change.** While it involves a great deal of instrumental activity it has to be much more than this. It has to be a transformation of the city as a designing event in time (that is, with urgency in the medium of time). None of this is possible unless the team given the task of moving the city undergoes, as said, an ontological transformation in order to overcome their taken-for-granted knowledge and practices (their habitus) so they may thereafter act otherwise.

Such transformation is not gained via a teaching programme in a classroom. Rather it needs to be situated and experiential, by means of simulated action research devoted to moving a city, wherein what is to be learnt is discovered from having identified the complexity of problems and understood them relationally. Thereafter, it becomes possible to discover or create appropriate knowledge to engage the problems (after action research) having made decisions about critical issues in conditions of uncertainty followed by failing, and trying again, then having to improvize and learn how to function as a collective, and gaining the means to be resilient in conditions of stress and hardship.

Conceptual team formation

Who to recruit is a key question – writers, researchers, architects/designers/ engineers, anthropologists/sociologists, psychologists, medical personnel, economists and political leaders to join and work as a cohesive transdisciplinary group. The team's membership not only prefigures action but also requires review at a very early stage of the induction process – thus it is also a selection process. The major task at the start of this process is the rewriting of the provided design fiction in the context of the actual planned city move, and thereafter its review. This design fiction will be used as a source of scenarios to be critically serially tested, developed and employed during the course of the creation of iterative briefs. This process can be seen as a substantial part of the unlearning and new learning programmes.

Team operation

Central to the team's operation is first, the development of a praxis that unifies situational analysis (another area of activity that would be developed in the induction process) and conceptual development (based on bringing the situational analysis together with an evaluation of the research done) to constitute a provisional vision. This activity can be seen as an initial stage of the project. The second stage is political. It publicly presents the vision as a way to communicate to communities the ambition and complexity of the move and to open up specific areas for autonomous design contributions by them within negotiated conditions of constraint and under the imperative of sustainment. For example, medical communities of interest would be invited to conceptualize the city's health facilities, as would the sporting, industrial, parks and urban agriculture, and educational communities. Transition team membership would support all these groups in this design action.

What this process recognizes (subject to its contextual refinement) is that the complexity of the project cannot be grasped (gathered and understood) without a considerable amount of formally organized directed research across numerous fields. This cannot be done by conventional forms of 'community consultation'. Just presenting a 'vision' of a moved city is likewise not viable when its form is to be the product of an ontology predicated upon futurally changed circumstances that create an 'otherwise event' of the city beyond appearances. What is actually needed are means of disclosure of change, and its complexity, along with learnt and invested input into the vision. Besides providing valuable design directive, the transition team's support can also constitute a mediation process with levels of engagement that again conventional consultation, and co-design, lack. The entire basis of this approach is contra to public relations promotion, political spin and community management.

Project management is obviously essential and unavoidable. However, it begs careful consideration and planning. Once the project is conceptually resolved, a technical and economic group would need to be formed within a prefigured framework that is fully articulated to the transition team and local government. The implication here is for an integrated management entity and not an independent directive process of project control. This relation demands a conjunctural understanding of the challenges and critical delivery issues of the project, and a continually reviewable timeline for each project phase rather than fixed up-front 'deliverables'. Pragmatically, what would be required is the establishment of a process management plan that identifies flexible modifiable programmes reactive to working under conditions of crisis. For instance, materials recovery from the 'old city' and an associated inventory are activities needing care so that the maximum of reusable material is extracted, sometimes under unfavourable conditions. This is the obverse of a rapid destruction and minimal materials recovery demolition practice. Slow demolition effectively means more time, but less expenditure on new materials acquisition (even if available, which they might not be).

Beyond pragmatics: publications, events and presentation

Publications, progress report presentations, exhibitions and workshops are all needed to provoke discussion, develop understanding and keep communities informed, thereby prompting feedback. This is done with a focus on communicating what is being brought into existence by the new city as an urban environment, society, culture, economy and political order that is conceptualized to be more appropriate to the times than the old city was, while retaining and developing as many of its best features and qualities as possible. Without inflating what is promised, and recognizing conditions of constraint, the new city has to be created and presented as a place of desire, but not by public relations hype, for this works against the construction of trust between the transition team and the community at large. More specifically, it undercuts those people who would support the formation of the community's autonomous design action.

Phase Two: Research

As indicated, a comprehensive research programme is essential. It has to prefigure all action, planning and design – this to assess risk over time, technical problems and their resolution, appropriate futural forms of governance and the needed, desired and appropriate economic, social and cultural vision/ environment for the city.

Design and planning (with in-built review processes)

This divides into three stages. **Stage one,** the design of the destruction of the old city, that begins by asking: what structural elements could and should be moved? (statues, fountains, historical features of special buildings like windows, arches, doors, gates, and so on); what activities should/must be continued and when should they be moved? (industries, communication facilities, hospitals, emergency services, refuse collection, markets, festivals, etc.); which buildings need to be classified as having high material recovery status, including moveable components?; which buildings have a low status and, once de-roofed and de-timbered, can be viewed as a source of base materials to crush for road construction and aggregate? Indivisible from this activity is the design of the move process itself and its logistics. This especially involves transport planning, labour hire requirements, inventory storage of recovery materials on the new city site and new material manufacture, extraction and purchase. All of this design and planning occurs at the same time that research and conceptual design of the new city is under way – this after establishing the criteria for **site selection**, and thereafter the assessment of possible sites in consultation with the National Relocation Department. The issue of distance of the move is critical insofar as the further there is to travel the greater the logistical complexity, time and cost. Locating a scaled-down port is another significant selection factor.

Stage two starts when the concept design and surveying are finalized and agreed by the city council and a community majority. Thereafter soil is broken on the new city site and earth works begin. This, again, involves detailed design and planning, contract issuance (service and legal), labour hire, materials requisition and all other actions and purchasing requirements so that the works programme is able to start.

Stage three is the commencement of a directly linked destruction and construction process under the direction of a joint project management scheme. Alongside all of this activity is the need for a **social and commercial transition support programme** (to plan, support, assist and manage the movement of people, institutions, services and businesses to the new city). Plus, a **consultative council** should be formed to create and manage a consultative process that is truly participatory. This council also has responsibility for all forms of community communication.

Clearly the time frame for these stages is substantial and depends on the scale of the city move, the location of the new city and the conditions under which the move is being taken. The order of magnitude of stages one and two could be three or four years, while stage three, which ideally would be divided into sub-stages, is likely to be two decades or more. The overriding aim of these processes and their timing is, first, the continuity of everyday, economic and socio-cultural life, and giving people time to adjust/adapt. Second, it is to avoid a hiatus whereby the old city ceases to function and the new one fails to operationally commence. Clearly circumstances may mean that the process does not occur under ideal circumstances.

Overdetermining the instrumental

It is essential that the project conception team understands that the instrumental action of moving the city has to be overdetermined by the concept that the city to be created is socio-culturally and economically appropriate to the immediate circumstances, and those projected to change over time. As such the project is not merely technical. The end result of moving the city, as directed by circumstantial change, is the transformation of the form of the urban and the society that occupies it. To do this means the transition team's undoing of given knowledge of the form and function of the high-impact climate-changed old city and using this new knowledge to direct the development of the new city based on a rigorous analysis of the extant situation and futural risk studies. This process directly connects to the team mission ethos.

To give an indication of the dispositional approach to the formation of the transition team, the initial period of their induction could look like the following: a reading of an introductory orientation document (like the draft below) followed by an extrapolation and review workshop to ensure individual and collective understanding. The sensibility that this exercise aims to develop would then be brought to a draft project brief (a document containing a more developed form of much of the information outlined above).

There would be a requirement for the team to organize, undertake and submit a return brief that confirms an understanding of the draft brief, and then raises questions of clarification and proposes options and suggestions. In addition, each member of the team would be required to reflect on the process as outlined, which would take four or five weeks, and then identify the particular learning needs that they require so they can fully contribute to the team. These needs are put to the team so a system of mentors/learning partners can be established. The assumption of the action is that everyone will have shortcomings while equally having an ability to respond to the shortcomings in others.

1. An orientation towards brief review and development

Writing a brief for moving a city is a substantial and complex task. There can obviously be no universal template as the nature and circumstances of any particular city will demand that the moved city be tailored to the specific needs of place and circumstance.

The driving force for producing a brief to move a city is not how to do it – an instrumental imperative – but what is to be created, why and with what desired consequences. This means the move is conducted on the basis of meeting practical ethical imperatives as well as community and economic needs. The second order design fiction provides the means to address both of these imperatives in an elaborated narrative form, but not on the basis of identifying and resolving all problems. Rather it will assist in the identification of problems through the process of its review. At the same time, the review of the fiction itself is open to a similar interrogation. Hence this doubled task manifests the 'observation of observation' trope of the process. Obviously a brief for moving a city would not be completely directed by the fiction, but the fiction would make a substantial contribution to the critical framing of the brief.

So contextualized what this process does is to go beyond the fiction and its review to get to the fundamental issues that a transitional team has to grasp in the production of a really sound and effective brief. In doing so the team, if they are to succeed, cannot avoid the development of a well-conceived, clearly written and illustrated brief that the political leadership directing the move can understand and support. It also has to be able to be summarized appropriately to 'the community at large' so as to understand the process and engender enthusiasm for the new city. The complexity of the project needs to be exposed and go beyond the pragmatics of moving and give a sense of what would make a new city a place in which people would want to work, play and live in.

Critical issues in focus

Consideration needs to be especially given to two critical issues – contingency and breakdown – as implicit in the fiction and addressed in its review, as well as the commanding ideas directing and explicated from them.

Moving a city is contingent upon two factors that are absolutely a directive of the brief: the impending destruction of the city and the remaking of a city by human fabrication, as a world within the world, that is seen and felt to be futural. Neither of these factors are necessarily self-evident. They would require elaboration in the context of a specific city. Impending destruction would not only come from environmental threats but also from civil unrest or social breakdown in the face of a mass exodus of capital and people. Likewise, the notion of 'remaking the world within the world of human fabrication' does not imply making it as it was. The brief would therefore need to prompt the asking and answering of fundamental questions about the form and function of the new city as an agent and event of 'world remaking'. The second issue – breakdown – goes to the old city and links to the condition that follows from the forces of its environmental and directed destruction needed to take the city from partial dysfunction to complete inoperability (with the exception of older people staying in community housing and facilities). Again, the brief requires this process being understood in relation to the specificity of the risks and the actual impacts of particular modes of destruction and how they affect design and the timing of the extraction of the material resources of the city.

Last, and importantly, the relation between the commanding ideas that framed the fiction, and which were elaborated in its reflective review, need to be seen as feeding the formation of the brief as factors directing the process of moving a city, but only after being evaluated as relevant or not.

Commanding ideas

These ideas, like opening worlds, ground and groundlessness and cosmotechnics, informed the fiction and were elaborated in Part 3. What the commanding ideas do is to set the moving of a city in a world of crisis, and as such places it as a city among cities in a similar critical condition. What this implies is the formation of collective knowledge to identify and draw upon, while understanding the specificity of the particular city being moved, including its situated conditions in life now lived in a world of overt crisis, and acknowledging that our species' actions have been causally generative of this situation. Futurally, three perspectives are likely to affect the thoughts and feelings of people facing the moving of a city in a world where the economic impacts of environmental destruction, in all its relational forms, are massive. Conflict ever proliferates, and political dysfunction exists in the extreme. For all but the self-deluded and very privileged, seeking a way forward means rejecting technology as a saving power, together with questioning a belief in the sufficiency of reason to comprehend the complexity of the crisis of the crisis. Another substantial need is to deal/cope with a widespread withdrawal of a large percentage of the global population into a nihilism wherein nothing has value except the pleasures of the moment. Likewise, there is the fatalism of transhumans wanting to withdraw from the physical world into a space of techno-cognitive artificial consciousness, and of those who want to abandon planet Earth altogether to create life somewhere else in the universe.

Life lived with an acute sense of crisis produces an unavoidable encounter with **groundlessness** which is the ontological 'nature' of being-in-the-world now. Recognized or not, this is as present as the arrival of the eventual fate of the world (such as impending extinction due to a distant solar disaster) to a proximate present. This implies the lack of an epistemological foundation for a functional (if not absolute) condition of certainty. Thus truth becomes relative, and existentially this means all knowledge is felt to be uncertain and insufficient to deal with the situation. As a result a crisis of values and sense of insecurity follows, that itself creates an embrace with nihilism. Equally, crisis and insecurity occur with the acquisition of the knowledge that it is 'we', our values and actions that are the fundamental cause of the crisis. Again a prospect of a slide into nihilism arrives based on a conclusion that even if 'we' could change ourselves, it is too late. To act futurally against this backdrop means understanding that groundlessness is not an abstraction but the concrete state of our being that is eternally present, made proximate by crisis as an evident removal of certainty of ground (in its most overt forms by a ecological collapse, extinction or a nuclear apocalypse, all of which are actual conditions of possibility). Action in this situation means acting on the basis of retained values and recognized imperatives but without certainty.

The creation of a city demands **a provisional ground**, a foundation, to be taken literally and epistemologically as the means that makes action possible – the essence of ground can be thought as structure. The relation between ground and groundlessness is an unavoidable issue for moving a city and its brief.

The determinants of moving a city are created by localized conditions of groundlessness insofar as the new cannot simply replicate the groupings of the old city; it has to be constructed in a changed world of overt uncertainty under new conditions in the present and future. This situation demands prior and new thinking, and implies a rethinking of being ungrounded, which means thinking terms of impermanence, change, adaptation and movement when forming the brief and designing the city. To illustrate, three terms will be considered: future, systems and technology.

Many philosophers of different cultures over a number of centuries have contested the relation between past, present and future as a linear progression. Likewise, the notion that the **future** is a void has been shown not to hold when critically questioned. Consider, for example, that climate change of the present is a consequence of greenhouse gas emissions of the past combining with those of the present to constitute future climate impacts that progressively arrive in the 'everlasting now' (the only moment in which we can exist). And then there is the disjunctural time of global communications. An international phone call creates a conversation in the same moment of a different time – e.g. my day may be your night, my present may be your past, but we share the same moment. Time is thus confirmed as that in which events occur (Aristotle), thus making global events experiences that are present at the same moment in a different time. Time also cannot be seen as circular, repeating like a clock, nor is it accumulative. Rather it is the duration of singular moments (Bergson). No discipline commands time, it is not under the ownership of science; 'things' have their own time, as do cultures.

Systems are a construct of an epistemology, as are their differences and hierarchy. Autopoietic systems (that recreate themselves) and allopoietic systems (that require external inputs) all exist within systems. Neither they, nor any system, can be viewed outside the epistemological means by which they are made present and recognized. Evoking a system does not necessarily mean a common understanding; however, it does trigger an assumption of a particular set of animated structural functional relations. Cities function by virtue of multiple systems. For instance, in the context of a brief for moving a city, the old city would have a metabolic system that evolved over time without an overall conceptualization ever having been created. But this system of the old city cannot be transposed to the new – it needs a transformation based on the conceptual model and dynamics of the form of the new city, its projected population and expected change over time. A new metabolic system (and its subsystems, like sewage and solid, liquid, putrescent, toxic and green waste) needs to be designed and constructed; the same applies to energy, reticulated water, street lighting and so on. The point to be noted at this juncture is that there is a direct correlation between the descriptive language of the brief and the character of what is actually designed. What this means is that there is a political dimension to how systems are (epistemologically) defined and designed.

Technology: this last of the three terms is the most complex. The critical observations of the fiction addressed several technological issues explicitly and implicitly; and there were those not expressed which should be acknowledged. The brief for moving a city would need to register the relations between technology and: (i) changing world conditions; (ii) breakdown; and (iii) a realizable and appropriately situated form for the moved city. The starting point is acknowledging that our species has always been technological, commencing with the use of stone tools (already in use by earlier hominoids), and the wooden and bone tools they shaped, forming a lifeworld of artifice into which 'we' Homo sapiens arrived (Fry 2012).

As technologies became more complex, so did their ontological designing impact on us. As we designed them, they designed us (bio-mechanically in use and in the tasks they enabled to be undertaken, cognitively), but unevenly in the context of global population distribution and environmental difference. The result has been twofold: first, the environmental impact of technology progressed from being undetectable to becoming terrestrially and climatically enormous. And second, differentially, the extremes between the technologically disadvantaged and the most advantaged are so great that the ontological changes have resulted in the fragmentation of our species.

Three particular transformations are recognized that support these claims. The first is the breakdown of the binary distinctions of technology/ nature and machines/organisms. Nature and technology have converged to constitute the 'naturalized artificial', most evident in the process and products of biotechnology. Argument on the machine/organic relation has been part of this convergence (Canguilhem [1952] 1992) and predated this technology. The second force of transformation has been another convergence, that between electronics, systems and cybernetics, this not only by the internet's transformation of communications, but via social media, social mores and psychologies (especially of younger generations). In the process of gaining such capabilities, psycho-technologies were formed. These continue to fundamentally alter 'our' being at an ontological level and mark a mind/ technology nexus. Lastly, is the importance of cosmotechnologies. In relation to the brief, they need to be understood, recognizing that different cultures can and, especially in the past, have, produced their own and very different technologies, mostly excluded from the history of technology. More than this, in changing world conditions, as contextually linked to moving cities, greater cultural technological difference is needed in combination with more resistance to the defuturing of universal hegemonic instrumentalism, which is now at the very core of current technological development. Hence, cosmotechnologies will become of increasing future importance. Noting this registers an absence in the fiction.

These last remarks lead us to recall that technology and economic development were pathfinders of modernity, the negative consequences of which have delivered the 'end times' (which can now be understood as the end of the modern world marked by the claims of the Anthropocene and the commencement of the planet's sixth extinction event) now being experienced as the regression of post-development and the growing negative experiences of a changing climate. This moment is not just of the world around us but *is of us who are post-moderns*. As indicated, we, as a species, are changing. Not only is what it means to be human becoming more plural but so is 'our' relation to the inhuman and non-human. A problematic divide is opening between the transformations of our being and the language of designated changes (non-human, posthuman, trans-human and inhuman). In this setting, the most basic and critical observation to make is that the end-times are of our own species' making: defuturing comes from 'our' actions. Therefore, it follows, as already said, that nothing affirmative will change unless we change. Postdevelopment, positioned by these observations, denotes and declares the need for another direction, another mode of world making. While still inchoate, the thinking of postdevelopment in formation, and the circumstantial changes now under way (of which moving cities will be a significant example) are contracting globalism and expanding national self-interests. Again, such thinking needs to infiltrate the brief, the complexity of which should now start to become clearer, in that the way cities are positioned in the world is already being transformed.

The question of epistemology raised by the fiction's review puts the issue of grasping the theoretical and strategic importance of 'the event' (as concept) firmly in place as a key element that the brief has to evoke a clear understanding of and thereafter directly engage with and extrapolate from in **informing the action it identifies** to be taken.

For the moment the move event can be qualified as the union of *the temporality of becoming within the designated locus in which things occur.*

The city so viewed can be deemed as a theoretically informed conceptually directed event in its process of arrival, in the nature of its nascent being, and in the form of what its being brought into being. The concept translated into the being of a moved city is: its constitution is an event; its operationality is an event; and all that the city brings into being is an event in which things happen, that are not merely technical. What the brief therefore demands is a comprehensive response to a stated imperative to design the moving and moved city as an event of the 'now' viewed futurally and ontologically, meaning that the event is both designed and designing. To enable this, the review listed a series of considerations able to open a new epistemological horizon to know that:

- Breakdowns of different orders are treated as opportunities to embrace, in contrast to being seen as irrecoverable conditions of 'collapse';

- Destruction/creation as an absolutely overlooked dialectic (acts of creation as fundamentally bonded to acts of destruction, for example: world making is equally world unmaking; the home is a place of both life and waste making; new ideas arrive by overpowering the old);

- The compound problem of defuturing, as the effect of unsustainability, drives life lived with displacement, unsettlement and destruction, all producing loss, abandonment and the unknown.

Futural ongoing designing consequences of all actions designated by the brief require identification and questioning so as to be directive of action. Such an exercise of ethical responsibility does not guarantee that all possibilities will be recognized and all decisions will be correct. But it does mean that the extent of defuturing impacts will be far less than if action is taken without any attempted foresight of consequences. This means being aware that ongoing geopolitical instability is the deepening condition of world affairs with serious implications everywhere – this especially as nations and international organizations fail to have sufficient means to deal with the scale of the environmental, social and international security problems that are arriving.

Knowing, understanding and engaging events in these circumstances demands the creation of a huge amount of new knowledge able to grasp the emergent order of worldly unsettlement, settlement under stress and resettlement. All of these events are often unstable, occurring as action and movement in time (that is, action in the medium of time and with urgency). Such action requires being recoded as futuring or defuturing, with every associated event being made present and projected as sign (visual/meme, audio, written/published). What is being said here is that our actions are taken with a certain sense of the world, but 'the world' itself is an imaginary. The faster 'the world' changes the greater the disjuncture between it and our imagined 'world picture' – world in both cases is only present as representation, yet 'we' act upon it. To act from a more informed perspective the disjuncture between worlds requires correction, hence the imperative to recode world as sign. The context of moving a city is not just something that is functionally done, informed by immediate environmental circumstances. It is also done with *a sense of the world* and a prospective future. The local is a point where *the being of the world* arrives for 'us' in our event of *being in the world*.

Knowing the city – **researching and profiling** it in the conditions directing the need for it to move – is a key research action. While the need to move comes from some kind of objectification of environmental encroachment, it is also an existential condition that in turn generates social, economic and political influences and pressures. As people become concerned, and see that the future of the city is foreshortened, the pressure on politicians to take action increases, investment in the city ceases, capital starts to be withdrawn and businesses start to plan to move, all of which adds to the pressure to abandon or move. While abandonment can be measured, and will be marked by early leavers, it can also portend crisis. Seen in this context, moving the city is not just a response to crisis but also a means of managing it. Most fundamentally it allows all communities, organizations, institutions and businesses that constitute the city to plan a course of action out of crisis. Notwithstanding the hardship experience, the prospect of the move can provide the possibility of an affirmative future. The brief has to capture this prospect and communicate the means of its realization.

Confronting the environmental issues starts with a risk profile, and this would need to be developed on two levels. First is the speed and seriousness of the encroachment risks prompting the city to be moved. For example, exposure to flood, heat, drought and fire, or non-availability of potable water (or means to create it), can all obviously drive a need to move. Second are the specific risks created by this situation as projected over time, including impacts upon, for instance: the built fabric of the city and its infrastructure; its socio-cultural environment across the full demographic spectrum; public health; the ability of the local economy to function; and the ability of the political regime to manage the city and administer its services. Until this information is gained it is not possible to establish the degree of urgency and the complexity of the 'always complex' move process. Clearly the need to move coming from a high-impact disaster likely to be repeated (thus making rebuilding unwise) is very different from a graduated risk like rising sea levels. Another influential assessment factor is the disaster response capability of the city in relation to projected impacts. Indivisible from this substantial research exercise is the research associated with the location to which the city will move.

Here the issues begin with establishing the criteria for **site selection**, and thereafter the assessment of possible sites. The issue of distance of the move is critical insofar as the further there is to travel the greater the logistical complexity, time and cost.

Linking the research on the managed destruction of the old city and the mode of creation of the city to be built determines **the move process** as a unified project. The starting point here is an audit of all material resources (formal and informal), followed by the itemization of disassembly, transportation and new construction processes that all demand handling and managing a huge volume of material resources, inventory creation and administration. Even when a labour force has been hired, its organization and training are significant tasks. While people would be recruited who have the needed technical skills, they will be mostly working with recovering (with care), or recovered, materials in ways that are innovatory. In almost all cases this means a short training programme would be needed.

Strategic design and planning for moving a city is another huge task to be done in a dynamic environment. The directed forces of disassembly of the old city, and 'mining' of resources, by degrees of time and speed, will be competing with the process of environmental encroachment and destruction.

Moving people with regard to their well-being, and the coordination of all services, agencies and organizations needing to be moved are also challenging tasks. All this requires a coordinated exercise mapped onto a raft of other critical political, practical, social and economic factors aiming to maintain a level of functionality of the city while the material process of defuturing continues. As change occurs and as negotiation takes place, uncontrollable things happen: key people pre-emptively move to other cities, as do some companies; people lose their jobs; economic pressures increase; and environmental impacts may unexpectedly escalate. In this fluid situation, plans are modified, positions change and budgets alter, while objectives have to remain as firm as possible. Conventional project management methods simply do not work with high levels of variables. This means that what has to be designed is not just a strategic disposition of project elements over time, but also contingencies and a social ecology able to cope with the breakdown of the city happening at the same time as its material fabric is being disassembled. Concurrently, the material and socio-cultural framework of the new city is starting to be created.

Central to this transitional situation is the formation of a supportive structure of social power and relations able to adapt to changing circumstances. Vital to this, as illustrated by and in the fiction, is good and clear political and practical leadership and social cohesion, unified by a common goal at every level, so that even in conditions of confusion there remains a shared understanding of the overall direction to be followed.

Politics and the political imagination

Moving a city is a profoundly political project in three respects. The first centres on bringing all the social, cultural, economic and political factions of the city to be moved into a cooperative, if not consensual, working relationship that allows for the collective forces of the city to be mobilized to support the process in a well-planned and organized manner. The second is getting a common vision produced and agreed upon by the same constituency. The third is gaining an agreement on the form of governance for the new city, which may be markedly different from the old city's system (this because of a liberation from structures inherited from the political history of the old city, changes in the form of the new city and, above all, challenges coming to the city from the future). All the creators of the brief need to fully understand this political dimension.

The political, so presented, overarches institutional party politics. To gain the level of cooperation needed equanimity among all parties during the process is essential. The wider crisis, in which moving the city is occurring, needs to be well communicated locally, done with integrity. Both actions directly connect to establishing and maintaining a dominantly unified community. Without this the move process is at risk.

Anthropocentrism, as indicated earlier, is at the causal core of this crisis. The Anthropocene is one way its effect is named. The new city in its form, economy, social structure and political institutions, and mode of governance would all need to be constituted from, and informed by, sound knowledge that unconstrained human self-interest is now antithetical to our species' ability to become futural. Rather that idealistically believing this can be attained by acts of will, more realistically it begs to be seen as possible by redirection from the imperative of sustainment. Without a self-interested commitment to sustainment 'we' (as the sum of our differences) are en route to losing everything that sustains us. This truism is one that global and national political leadership still fails to understand. The advancement of hyper-consumerism as a driver of economic development, however fuelled, is anathema to the long-term consequences of climate change already unrolling, alongside the combined impacts of all global eco-environmental problems and growing geopolitical instability. The implication is that the economies, and extant politics, of all regimes are structurally embedded in the unsustainable. Part of the breakdown in which the moving of the city is situated will show that hyper-consumption will become impossible to sustain.

Bringing the issue of the political to the creation of a city move brief is not to suggest that the design of its mode of governance should be part of its remit, although this is a task for local political leaders. However, designating an organizational structure enables a process to be created that is political. Such a structure is more than informational and operational, for it also creates ontologies that can constitute the political environment with which a politics of governance would have to deal. Implicit in the situation are two complex additional factors, again beyond the brief, that would in different ways exercise a great deal of influence over the formation and development of the political life of the city.

One is how forms of resistance to threats to the city are conceived (be they socio-political from internal forces or by incursions from external forces). On this, the design fiction could be considered as instructive. The other factor is far more intangible. It is the making of a cultural and intellectual investment in creating a political imagination able to establish the kind of culture that will deliver the type of governance to cope with the future that the city and its population will face. While these issues are outside the brief they are not external to the formation of the culture of the new city to which enacting the brief will contribute.

The last item in an initial thinking of what a city move brief might look like goes to the leftover fragments of the old city occupied mostly by the elderly who refuse to move to the new city. This is a problem certain to exist. It is likely, as the fiction indicated, to be linked with supporting family members or carers and a few small businesses. While much of the old city will have been destroyed and would by now be under water, perhaps some of these fragments could be clustered and metrofitted (in this context meaning 'urban scale retrofitted': Fry 2017) effectively turning them into villages with a post-first life future. If this were deemed viable (by research) it might form part of the brief.

Placement and design as politics

All that is future directive can be deemed to be political. For this to become visible there have to be discernible effects/affects. Initially the agenda of **design as politics** (Fry 2011) was defined in three ways. Basically, in confrontation with design as defuturing, the agenda argued that so much of what is brought into being by design takes time away, thus reducing the finitude of (our) being. Then, with this recognition, it argued that redirecting the 'things' that are designed and made, as well as the 'things' of the extant designed world, is political action. In taking such action design(ers) are effectively re-framing design as politics itself, and at a most fundamental level. In doing this, design is being taken beyond the limits of its institution and discourse. From this redefined position design can start to displace itself as defuturing with a new mode of learning (of, by and for) futuring practices. Hence this action was marked by the arrival of **design futures** (Fry 2009) as a specific kind of practice with directional agency that requires redirection professionally, socio-culturally and economically. This requires a form of strategic design thinking that has an informed understanding of the future, of effective means of change and a redefined role for the designer. Design redirected and rethought hereafter is devoted to responding to the imperative of sustainment (the project and condition of being futural). **Design fiction** comes into 'the picture' as a particular kind of design futuring that takes design beyond design as the realm a of professional practice and gatekeeping discourse and returns it to anthropological and post-disciplinary domains (Fry 2012). What this means is grasping design (prefiguring it as going ahead of what is brought into being) as a fundamental element of our being that cannot be contained by any disciplinary claim.

Design fiction has been placed in this contextual frame and thus articulated to design (as politics and futuring). Second order design fiction is a nascent practice, able to direct the form of a primary design agent: the brief. As such, it is open to be authored by any individual, community or organization with a need for something futural to be brought into being by design.

Advancing the practice of the autonomous design

More specifically, design fiction can act as an extension of autonomous design in designing with others, especially as a means of enabling the design power of a community to be materialized. Autonomous design resituates the conceptualized form of collectively authored material change by an organic community as striving for futural means of their sustainment. Collective talking, writing and visualized ideation are designing agents that go ahead of themselves that prefigures and directs how the appearance of designing arrives in the world. So posed, autonomous design is a taking back of the power of design, and a negation of the universal erasure of the local and Indigenous. There is a direct correlation between design and power – the lack of ability to design (as a prefiguration of the conditional circumstances directive of one's life) equates to a lack of power itself.

Advancing the practice of the autonomous designer

Autonomous design is a taking back of power by the designer. By degree, to design is to have power. But to be a provider of professional design services is to be circumscribed because the power to direct what is designed is dominantly vested with the client, the brief and, in most cases, 'the market'. Working with a community on an autonomous design project, a designer distributes their power and facilities to a community's designing power. Their role becomes more akin to enablement rather than origination. Working independently, an autonomous designer conceptualizes projects, authors briefs and enables their realization, all by design. But to be an autonomous designer requires gaining new knowledge and skills that significantly expand what it means to be a designer, and for design to be an independent entity. For an already qualified and working designer it means a process of unlearning, relearning and new learning. For someone wishing to become an autonomous designer the need is for a new and different kind of design education to be established. Currently, neither possibility exists in a fully developed form, but the formative process has started and it will arrive. Second order design fiction can be placed in this context as one example of the 'to be learnt'.

A comprehensive fiction (as with the example of 'moving a city') requires a certain level literary skill, and the ability to inject critical reflective observation of the observed into the input of the character, context and form of the narrative. The process of reflection is not just an intuitive exercise but one that demands self-ethnographic, hermeneutic and theoretical knowledge, as does the writing of the project brief as the key output of the fiction. There are obviously a range of other areas of knowledge and skill that are needed for someone to become an autonomous designer, including being entrepreneurial and organizational.

A politics of scale

Design as politics, design futuring, second order design fiction, autonomous design and the autonomous designer, informed by the imperative of sustainment, are all elemental to advancing (the) sustainment as a project. This project is an endless process toward relationally linking economic, political, social and cultural action to establish conditions of difference that are futural. This occurs by the negation of the defuturing propensity of all that is demonstrably unsustainable. In advocating all of this, there is one absolutely critical qualification to make. The ambition is huge, and must remain so, but action taken always has to be proportionate to resources and the capability of situated conjunctional limitations. Thus, the project scale needs to be determined by a sense of what would be circumstantially successful. Idealism must be held in check. The measure of success is not defined by the immediate impacts of the event 'in place' but the extent to which it can be appropriated with transformational agency – this is a major factor in design as politics.

Appropriation has to be understood as an action over time. Strategically the creation of ideas, thinking, events, texts, images (moving and still) and futural 'things' invite appropriation, get appropriated, and therefore take on an efficacious 'life of their own'. This is how a multiplicity of small actions can, in time, realize a large ambition. 'Viral transmission' is never enough – whatever is encountered has to have transformative agency.

Concluding remark

From setting up the case for second order design fiction, providing a sample fiction, presenting a reflection of it and then showing how the process can be directive of writing a brief for autonomous action, *a tentative start has been made toward a developable method*. It will continue to be refined by myself, and others. The case for the practice does not need to be endlessly repeated, for its efficacy in use should communicate its value.

Appendix

The choice made of using moving a city as an example of second order design fiction is based on numerous urban design projects over three decades, but more specifically my own experience of a city move and related projects. The fiction was also informed by research for two books: the first was *City Future in the Age of a Changing Climate* (Routledge, 2015). It centrally addressed the issue of moving cities as a result of climate change impacts underway. The second book, *Remaking Cities, An Introduction to Metrofitting* (Bloomsbury, 2017) likewise enabled the development of city move theory and practices. Relevant experience was also gained from research undertaking to direct two intensive courses taught at the School of Design at the Polytechnic University of Hong Kong in 2016–17. Both explored design responses to the impact of climate change on the cities of the Pearl River Delta.

The specific city move project I worked on was in 2009 as a member of an international workshop organized by the Swedish Industrial Design Council in the northern Sweden city of Gällivare. Forty designers from around the world were selected to work for two weeks on concepts to move the city. The reason for the move was because over a century ago the city was built above an iron ore mine, but over recent decades old mine workings subsided and created a massive and growing sinkhole into which areas of the city were falling. As a result a major local crisis had developed. Many houses had been lost, attempts to physically move built structures had failed and the relationships between the local community, the mining company and local government had become very bad.

One of the first things that was recognized by workshop members was that the issue of where to move to had not been given sufficient attention. Without this being clear and desired, the chances of motivating people, especially those who were not immediately under threat to move, would be low. As a result the new location, and a new city concept, became a design priority. Another important design factor considered was that many older people did not want to move, this irrespective of the conditions of their circumstances; in contrast, young people were keen to move if there was somewhere and something better to move to.

The event was a success – this not because the workshop solved all the problems or presented a single design solution, but because it provided many new design ideas to review. As such it created a conversation in the community that gave all parties ideas, options and possibilities to consider. The presented design concepts were all drawn upon by everyone concerned, and used in developing a dialogue between the local authority, the mining company and the community. As a result the relations between the three factions improved and they all started to work together. From then on significant progress was made. Retrospectively, the project shared some features of autonomous design practice: specifically, the community designed with the design ideas generated by the workshop.

Two other design projects that advanced relevant city move knowledge are worth mentioning. The first was the design of a sustainable city for fifty thousand people. This project was undertaken for a global design completion (2007) organized by the California chapter of the Royal Institute of British Architects and the America Institute of Architects. The submission that Jim Gall, an architect colleague, and I put forward was based on transforming an existing town of a few thousand people into a relocation destination for communities from Central Australia expected to be displaced by heat and drought (this problem which has continued, worsened and is now moving toward a crisis). Fourteen teams from nine countries were shortlisted and invited to present at the Architectural Museum in Los Angeles. Our submission centred on a detailed illustrative linear narrative based on designing back from the future to the present (a key design concept that has been subsequently developed). The submission was non-compliant, all other teams presented master plans – even so the submission won second place.

The other competition (in 2009) was national. I led the submission together with my architect colleague, plus a small group of masters' students. The brief was for the design of a new civic centre for the City of the Gold Coast in Queensland, Australia – a city with a high-risk exposure to sea level rises. The submission, again non-compliant, was to move the city. It had three elements: a relocation satellite city, a floating suburb and a bridging scheme linking elements stranded by inundation: thus fragments of the original city were retained and made viable. To the team's great surprise it won joint first prize

None of these projects and their approaches were seen as purely technical, but recognized as being indivisibly economic, social and cultural. Moreover, they were also understood as learning towards design for the coming climate future.

Notes

Part 1

1 See for example Ursula Le Guin, *The Left Hand of Darkness* (1969), *The Lathe of Heaven* (1971), *Four Ways of Forgiveness* (1994); and Margaret Atwood, *The Handmaid's Tale* (1985), *Oryx and Crake* (2003), *The Year of the Flood* (2009).

2 An account of *Somehow Crystal* by Norma Field is featured in Masao Miyoshi and H. D. Harootunian (eds), *Postmodernism and Japan* (1989: 169–87).

3 This absence was corrected in 2012 as 'the deliberate use of diegetic prototypes to suspend disbelief' (Bosch 2012, cited by Levin 2016).

Part 3

1 IPPC (2019), *The Ocean and Cryosphere in a Changing Climate* (Monaco). It should be noted that since the onset of reporting of climate change sea level rises, revised figures have always been upward.

2 This is confirmed, for instance, with the moving of the Swedish cities of Kiruna and Gällivare.

3 By the time of our arrival some 200,000 years ago, earlier hominoids were using about seventy stone tools, and an unknown number made in bone and wood (Fry 2012).

4 A saying in Indigenous Timorese culture.

5 Individuation is defined by a series of related concepts by Simondon: pre-individuation (prefiguration out of a situated state that transcends conditions of instability/stability); individuation (the genesis of individuality of the thing in itself); transduction (the realization of the individuation of the 'real self'); and psychic-individualism (the emergent non-physical means by which individuals deal with their individuation). Simondon also wrote of the misplaced fear of 'the cultivated man' directed at 'machines that threaten mankind' (1958: 3).

6 Bringing the problem of a lack of ability to attend to a condition of mind, Stiegler comments on attention deficit disorder, and of everything stemming from the destructive effects of the exploitation of attention.

7 Primary retention is the retaining of experience in the conscious present, while secondary retention is the assembly of what is remembered to constitute the composite which is memory.

8 Traditionally 'tias' weaving in every Timor village has its own brightly coloured pattern. The weavings are rather like a long scarf – their width marks the passage of time, every major event in village life requires that the pattern is changed, with reading of the pattern being knowledge that passes from one generation to another. One can perhaps view these woven objects as pre-literate 'texts'.

9 Techne+logia (from logos) = craft (knowledge) + word which can be translated with a little creative licence as 'the naming of making'.

10 Published in German in 2009 and then in English in 2013 under the title, *The Event*.

11 Not least by its reductive figure of the anthropos and its: positing in linear time; problematic bonding to history; lack of acknowledgement of the post-natural/naturalized-artificial; exclusions of futural forces of auto-destruction external to inscribed processes of negation that will be created by breakdown.

References

Adas, M. (1989), *Machines as the Measure of Men*, New York: Cornell University Press.

Adorno, T., and M. Horkheimer ([1944] 1969), *The Dialectic of Enlightenment*, London: Verso.

Agamben, G. (2006), *The Open* (trans. K. Attell), Stanford: Stanford University Press.

Amin, S. (1976), 'Unequal Development: An Essay on the Social Formations of Peripheral Capitalism', New York: *Monthly Review Press*.

Atwood, M. (2003), *Oryx and Crake*, London: Bloomsbury.

Badiou, A. (2007), *Being and Event* (trans. O. Felham), London: Continuum.

Barrat, J. (2013), *Our Final Invention*, New York: St Martins Press.

Barthélémy, J-H. (2008), 'Du mort qui saisit le vif', (trans. Justin Clemens), *Parrhesia*, 7: 28–35.

Baudrillard, J. (1983), Simulations (trans. Paul Foss, Paul Patton and Philip Beitchman), New York: Semiotext(e).

Benjamin, W. (1973), *Illuminations*, London: Fontana Collins.

Bertalanffy, Von L. (1969), *General Systems Theory*, New York: George Braziller.

Bleecker, J. (2017), 'Props make the future', in T. Durfee and M. Zwiger, *Made Up*, 27–8, New York: Arts Center Graduate Press/Actar.

Canguilhem, G. ([1952] 1992), 'Machine and Organism', in *Incorporations*, J. Carry and S. Kwinter (eds.), 45–69, New York: Zone Books.

Castoriadis, C. (1997), *World in Fragments* (trans. D. A. Curtis), Stanford: Stanford University Press.

Cockcroft, J. D., A. G. Frank, and D. L. Johnson (1972), *Development and Underdevelopment*, New York: Anchor.

Cohen, T., C. Colebrook and H. J. Miller (2016), *Twilight of the Anthropocene Idols*, London: Open Humanities Press.

de Chardin, T., ([1959] 1976), *The Phenomenon of Man*, New York: Harper Books.

Deleuze, G. (1993), *The Fold* (trans. Tom Conley), London: The Athlone Press.

Diprose, R. (2017), 'Speculative research, temporality and politics', in A. Wilkie, M. Savransky and M. Rosengarten (eds.), *Speculative Research*, 39–51, London: Routledge.

Dunne, A., and F. Raby (2014), *Speculative everything: Design, fiction and dreaming*, Cambridge, MA: The MIT Press.

Durfee, T., and M. Zwiger (2017), *Made Up*, New York: Arts Center Graduate Press/Actar.

Ellul, J. (1964), *The Technological Society* (trans. J. Wilkonson), New York: Knopf.

Escobar, A. (1995), *Encountering Development*, Princeton, NJ: Princeton University Press.

Field, N. (1989), *Somehow Crystal*, in Masao Miyoshi and H. D. Harootunian (eds.), *Postmoderism and Japan*, 169–88, Durham, NC: Duke University Press.

Fry, T. (2009), *Design Futuring: Sustainability, Ethics and Practice*, Oxford: Berg.

Fry, T. (2011), *Design as Politics*, London: Berg.

Fry, T. (2012), *Becoming Human by Design*, London: Berg.

Fry, T. (2017), *Remaking Cities,* London: Bloomsbury.

Fry, T. (2020), *The Urmadic University*, Launceston: DPPP.

Fry, T., and M. Tlostanova (2021), *A New Political Imagination: Making the Case*, London: Routledge.

Fukiyama, F. (1992), *The End of History and the Last Man*, New York: Free Press.

Gibson, W. (1984), *Neuromancer*, New York: Ace Books.

Haar, M. (1993), *Heidegger and the Essence of Man*, New York: SUNY Press.

Haraway, D. (2003), *The Companion Species Manifesto: Dogs, People and Significant Otherness*, Chicago: Prickly Paradigm Press.

Haraway, D. (2007), 'When Species Meet', *Posthumanities*, vol. 3, 1–25, Minneapolis, MN: Minnesota Press.

Harding, S., ed. (2011), *The Postcolonial Science and Technology Reader*, Durham, NC: Duke University Press.

Harris, R. (2019), *The Second Sleep*, London: Hutchinson.

Heidegger, M. (1962), *Being and Time* (trans. J. Macquarrie and E. Robison), Oxford: Blackwell.

Heidegger, M. (1968), *What is Called Thinking* (trans. J. Glenn Gray), New York: Harper and Row.

Heidegger, M. (1971), *Poetry, Language, Thought* (trans. A. Hofstadter), New York: Harper and Row.

Heidegger, M. (1975), *Poetry, Language, Thought*, New York: Harper and Row.

Heidegger, M. ([1967] 1998), 'On the Essence of Ground' (trans. W. McNeill), in W. McNeill (ed.), *Pathmarks*, 97–135, Cambridge: Cambridge University Press.

Heidegger, M. (2013), *The Event* (trans. Richard Rojcewicz), Bloomington: Indiana University Press.

Hui, Y. (2016), *The Question Concerning Technology in China: An Essay in Cosmotechnics*, Falmouth: Urbanomic Media.

Hui, Y. (2019), *Recursivity and Contingency*, London: Rowman & Littlefield.

Huntington, S. (1965), 'Political Development and Political Decay', *World Politics*, 17 (3): 386–430.

Ingold, T. (2013), 'Anthropology Beyond Humanity', *Suomen Anthropologi*, 38(3): 5–23.

IPCC (2019), *IPCC Special Report on the Ocean and Cryosphere in a Changing Climate*, ed. H.-O. Pörtner, D. C. Roberts, V. Masson-Delmotte, P. Zhai, M. Tignor, E. Poloczanska, K. Mintenbeck, A. Alegría, M. Nicolai, A. Okem, J. Petzold, B. Rama and N. M. Weyer.

Jullien, F. (2014), *On the Universal*, Oxford: Polity.

Kearney, R. (1988), *The Wake of Imagination*, Minneapolis, MN: University of Minnesota Press.

Kinsley, S. (2014), 'Memory programmes: The industrial retention of collective life', *Cultural* Geographies, 155–75. Available online: https://doi.org/10.1177/1474474014555658 (accessed 31 October 2019).

Kurzwell, R (2005), *The Singularity is Near*, New York: Penguin.

Latour, B. (1993), *We Have Never Been Modern* (trans. Catherine Porter), Cambridge, MA: Harvard University Press.

Levin, M. (2016), 'Design Fictions'. Available online: https://medium.com/digital-experience-design/tagged/design-fiction (accessed 29 May 2021).

Luhmann, N. (1989), *Ecological Communication* (trans. John Bednarz Jr), Chicago: University of Chicago Press.

Lyotard, J-F. (1988), *The Postmodern Condition: A Report on Knowledge* (trans. G. Bennington), Manchester: Manchester University Press.

Lyotard, J-F. (1991), *The Inhuman*, Stanford: Stanford University Press.

Mander, M. (2010), *Groundless Existence*, London: Continuum.

Maturana, H., and F. Varela (1973), *Autopoiesis and Cognition*, Dordecht: Reidel Publishng.

McDowell, J. (1994), *Mind and World*, Cambridge, MA: Harvard University Press.

Meillassoux, Q. (2012), Interview with Rick Dolphijn and Iris van der Tuin in *New Materialism: Interviews & Cartographies*, Ann Arbor, MI: Open Humanities Press.

Mignolo, W., and C. E. Walsh (2019), *On Decoloniality*, Durham, NC: Duke University Press.

Moffat, L. (2019), 'Putting speculation and new dialogue in dialogue', *Palgrave Communications* 5, Article 11. Available online: https://www.researchgate.net/publication/330890628_Putting_speculation_and_new_materialisms_in_dialogue (accessed 28 May 2021).

Quijano, A. (2007), 'Coloniality of Power, Eurocentrism in Latin America' (trans. Michael Evans), *Napantla: Views from the South*, 1 (3): 1–45.

Richardson, B. (2000), 'Recent Concepts of Narrative and the Narratives of Narrative Theory', *Style*, 34 (2): 168–75.

Roden, D. (2015), *Posthuman Life*, London: Routledge.

Rostow, W. W. (1960), *The Stages of Economic Growth: A Non-Communist Manifesto*, Cambridge: Cambridge University Press.

Ruggeri, A. (2017), 'Miami's fight against rising sea levels', *BBC Future*. Available online: https://www.bbc.com/future/article/20170403-miamis-fight-against-sea-level-rise (accessed 3 January 2020).

Salih, T. (2009), *Season of Migration to the North* (trans. Denys Johnson-Davies), New York: NYRB.

Sauvy, A. (1952), 'Société Démographie – En vrac', *Trois Mondes, Une Planète*, L'Observateur, 14 August.

Schmitt, C. ([1919] 1986), *Political Romanticism* (trans. Guy Oates), Cambridge, MA: MIT Press.

Shelley, M. ([1818] 1994), *Frankenstein; or, The Modern Prometheus*, New York: Dover.

Simondon, G. ([1958] 1980), *On the Mode od Existence of Technological Objects* (trans. N. Mellamphy), London: University of Western Ontario.

Stambaugh, J. (1992), *The Finitude of Being*, New York: SUNY Press.

Sterling, B. (2005), *Shaping Things*, Cambridge, MA: MIT Press.

Sterling, B. (2011), Symposium Keynote, reprinted in T. Durfee and M. Zwiger, *Made Up* (2017), 18–26, New York: Arts Center Graduate Press/Actar.

Stiegler, B. (1998), *Technics and Time 1* (trans. Stephen Barker), Stanford: Stanford University Press.

Stiegler, B. (2012), 'Care', in T. Cohen (ed.), *Telemorphosis: Theory in an Era of Climate Change*, vol. 1, London: Open Humanities Press.

Stiegler, B. (2018), 'Within the limits of capitalism: economizing means taking care', Ars Industrialis. Available online: https://arsindustrialis.org/node/2922 (accessed 18 June 2018).

Thorne, T. (2014), The *Singularity is Coming*, New York: Etcetera Press.

Tonkinwise, C. (2014), 'How We Intend to Future: Review of Anthony Dunne and Fiona Raby', *Speculative Everything: Design, Fiction, and Social Dreaming*, DesignPhilosophy Papers, 12 (2): 169–87. Available online: http://www.thestudioattheedgeoftheworld.com/uploads/4/7/4/0/47403357/6tonkinwisedunne-raby.pdf (accessed 10 August 2020).

Ulmen, G. L. (2006), in Carl Schmitt, *The Nomos of the Earth* (trans. G. L. Ulmen), 9–36, New York: Telos Press.

Vernadsky, V. I. (2005), 'Thee Biosphere and the Noosphere', *Executive Intelligence Review*, 18 (02): 4–5.

Weiner, N. (1948), *Cybernetics: Or control and communication in animals and machines*, Cambridge, MA: MIT Press.

Whitehead, A. N. (1978), *Process and Reality*, New York: The Free Press.

Wilkie, A., M. Savransky and M. Rosengarten, eds. (2017), *Speculative Research*, London: Routledge.

Willis, A-M. (2007), 'Ontological Design – Laying the Ground', *Design Philosophy Papers Collection*, Ravensbourne: Team D/E/S.

Yasuo, T. (1980), *Nantonaku Kurisutaru* (Somehow Crystal), Tokyo: Bungei.

Index